Modern Music

The avant garde since 1945

Paul Griffiths

Modern Music
The avant garde since 1945

George Braziller
New York

Published in the United States in 1981
by George Braziller, Inc.
Originally published in England, 1981 by J.M. Dent & Sons Ltd.,
Aldine House, Welbeck Street, London W1M 8LX

Cover: extract from Cornelius Cardew's *Treatise,* © 1960,
Hinrichsen Edition, Peters Edition Ltd., London.

For information address the publisher:
George Braziller, Inc.
One Park Avenue
New York, NY 10016

Library of Congress Cataloging in Publication Data

Griffiths, Paul.
Modern music.

1. Music—History and cirticism—20th
century. I. Title.
ML197.G76 1981b 780'.904 81-10123
ISBN 0-8076-1018-6 AACR2

Printed in the United States of America
First Printing

for my son Edmund Patrick

with whom this book had a race to delivery
and lost

Contents

Music Acknowledgments

Permission to reproduce the following music examples is gratefully acknowledged.

1	Boulez: Sonatina for flute and piano (Amphion/United Music Publishers)
2–4	Boulez: Piano Sonata no. 2 (Heugel/United Music Publishers)
5	Cage: *Sonatas and Interludes* (© Copyright 1960 Henmar Press Inc., New York)
6–7	Babbitt: Three Compositions for Piano (Boelke-Bomart/Alfred A. Kalmus)
8	Babbitt: Composition for Twelve Instruments (Associated Music Publishers/Schirmer)
9	Messiaen: *Mode de valeurs et d'intensités* (Durand/United Music Publishers)
10	Webern: Piano Variations (Universal Edition, Alfred A. Kalmus)
11–12	Stockhausen: *Kreuzspiel* (Universal Edition, London)
13–15	Boulez: *Structures: premier livre* (Universal Edition, London)
16–17	Barraqué: Piano Sonata (Bruzzichelli)
18	Cage: *Music of Changes* (© Copyright 1961 Henmar Press Inc., New York)
19	Wolff: Serenade for flute, clarinet and violin (unpublished)
20	Feldman: *Projection II* (© Copyright 1951 Henmar Press Inc., New York)
21	Brown: *December 1952* (Associated Music Publishers/Schirmer)
22	Stockhausen: *Studie II* (Universal Edition, London)
23–4	Stockhausen: *Kontra-Punkte* (Universal Edition, London)

25 Stockhausen: Piano Piece III (Universal Edition, London)
26 Zimmermann: *Perspektiven* (Schott)
27 Pousseur: *Exercices* (Universal Edition, London)
28 Babbitt: String Quartet no. 2 (Associated Music Publishers/Schirmer)
29–30 Boulez: *Le marteau sans maître* (Universal Edition, London)
31 Nono: *Il canto sospeso* (Ars Viva/Schott)
32 Kagel: *Anagrama* (Universal Edition, London)
33 Stockhausen: *Gruppen* (Universal Edition, London)
34 Babbitt: time-point set
35 Stockhausen: *Zeitmasze* (Universal Edition, London)
36–7 Boulez: Piano Sonata no. 3 (Universal Edition, London)
38 Boulez: *Improvisation sur Mallarmé II* (Universal Edition, London)
39 Bussotti: *Per tre sul piano* (Universal Edition, London)
40 Stockhausen: *Refrain* (Universal Edition, London)
41 Berio: *Circles* (Universal Edition, London)
42 Penderecki: *Threnody* (© 1961 Deshon Music Inc./PWM Editions. Reprinted by permission of Belwin-Mills Music Ltd. International copyright secured. All rights reserved.)
43 Stockhausen: *Kontakte* (Universal Edition, London)
44 Babbitt: *Post-Partitions* (© Copyright 1975 Henmar Press Inc., New York)
45 Westergaard: Quartet (Schott)
46 Wuorinen: *The Politics of Harmony* (© 1967 by Charles Wuorinen. Copyright assigned in 1971 to C. F. Peters Corp., New York)
47 Cage: *Atlas eclipticalis* (© Copyright 1961 Henmar Press Inc., New York)
48 Riley: *In C* (unpublished)
49 Glass: *Music in Similar Motion* (unpublished)
50 Reich: *Violin Phase* (Universal Edition, London)
51 Cardew: *Treatise* (© Copyright 1960 Hinrichsen Edition, Peters Edition Limited, London)
52 Cardew: *Soon* (Cardew)
53 Davies: *Taverner* (Boosey & Hawkes)

Introduction

To every age it may appear that artistic development is unprecedentedly rapid, unforeseeably strange, and yet there seems good reason to believe that the changes which have taken place in music since World War II have been quite unusually radical. In the first place, Pierre Schaeffer's invention of *musique concrète* in 1948 made electronic composition at last a practical possibility. Within a few years the usefulness of the new medium had been greatly enlarged by the introduction of purely electronic sound synthesis, due to Karlheinz Stockhausen and Herbert Eimert; and subsequent advances in the field, including the development of electronic music synthesizers, the progressive refinement of computer techniques for handling sound, and the growth of live electronic music, have all opened wide new areas to the composer. Secondly, the evolution of serialism, and in particular the application of the method to rhythm, loudness, timbre and other parameters, precipitated a rapid advance in musical thought during the years 1947–53. The new directions then taken by such composers as Milton Babbitt, Pierre Boulez and again Karlheinz Stockhausen have continued to have a determining influence on musical composition. Thirdly, the work of John Cage, especially, has stimulated a variety of approaches to the use of chance or choice, ranging from the creative abdication of Cage himself to the elaborate aleatory thinking of Boulez. And there have been other revolutions of narrower scope: new ways of joining music with language and with theatre, the discovery of new potential in medieval and Renaissance music, the use of quotations in collages, a deep and sympathetic involvement with the musical traditions of Asia and Africa.

All these developments have contributed to the extraordinary diversity of music in the 1980s and in many cases, to a sharp divergence from the music of earlier periods. The year 1945 provides a convenient starting-point for a study of recent musical history, not only by virtue of its political significance but also for reasons more closely connected with the art. Of the composers who had had a part in the century's earlier musical revolutions, Webern and Bartók both died in 1945. Berg had been dead for a decade, Ives had long completed his work, and Varèse had been silent since the early 1930s. Schoenberg, with only a few years to live, wrote no more than a handful of important works after the war. Only Stravinsky remained, and it was now his role more to follow, with however much brilliance and originality, than to lead. 1945 marks the end of one era and the beginning of another, for the composers who have shaped music in more recent times – Boulez, Stockhausen, Babbitt, Berio, Nono, Ligeti and the rest – all produced their first acknowledged works in the crucial early years of peace. Even those who, like Messiaen, Cage and Carter, belonged to an intermediate generation and had begun their careers in the 1930s, found themselves in the late 1940s at irrevocable turning-points in their work. Without doing too much violence to history, therefore, it has been possible here to confine discussion largely to those composers who have emerged since World War II, though a few others, principally Cage and Messiaen, have been so influential as to demand admittance too.

It has seemed appropriate to divide the course of music since 1945 into two parts. The first, which is concerned with the advent and transcendence of total serialism and with the rise of an international avant garde, covers the years up to around 1960. At that point the history of music may be considered to have reached an end. There was a dissolution of the creative fellowship among composers which had been fostered in the early 1950s by the existence of common goals, or supposed common goals, and it became no longer possible to speak of a unified thrust of musical endeavour; only the most tenuous links of aim and method exist among the composers who dominated the 1960s and 1970s. Plurality, which is the single distinctive feature of contemporary music, calls for a different method of treatment, by aesthetic rather than chronology, and this is the method adopted in the traverses which constitute the second part of this study. In both parts each chapter concludes with a 'repertory' listing relevant works, with details of publishers and recordings where these exist. Music examples are notated at sounding pitch.

Prelude: Music in 1945

'In 1945 or 1946', Pierre Boulez has written, 'nothing was finished, everything was still to be done. We had the privilege of making those discoveries, and that of finding nothing in front of us, which may sometimes be testing, but which facilitates a lot of things.'[1] Boulez saw himself as confronted by a virgin field because, according to his unyielding demand for progress in musical composition, there had been little advance since the great days before World War I, when within the span of a few years Schoenberg, Webern, Debussy and Stravinsky had produced their most revolutionary works. Schoenberg's invention of serialism had been a momentous contribution, but Schoenberg had compromised with history by using the method to shore up the outdated forms of tradition, the outworn aesthetics of German Romanticism. Stravinsky, in similar fashion, had failed to pursue the new rhythmic possibilities so abundantly exposed in *The Rite of Spring,* but had instead become a pasticheur and assembler of musical curios. The time was ripe, with the end of the war bringing its own needs for physical and psychological rebuilding, for a new adventure in musical thought.

That adventure will be the principal matter of the chapters which follow, but first it may be useful to indicate something of the state of music in 1945, bearing in mind that no composer in that year could have had a complete picture of what his colleagues were doing: communications had been impeded not only by the inevitable wartime disruption of concert life and of the publishing industry, but also by Nazi cultural policy, which had anathematized almost every kind of musical innovation, and equally by the fact that many prominent European musicians had been driven to seek refuge in the U.S.A. Schoenberg, sole surviving member of the 'Second Viennese

School' after Webern's death in September 1945, was living in Los Angeles and proving in his last works, which include the String Trio op. 45 (1946) and *A Survivor from Warsaw* op. 46 (1947), that while adhering to serial principles he could recover the fierce tension and the rapid shifts of colour and emphasis that had marked his atonal, expressionist compositions of nearly 40 years before. During this late phase he was also able to see the beginning of a revival of interest in his music in Europe. Soon after the end of the war Karl Amadeus Hartmann, who had been a pupil of Webern, began a series of 'Musica Viva' concerts in Munich with the aim of bringing musicians and audiences up to date with the developments stifled during the Nazi years, and Schoenberg's music featured in the programmes from the first. Hartmann's example was widely imitated in Germany; meanwhile in Paris one of Schoenberg's own pupils, René Leibowitz, was conducting performances of works by the master and his followers, and was instructing a new generation in the methods of serialism.

Stravinsky, also resident in Los Angeles, had entered on the final phase of his neo-classical investigations with the Symphony in Three Movements (1942–5). In relating to the experience of war – Stravinsky himself referred to films of 'scorched-earth tactics in China' in connection with the first movement and of 'newsreels and documentaries . . . of goose-stepping soldiers' lying behind the third[2] – the work bears comparison with Honegger's Third Symphony, or *Symphonie liturgique* (1945–6), whose three movements have the significant titles of 'Dies irae', 'De profundis clamavi' and 'Dona nobis pacem'. At the same time other composers who had fallen under the spell of neo-classicism were now setting their sights at the highest symphonic grandeurs, particularly Aaron Copland in his Third Symphony (1946) and Roger Sessions in his Second (1944–6). For such men as these the symphony perhaps held greatest promise as a form in which divisions might be reconciled and new hope forged; certainly the implicit programme of Honegger's work and the public rhetoric of Copland's suggest as much.

In the U.S.S.R., too, the symphony was being cultivated assiduously, though as a genre suited to the optimistic and aesthetically conservative doctrine of socialist realism and to official requirements for music to celebrate the defeat of Hitler. Vano Muradeli's Second Symphony (1945), for instance, is dedicated 'to the victory of the Soviet people over Fascism', and Shostakovich's Ninth (also 1945) is a light and joyous piece thrown off within the first weeks of peace. Prokofiev's Sixth Symphony (1945–6), a much weightier work concerned more with the remembered nightmares and privations of war than with victorious exulting, was denounced at its first Moscow performance as 'formalist', along with Shostakovich's Eighth Symphony, and banned for a decade. The newly severe interpretation of socialist realism, announced to musicians by Andrey Zhdanov in January 1948, obliged composers not only in the U.S.S.R. but throughout the communist bloc to address their music to the people in the simplest and most direct terms. Thus musicians from eastern Europe were effectively prevented from participating in avant-garde movements for some years: Witold Lutosławski, for instance, could not follow up his exploratory First Symphony until the cultural thaw came to Poland in 1956. But equally and more widely significant was the tension set up between musical radicalism and commitment to political revolution.

In western Europe, where restraints were being released rather than imposed, the new freedom of information about serialism encouraged several composers to investigate the usefulness of the technique. Wolfgang Fortner, perhaps stimulated in his inquisitiveness by his young pupil Hans Werner Henze, began in his Symphony of 1947 to accommodate his vigorously contrapuntal, neo-classical style to serial methods, seeking a compromise of the kind which had already been achieved in different ways by Frank Martin and Luigi Dallapiccola. These last had been among the few outside the Schoenberg circle to interest themselves in serialism before the war. Martin, who had begun to do so in the 1930s, produced in his *Petite symphonie concertante* (1945) a notably winning fusion of serial practice with quasi-Baroque writing and clean, fresh colour, the work being exquisitely scored for harp, harpsichord, piano and two string orchestras. Dallapiccola had adopted serial methods in 1942, and used them in an entirely individual manner in his most important work of this period, the powerful opera *Il prigioniero* (1944–8), deploying a variety of serial transformations in a style which adapts Verdian effusion to the harmonic world of Berg and the dense thematic working of Schoenberg.

But serialism was by no means yet in the ascendancy. An observer in England might have supposed that the future lay with Vaughan Williams, at work on his Sixth Symphony (1944–7), or with Benjamin Britten, whose opera *Peter Grimes* (1942–5) was first performed in the early summer of victory; while in Paris, the city where Boulez was completing his studies as liberation came, Poulenc was continuing to produce songs, orchestral works and piano music much as before, and Messiaen, Boulez's teacher, was bringing his style to a point of culmination rather than change in the Tristan trilogy he began with the song cycle *Harawi* (1945).

As for those others who were to have a decisive influence on the course of music during the next decade, Cage was in New York, continuing to exploit the potential of the prepared piano he had invented in 1938; his works of 1945 included a substantial set of Three Dances for two such instruments. In the same city Babbitt was completing his studies of the serial system while earning his living as a composer for Broadway, where in March 1945 Kurt Weill's latest work, *The Firebrand of Florence,* had its première. Luigi Nono was embarking on his career under the tutelage of Malipiero, and in Germany a boy called Karlheinz Stockhausen was working on a farm to earn enough money to continue his education.

Part I

The Serial Ascendancy

1 Paris, 1945–8

Several factors determine the choice of Paris in 1945–8 as a first point at which to test the developments in music since the end of World War II. It was at this time that Messiaen composed his largest and most elaborate work so far, the *Turangalîla-symphonie,* a composition which crowns his earlier achievements and at the same time displays new concerns which he shared with the young pupils who had gathered around him. It was also at this time that the most gifted of those pupils, Pierre Boulez, produced his first works, graduating from the miniature *Notations* for piano (1945) to the four-movement Second Piano Sonata (1947–8), which brought his early style to a climax of intellectual sophistication and expressive vehemence. Finally, the year of the sonata's completion also saw the creation by Pierre Schaeffer, working in the studios of Radiodiffusion-Télévision Française, of the first essays in *musique concrète,* music using transformations of natural sounds and composed not on to paper but on to gramophone records.

MESSIAEN'S CLASS

In seeking the source of the great revolution in French music which came in the late 1940s it is necessary to consider first the class which Messiaen directed at the Paris Conservatoire, for it was there that most of the young French composers of the time received the stimulus to press forward with a radical rethinking of the art. Boulez, who studied with Messiaen during the academic year 1944–5, later wrote an appreciation of his teacher which eloquently conveys the feeling of the time: 'In the desert, the solitude of the Conservatoire one man seemed to us the only sheet-anchor. He was only a teacher of harmony, but his reputation was rather notorious. To choose to study with him already meant a great deal: it was as if one were withdrawing oneself from the mass and electing for obstinacy. . . . It was truly an epoch of exploring and freedom – fresh air and openness amidst the stupidity which surrounded us. Secretly, or almost so, we grew to a total admiration for unwhispered names, unknown works which aroused our attention; meanwhile we moved forward together. And our investigation was not confined to Europe: acquaintance with Asia and Africa taught us that we were not alone in having the privilege of "tradition". They brought us to a stage at which music was not just an art object but truly a way of life, a permanent branding.'[1]

Messiaen had been appointed to the Conservatoire in 1942, but, as Boulez notes, his official duties comprised only the teaching of harmony, for he was regarded as a potentially dangerous influence. Response, for instance, to the first performance of his *Trois petites liturgies de la Présence Divine,* which took place in April 1945, when Boulez was a member of his class, included a large measure of fierce condemnation for the outrageous audacity he had shown in creating an act of worship and for his vulgarity in clothing it in perfumed harmonies. In 1947 he was given a class in analysis, aesthetics and rhythm, but not until 1966 was he to be made professor of composition. However, he had begun teaching composition privately in 1943 at the home of Guy Delapierre, and it was in these extracurricular classes that Boulez and his confrères learned their admiration for 'unwhispered names', which meant far more to them than did the supposed sacrileges that had scandalized Messiaen's critics. Isolation, none the less, played its part in giving the class the strength and the single-minded determination of a secret society.

Many of Messiaen's disciples also went to Leibowitz for lessons in 12-note technique. Boulez heard Leibowitz direct a performance of Schoenberg's Wind Quintet op. 26 in 1945, and this proved a determining experience: 'It was a revelation to me. It obeyed no tonal laws and I found in it a harmonic and contrapuntal richness, and a consequent ability to develop, extend and vary ideas, that I had not found anywhere else. I wanted, above all, to know how it was written, so I went to Leibowitz and took with me other students from Messiaen's harmony class.'[2] In retrospect it is surprising that Schoenberg's Wind Quintet should have been the work to reveal to Boulez the scope of serialism, for he was soon to criticize its adherence to Classical models of form, but clearly he was sufficiently impressed by its technical virtues to ignore for the moment aesthetic misgivings.

Among the fellow pupils of Messiaen who joined him in Leibowitz's classes were Serge Nigg and Jean-Louis Martinet. Under Messiaen the young band had gained a sense of mission in pursuing aesthetic renewal; now they received the tools with which to carry out their reform, and their intransigence grew. Boulez has recalled how, at the Paris première of one of Stravinsky's latest works, they demonstrated in no uncertain terms their dissatisfaction with pre-war aesthetics, their impatience with anything that proposed return or compromise.[3]

Nevertheless, Boulez appears to have been alone among his colleagues in the ruthlessness with which he pursued the goal of creating a new musical language. Nigg and Martinet, in their respective symphonic poems *Timour* (1944) and *Orphée* (1944–5), underwent the direct influence of Messiaen, whereas Boulez in works of the same period was already distancing himself far from his teacher. The title of his *Trois psalmodies* for piano (1945) inevitably calls to mind the *Trois petites liturgies*, of which the last movement is a 'Psalmodie de l'uniquité par amour', and Antoine Goléa has said that these early pieces 'lie on the confines of the modal writing dear to Messiaen and of atonality'.[4] Boulez himself has recalled that at the time when he wrote the *Psalmodies* he 'scarcely knew of the existence of serial music but very clearly felt the necessity of atonality';[5] the extent to which the pieces also show signs of Messiaen's modality must remain in doubt while the music remains inaccessible. To judge from the *Notations*, the only pre-serial work by Boulez to have been performed since the late 1940s, Messiaen's influence extended to certain details of pianistic style but not to matters of harmony. Boulez was evidently impressed in his early piano writing by the *Vingt regards sur l'Enfant Jésus*, which Messiaen was completing when his young pupil arrived at the Conservatoire. As an example, the Tempo II material in the first movement of the Second Sonata has its ancestry in the 'chord theme' of the Messiaen work. More important, as will appear, Boulez drew on his teacher's methods of rhythmic manipulation, but he was much more discreet and selective when it came to borrowing from Messiaen's harmonic world. There is, for instance, something Messiaen-like in his fondness for a motif constructed from a tritone and a perfect 4th or 5th, a unit which has an important functional role in the Sonatina for flute and piano (1946) and to a lesser degree in the cantata *La soleil des eaux* (1948), but Messiaen's modes pass only as fleeting shadows within the vibrant atonal universe of these works.

The other great influence on Boulez at this time was that of Schoenberg, to whose atonal compositions he had been attracted even before he heard the Wind Quintet. As his piano works from the *Notations* to the Second Sonata clearly show, the piano style adopted by Schoenberg in the Three Pieces op. 11 and in *Pierrot lunaire* was even more important to him than Messiaen's example. What he was emulating was a style that had 'considerable density of texture and a violence of expression because the piano is treated not as Stravinsky treated it, as a percussion instrument, but as a percussive piano which is at the same time remarkably prone to frenzy'.[6] However, he was of course more lastingly indebted to Schoenberg as the promulgator of serialism, which he used for the first time in the Sonatina, though even this début piece goes well beyond accepted canons.

Unlike André Casanova, a fellow member of Leibowitz's class (though not a pupil of Messiaen) who followed Leibowitz in technical matters and found a way, via Berg, to give serial music a typically French grace,[7] Boulez set out with characteristic intemperateness to push serial construction as far as might be. Where the *Notations* of the previous year had been the tiniest miniatures, comparable in length with the pieces of Schoenberg's op. 19, the Sonatina is a continuous movement of 510 bars. That Boulez could so rapidly proceed to a work of such dimensions testifies to the potential for transforming musical ideas which he had immediately recognized in serial technique, and demonstrates too the stimulus he had discovered in Schoenberg's union of four movement-types in the Chamber Symphony op. 9, the declared formal model for the Sonatina.[8] His serial practice is not Schoenberg's, nor indeed is it Webern's, even though he had been greatly impressed by the motivic methods of the latter's Symphony op. 21 when he heard Leibowitz direct the work in December 1945.[9] To be sure, his use of the series as a source of smaller units may be regarded as Webernian, but these units are generally deployed and developed quite independently, without any respect for the integrity of particular serial forms. Moreover, he often shuffles the pitch succession within his privileged motifs, among which the tritone-4th or tritone-5th element has pride of place.

Ex. 1

Example 1, from the opening of the 'first movement' of the Sonatina, shows a rare complete linear statement of the series, in the flute part: there are two occurrences of the above-mentioned element (B flat–E–A and D–A flat–E flat). One may note also that the series has no intervals of a major 2nd or a minor 3rd, or their various inversions and octave transpositions, though this is not much of a limitation given Boulez's cavalier handling of the series, some indication of which may be gleaned from these few bars. The piano does not provide complementary support, as one might have expected if the work had been by Schoenberg, nor is it related to the flute by contrapuntal engineering, as it might have been if Webern had been the author; instead it presents a distorted alternative. There are places where the piano gives a close approximation to the pitch succession of the series (see, for example, the sequence E–F–. . . B–B flat, in bars 35–7, almost a statement of the series transposed down a semitone), but equally its minor 3rd in bar 33 is a flagrant violation. Further inspection of the example will reveal numerous other points of imitation, rhythmic and intervallic, between the piano and the flute (compare, for instance, the flute in bar

35 with the piano's right hand in bar 40), but the derivations are most usually hazy and remote. The work does not have a serial logic of the kind which may be discerned in compositions of Schoenberg or Webern, but rather it offers an overflowing stream of momentary allusions and reminiscences.

Where the Sonatina is most thematic, in the extraordinarily symmetrical and playful 'scherzo', it is least serial,[10] and indeed Boulez seems to have reacted at once against any thematic use of the series. The initial five-note fragment in the flute part of Example 1, though a recurrent gesture, functions not as a theme but rather as a periodic call to attention, a reminder of serial proprieties when the music's heterogeneous divagations are threatening to get out of control. And though the whole series does appear in the 'slow movement', it is buried as a trilling cantus firmus, overlaid by elements whose serial origins are often obscure. At other points, as in the section beginning at bar 296, Boulez destroys the series utterly, splitting it into dyads which he engages in a purely rhythmic development without reference to the pitch orderings of the series. This is typical of a work whose strident power is fuelled by the antagonism between serial regulation and the perpetual quest for ways of transforming and even disintegrating the series, as also by those metrical dislocations which result from the use of rhythmic cells inherited from Messiaen and *The Rite of Spring*. Boulez's achievement here, in combining the lessons of his predecessors, in bringing about a quite original expansion of serial technique and in conveying his unmistakable determination, is extraordinary for a composer of 21.

It was an achievement without parallel among the works of his contemporaries. Perhaps Nigg might have come closest: his Variations for piano and ten instruments (1947) show a more traditional handling of serial methods but with something of Boulez's violent brilliance. However, Nigg was soon diverted into support for political rather than musical advance, a turn of events marked by his Eluard songs of 1948 and by his joining a 'progressist' organization. His cantata *Le fusillé iconnu* (1949) was intended for first performance in East Germany, but in the event the authorities would have no truck with a serial composition, and Nigg elected to accept the party line: his First Piano Concerto (1954), for instance, is based not on a series but on a French folksong.

Among the rest of the group, Martinet shared Boulez's taste for the poetry of René Char, his Six Songs (1948) and Six Poems (1951–2) following *Le soleil des eaux* and *Le visage nuptial,* but his musical allegiances are more overtly exposed. Unable to match Boulez's synthesis of the recent past, he produced in his 'symphonic fragments' *Promethée* (1947), for example, what is virtually a catalogue of orchestral devices taken from Berg, Stravinsky and others, and before long he had left the avant garde altogether to pursue a tonal style influenced by Bartók and Messiaen. As for Michel Jarre, the young colleague who joined Boulez when the latter was appointed in 1946 as musical director of the Renaud–Barrault theatre company, he eventually achieved fame for such scores as *Lawrence of Arabia* and *Dr Zhivago*.

BOULEZ'S SECOND PIANO SONATA

The position held by Boulez as leader of the young Parisian serialists was definitively established by 1948, the year in which he not only completed the Second Sonata and the first version of *Le soleil des eaux* but also published two articles in the new journal *Polyphonie*. In 'Incidence actuelles de Berg'[11] he attacked the examples of 'Romanticism' and 'attachment to tradition' he found in various works by the composer, being exercised largely by a contemporary tendency to praise Berg at the expense of Schoenberg and Webern as the purveyor of atonality with a human face. In 'Propositions',[12] having asserted the uselessness of compromise, he pointed to ways in which music might be made to advance, particularly in the field of rhythm.

The article briefly surveys the contributions of Stravinsky in manipulating rhythmic cells, of Bartók in introducing complex metres and syncopations, of Jolivet in allowing irrational values, of Messiaen in transforming rhythmic units by augmentation, diminution and extension, and of Webern in concealing regular metres. But while acknowledging the value of these ventures, Boulez criticizes the music of his predecessors for 'a lack of cohesion between the elaboration of the polyphony in itself and that of the rhythm'.[13] If one may interpret his need as that for a coherence between pitch organization and rhythm – and such an interpretation is supported by his works of the period – then it is clear that the path towards total serialism, eventually attained in 1951–2, had already been chosen. The early landmarks on that path are the principal subject of the article, which makes reference to the works its author had recently composed: the Sonatina, the cantata *Le visage nuptial,* the *Symphonie concertante* and the Second Piano Sonata.

The Second Sonata, a much weightier work than the Sonatina or the First Sonata, is conceived on the Beethovenian scale of four movements and shows, besides an extraordinary further development in the complexity of Boulez's divergent serial technique, a deeper involvement of rhythm as a functional participant in the musical fabric. If there was to be a coherent relationship between pitch and rhythmic structures, then, as Boulez saw it, the rhythm had to obey similar laws of instability and non-repetition to those which obtained in his serial universe: as he wrote in 'Propositions', 'the principle of variation and constant renewal will guide us unpityingly'.[14] The most usual result of this principle in the Second Sonata is a tangled counterpoint of cells, frequently in three or four parts, ceaselessly reinterpreting the proportions of a few basic motifs. Example 2*a* shows the first two bars of the sonata and Example 2*b* a

Ex. 2a

Ex. 2b

passage from later in the first movement, the latter redrawn in order to make the polyphony clearer (the division into parts adopted here is arbitrary). Among other correspondences, the semiquaver repeated-note element of Example *2a* appears in Example *2b* in units of semiquavers, triplet quavers, quavers and triplet crotchets, with various transformations of its pitch components. Cellular counterpoint of this kind is alternated in the first movement with vigorous chordal charges (Tempo II) which serve to re-inject the music with energy whenever it shows signs of flagging or of coming to a dead end, and they themselves strive towards an even quaver motion which, once achieved, is suddenly galloped into triplets before the counterpoint returns 'rapide et violent'.

If the underlying model for this dialectical movement is that of the classical sonata allegro, the fluid second movement provides a fascinating premonition of Boulez's later formal methods, its progress being interrupted by musical parentheses in faster or slower tempos. The first part, played without such interpolated commentary, is repeated in the second as the substrate for what Boulez calls a 'troped' development,[15] relating his technique to the medieval practice. Contrasting with this elaborate structure, the third movement is straightforwardly a scherzo with three trios, the last example in Boulez's music of a conventional formal scheme.[16] The finale is again a highly ramified construction. Starting with three and a half pages of desperate suggestion around the basic ideas, it plunges into the extreme bass for an ominous serial statement which gives rise to a quasi-fugal development in two sections, the themes being defined more by rhythm than by pitch.[17]

Boulez's technique of cellular working, already demonstrated in Example 2 and present in every movement of the sonata, is most rigorously applied in this finale, which shows the first tentatives towards a specifically serial handling of duration. Example 3 is particularly interesting in this respect, since here the cells have been conjoined to produce a polyphonic unfolding in durations which are all multiples of a semiquaver. The idea of creating rhythmic counterpoint from lines made up of semiquaver multiples probably came from Messiaen's *Turangalîla-symphonie,* where this technique is employed in the movements 'Turangalîla II' and 'Turangalîla III'.[18] Equally reminiscent of Messiaen's prototype is the mirror relationship which exists between the first line and the second, the former having the values 2–7–3–7–4–9–2–(6–4) where the latter has

Ex. 3

(8)–2–9–4–7–3–7–2, while the third line presents a fragment of this sequence, 9–4–7 (E–B flat–E flat). The technique is not of course yet serial, but Boulez would appear to be working his way towards a treatment of duration which can be assimilated to serial organization. It is noteworthy, and similarly significant in the light of Boulez's future development, that the pitch successions in this example do not share the relationships exhibited by the duration lines. Following the example of Messiaen, Boulez treats rhythm and pitch as separately composable elements, and as elements whose structures may even be placed in open conflict.

A clearer example of Boulez's cellular conception of rhythm is afforded by Example 4, which shows the rhythmic construction of a passage from later in the sonata's finale. The cells are again fused by ties, the requirement being here for a 'grisaille sonore', and yet the notation allows one to perceive that the structure is, if not yet methodical, then elaborately wrought. Instead of using 'arithmetical' rhythms, as in Example 3, Boulez draws on all the tech-

Ex. 4

niques of cellular variation he had developed from Messiaen, Jolivet, Stravinsky and Varèse. There are two basic cells, marked *a* and *b* in the example; *a* is distinguished by two equal values and a third which is dissimilar, *b* by its symmetry (it is, in Messiaen's terms, a 'non-retrogradable rhythm'). The modifications of these basic shapes are easy to follow: the first line continues, for instance, with a version of *b* in which the middle values are diminished, then with a doubled retrograde of *a*, then with a further variant of *b*, and so on. Here again Boulez is pressing towards a rhythmic method suited to serial organization, but his deployment of the cells scarcely suggests an intention to make the structuring audible: outlines are rendered indistinct and transformations obscured by their speed and density. The highly evolved construction is obliterated as it is established.

This is indeed characteristic of Boulez's early music, and in particular of the Second Sonata. The violence of the work is not just superficial rhetoric but symptomatic of a whole aesthetic of annihilation, and especially of a need to demolish what had gone before. As Boulez has said: 'History as it is made by great composers is not a history of conservation but of destruction – even while cherishing what has been destroyed'.[19] The massively powered developments of the sonata's outer movements bring an auto-destructive impetus to the classical moulds of sonata allegro and fugue in a determined refutation of Schoenberg's conservative practice with regard to form, and at the same time Boulez effaces his own constructive means, not only by piling up rhythmic cells so as to destroy their identities, as in Examples 2 and 4, but also by pressing his proliferating serial method so hard that the unifying power of the series is threatened.

Such a creative tempest is not limited to the Second Sonata but is to be found too in the cantatas *Le visage nuptial* and *Le soleil des eaux*, for which the choice of Char's poetry was dictated by 'the clipped violence of his style, the unequalled paroxysm, the purity'.[20] These are terms which could be applied equally to Boulez's music from the late 1940s, which is the music of a young man impatient with anything less than total engagement in advancing compositional thought, and also that of one who had been 'struck in a very violent way' by the beauty of African and Far Eastern music (to which, it will be remembered, he had been introduced by Messiaen), 'a beauty so far removed from our own culture and so close to my own temperament'.[21] He had found, moreover, a poetic model nearer home, as he acknowledged at the end of 'Propositions'. 'I think', he wrote, 'that music must be hysteria and collective spells, violently of the present – following the direction of Antonin Artaud . . . but I have a horror of treating verbally what people complacently call aesthetic problems . . . I prefer to return to my ruled paper.'[22]

The work which Boulez returned to his ruled paper to write was the *Livre pour quatuor* (1948–9), his first instrumental work without piano. The new medium inevitably imposed, as he has said, 'a certain reticence',[23] but it also made available a wider variety of tone colour, for he availed himself of the effects to be found in the quartets of Debussy, Bartók, Berg and Webern. Of the six movements, II and VI (and perhaps also IV, which has been neither published nor performed) are those in which attention is fixed most firmly on the development of rhythmic cells in an intensive manner proceeding from the Second Piano Sonata. The odd-numbered movements are freer in feeling and motion, and often touch an abstracted sensousness that also marks the first part of *Le soleil des eaux*. But rhythmic complexity is a feature throughout, and this perhaps accounts for the delayed and piecemeal première of the work: movements I and II were not heard until 1955, and III, V and VI followed only in the early 1960s. Partial performances are not, however, in contradiction with the nature of the *Livre*, for the players are invited to choose and order movements as they will, though there is some doubt as to whether this aleatory freedom was part of the original conception. In any event, by the late 1960s Boulez had decided that the work could not be performed adequately without a conductor, and so he withdrew it (except for performances by quartets who had already learned it) and set about a new version for large string orchestra, *Livre pour cordes*.

The *Livre pour quatuor* was not alone among Boulez's works in coming to notice only after a lapse of time, for none appeared in print until the beginning of the 1950s. The Second Sonata was generally known only by reputation until it was played in New York and at Darmstadt in 1952; *Le visage nuptial* was not heard until 1957; *Le soleil des eaux* was withdrawn after a Paris performance in 1950 and not heard again until 1958; and the Sonatina was not widely known until it had been played at Darmstadt in 1956. As far as the public and most of Boulez's colleagues were concerned, therefore, his early works existed only in their effect on his subsequent achievements, and there was little opportunity for them to wield much influence outside the Paris circle which he dominated so completely.

MUSIQUE CONCRÈTE

By comparison with works of the scale of Messiaen's *Turangalîla-symphonie* or Boulez's Second Piano Sonata, Pierre Schaeffer's *Etude aux chemins de fer* (May 1948) might appear a negligible contribution, consisting as it does of a mere three minutes of sound created by manipulating recordings of railway trains. And yet it was with this diminutive piece that the whole genre of *musique concrète* was instituted and that electronic apparatus was proved to have a useful role in musical composition.[24] Experiments with discs had been conducted before the war, notably (and independently) by Milhaud, Hindemith and Varèse, but it remained to Schaeffer to discover and to utilize the basic techniques of electronic transformation: reversing a sound by playing its recording backwards, altering it in pitch, rhythm and timbre by changing the speed of playback, isolating elements from it, and superimposing one sound on another. It was Schaeffer's aim to use these means in such a way as to free his material from its native associations, so that an event could become not just an evocative symbol but a 'sound object' amenable to compositional treatment: to have depended on the original associations would have been, in Schaeffer's terms, to create not music but literature, to make a drama of sound effects rather than a musical composition of rhythms and timbres. An important discovery was made when he noted that the removal of the opening instants of a sound, the 'starting transient', could transform its character, a bell stroke, for instance, being changed into something more like an organ tone. Armed with techniques of this kind, he hoped that he could employ an array of gramophone turntables as 'the most general musical instrument possible', providing facilities for the alteration of any sound derived from the real world (hence the term '*musique concrète*' to denote this music created from 'concrete' sound sources).

Schaeffer's early studies, which include not only the railway piece but also others derived from piano chords (played, incidentally, by none other than Boulez) and saucepans, were broadcast by French radio on 5 October 1948 in what was billed as a 'concert of noises'. The result was immediate interest from the public and from fellow composers. Several young musicians visited Schaeffer's studio, and one of them, the Messiaen pupil Pierre Henry, remained to collaborate with him on what was the first extended electronic composition, the *Symphonie pour un homme seul* (1949–50), which uses a wide variety of sounds – vocal, instrumental and orchestral, as well as many from everyday objects – in 11 short movements of diverse character, by turns erotic, whimsical and menacing. The work received its première at the first public concert of electronic music, given at the Ecole Normale de Musique in Paris on 18 March 1950. With the arrival of the tape recorder to revolutionize techniques later that year, and with the formal establishment by French radio of a Groupe de Musique Concrète in 1951, the path was open for electronic music to leave the kitchen of sound effects and make a decisive contribution to the course of the art.

REPERTORY

Boulez: *Notations* for piano (1945, unpublished), also orchestral version (1978–, unpublished).
—— *Trois psalmodies* for piano (1945, unpublished).
—— Sonatina for flute and piano (1946, Amphion). Adès 16005, Delta SDEL 18005, EMI C 061 268950, RCA VICS 2321, Véga C 30 A 139, VSM C 061 10914, Wergo 60052.
—— Piano Sonata no. 1 (1946, Amphion). CBS 72871, Guilde Internationale du Disque SMS 2590, Vox STGBY 637.
—— *Le visage nuptial* for soprano, contralto, two ondes martenot, piano and percussion (1946–7, unpublished), revised for soprano, contralto, women's chorus and orchestra (1951–2, Heugel).
—— Piano Sonata no. 2 (1947–8, Heugel, Mercury). DGG 2530 050, DGG 2530 803, Finnadar SR 9004, Véga C 30 A 309 (omits finale).
—— *Le soleil des eaux* for soprano, tenor, bass and orchestra (1948, unpublished), revised for soprano, tenor, bass, chorus and orchestra (1958, Heugel), further revised for soprano, chorus and orchestra (1965, Heugel). Argo ZRG 756, HMV ASD 639 (both 1958 version).
—— *Livre pour quatuor* for string quartet (1948–9, Heugel, movements IV and VI unpublished), recomposed as *Livre pour cordes* for string orchestra (1968–, unpublished). CBS 73191 (orchestral version, movement I), Erato STU 70580 (quartet version, movements I, III and V), Mainstream MS 5009 (quartet version, movements I, II and V).
Martinet: *Orphée* for orchestra (1944–5, Heugel).
—— *Promethée: fragments symphoniques* for orchestra (1947, unpublished), revised (1965, Heugel). Barclay 995 030 (1965 version).
—— Six Songs for chorus and orchestra (1948, Heugel).
—— Seven Poems of René Char for four voices and orchestra (1951–2, Heugel).

Messiaen: *Turangalîla-symphonie* for orchestra (1946–8, Durand). EMI SLS 5117, RCA SB 6761–2.
Nigg: *Timour* for orchestra (1944, unpublished).
—— Variations for piano and ten instruments (1947, Chant du Monde).
—— *Quatre mélodies* for voice and piano (1948, Jobert).
—— *Le fusillé inconnu* for two voices and orchestra (1949, unpublished).
Schaeffer: *Etude aux casseroles, Etude aux chemins de fer, Etude au piano II, Etude aux tourniquets* and *Etude violette,* all on disc (1948). Philips 6521 021.
Schaeffer and Henry: *Symphonie pour un homme seul* on disc (1949–50). Ducretet-Thomson DUC 9, London DTL 93121.

2 New York, 1948–50

It is a curious coincidence of musical history that, at the very time when Boulez was expanding the possibilities of serialism in his Second Piano Sonata and *Livre pour quatuor,* Milton Babbitt was undertaking superficially similar but in essence quite different extensions of the serial principle. In 'Propositions' Boulez had confirmed that his reason for seeking rhythmic complexity was 'to achieve a correspondence between compositional methods as varied as those of serialism and a rhythmic element which also has a perfect "atonality" '.[1] What he did not know was that Babbitt had already developed a subtle kind of rhythmic serialism. He may later have learned of Babbitt's work from John Cage, who visited Paris in 1949 and who had been fascinated by Babbitt's Composition for Four Instruments, though on that occasion he was very much more interested by what Cage himself had achieved.[2]

CAGE AND RHYTHMIC STRUCTURING

The principal score of his own that Cage took to Paris was his *Sonatas and Interludes* for prepared piano (1946–8), the largest work in which he adjusted the timbres of the piano by inserting foreign objects between the strings: the score includes a 'table of preparations' which gives instructions for the placing of screws, nuts, bolts and pieces of plastic and rubber to alter the sounds of 45 notes. Preparation of the piano, which Cage had introduced in 1940 with his *Bacchanale,* thus offers the composer the opportunity to work with and transform his sound material in a very direct manner, inviting an empirical mode of working more commonly associated with the electronic medium. Indeed, the prepared piano was perhaps consciously developed as a home-made substitute for the synthesizer of the future. In 1937 Cage had expressed his optimistic view of the potential electronic evolution of music,[3] and in 1942 he was more specific: 'Many musicians', he wrote, 'the writer included, have dreamed of compact technological boxes, inside which all audible sounds, including noise, would be ready to come forth at the command of the composer'.[4] He went on in this article to speak of the work he had recently done at a Chicago radio station, using electrical gadgets (buzzers, amplified coils of wire, a radio and a gramophone) in various pieces intended for broadcast as disc recordings.

If in their experimental approach to sound the *Sonatas and Interludes* relate to Cage's electronic essays, they connect also with his earlier works for his own percussion orchestra, notably the *First Construction (in Metal)* for six players (1939), since the prepared piano is effectively a one-man percussion ensemble, with defined pitches largely replaced by noises and complex sounds. But in works of both kinds, those for prepared piano and those for percussion, his concentration on percussive sonorities was not just a matter of taste but also the result of a need to obscure harmonic functions in order to emphasize rhythmic relationships. His 'Defense of Satie',[5] a lecture delivered in the summer of 1948, soon after the completion of the *Sonatas and Interludes,* charges Beethoven with the 'error' of defining structure by means of harmony, whereas Satie and Webern had correctly used durations: 'There can be no right making of music', he concludes, 'that does not structure itself from the very roots of sound and silence – lengths of time'.[6] He then insists that the purpose of a musical composition is 'to bring into co-being elements paradoxical by nature, to bring into one situation elements that can be and ought to be agreed upon – that is, Law elements – together with elements that cannot and ought not to be agreed upon – that is, Freedom elements – these two ornamented by other elements, which may lend support to one or the other of the two fundamental and opposed elements, the whole forming thereby an organic entity'.[7]

In the *Sonatas and Interludes* he provided the most comprehensive demonstration of this combining of 'Law' and 'Freedom' in rhythmic structure. Each of the 16 sonatas and four interludes is based on a number sequence which defines the durational proportions of the subsections and often appears also in smaller rhythmic units. In the case of Sonata I, for instance, the sequence is 4–1–3–4–1–3–4–2–4–2, and the movement, like all the sonatas, falls into two repeated sections which correspond in length to its sequence, the first being of four, one and three double-dotted semibreves, the second of four and two double-dotted semibreves. The choice of duration unit is also dictated by the sequence, for the latter sums to 28 and the double-dotted semibreve can be divided into 28 semiquavers; it is thus possible for the sequence to unfold within any subsection. For example, the first subsection, with a length of four double-dotted semibreves, can equally be considered as containing 28 crotchet units, and so can express the sequence as shown in Example 5, which shows only the rhythm of this subsection. Here, it

Ex. 5

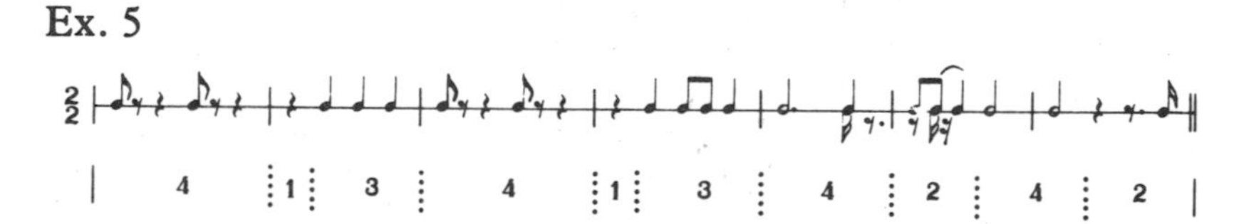

is clear, the proportions are to some degree masked by what one must take to be 'Freedom elements', though it is noteworthy that those elements themselves often state fragments of the 'Law' in miniature: the ratio 1:3, for instance, features in bars 1, 3, 5 and 6 as well as in its rightful places at bars 2 and 4.

The use of number sequences to determine rhythmic structures, which Cage had introduced in the *First Construction*, continued in the works that immediately followed the *Sonatas and Interludes*, including the String Quartet in Four Parts (1949–50) and the Concerto for prepared piano and orchestra (1950–51). In the former the sequence sets the relations of length among the four movements, which form a seasonal cycle from summer to spring. It is to these movements that the title alludes and not to the work's polyphonic nature, for Cage considers the music as 'a melodic line without accompaniment, which employs single tones, intervals, triads and aggregates requiring one or more of the instruments for their production.'[8] Thus the harmonies, reintroduced after a spate of works for largely percussive resources, are not to be interpreted as functional – and indeed the slow progress of unrelated chords defies an understanding in terms of harmonic consequence – but are rather single events, each chosen for its colour and caused to occupy the space allotted to it by the composer's numerical working. The string quartet thus becomes a kind of enlarged prepared piano, able to offer a different range of sonorities but similarly to be used as a reservoir of unconnected sounds. Cage pursues this mode of composition in writing for an orchestra of 22 soloists in the concerto, the players again contributing to a monorhythmic line of detached sound events.

As Cage recognized, his use of fixed-proportion rhythmic structures owed much to examples from the East, and indeed the *Sonatas and Interludes* irresistibly recall, in colour as much as in rhythmic style, the gamelan music of Bali, which the work of Colin McPhee would surely have drawn to his attention. At the same time the composition has deeper links with the orient, having been written during the period when Cage has said he 'first became seriously aware of Oriental philosophy'.[9] After reading the works of Amanda K. Coomaraswamy he determined in the *Sonatas and Interludes* 'to attempt the expression in music of the "permanent emotions" of Indian tradition: the heroic, the erotic, the wondrous, the mirthful, sorrow, fear, anger, the odious, and their common tendency toward tranquility';[10] and in the String Quartet he was stimulated by Eastern associations of summer with preservation, autumn with destruction, winter with peace and spring with creation.

For the moment Cage's allegiance to Eastern thought went along with a continuing adherence to elaborate pre-compositional schemes, and in particular to squared charts setting out the durational relationships to be employed in a work. Boulez was especially impressed by this innovation, as also by his American colleague's invention of new sonorities and his handling of complex sounds as units, which offered a pitch analogue for his cellular rhythmic technique. 'The direction of John Cage's research', he was to write in 1952, 'is too close to our own for us not to take account of it.'[11] But by that time, when Boulez had made the breakthrough into total serialism, Cage's retreat from Western rhetoric, to be observed progressively in the *Sonatas and Interludes,* the String Quartet and the Concerto for prepared piano, had set him on a very different path.

BABBITT AND GENERALIZED SERIALISM

Though Schoenberg had been active as a teacher in California since 1934, numbering Cage among his first American pupils, serialism did not find wide favour among composers in the U.S.A. until after World War II. It was then that Babbitt composed his first published works, which 'were concerned with embodying the extensions, generalisations, and fusions of certain techniques contained in the music of Schoenberg, Webern and Berg, and above all with applying the pitch operations of the twelve-tone system to non-pitch elements: durational rhythm, dynamics, phrase rhythm, timbre, and register, in such a manner as to preserve the most significant properties associated with these operations in the pitch domain when they are applied in these other domains'.[12] And that final clause, implying a search for congruence among the organizational means used for the different parameters rather than for separation or conflict, draws attention to the deep division between Babbitt and Boulez.

That division may be illustrated with reference to Babbitt's Three Compositions for Piano (1947–8), his earliest acknowledged work and one in which the techniques of rhythmic serialism differ fundamentally from those that Boulez developed from Messiaen's 'chromatic scale' of durations. Example 6 shows the opening of the first Composition, which has been analysed by George Perle.[13] The serial forms have here been marked in accordance with the following convention: P^0 = the prime form beginning on C (P^1 = that beginning on C sharp, etc), R^0 = the retrograde form ending on C,

Ex. 6

I^0 = the inverted form beginning on C, and RI^0 = the retrograde inversion ending on C.

Babbitt characteristically bases his pitch organization on bringing together fractions of serial forms to produce 'aggregates', or collections of all 12 pitch classes. In this case the fractions are simply hexachords, and it is easy to see how in each bar a pair of hexachords from different serial forms combine to create an aggregate. The principle in operation here, developed from Schoenberg's use of hexachords in complementary relationships, is that of 'combinatoriality', specifically of hexachordal combinatoriality. A 12-note set exhibits this property if one of its hexachords may be combined with a hexachord from another form of the same set to produce an aggregate (clearly, any prime form of any set will always be combinatorial with a particular retrograde form, and any inversion with a particular retrograde inversion; the possibilities are extended when a prime form is combinatorial with an inversion or retrograde inversion). The set chosen for the Three Compositions is particularly suited to combinatorial use, since a given serial form is hexachordally combinatorial with a transposition (the relationship of bars 1–2), an inversion (bars 3–4), a retrograde form (bars 5–6) and a retrograde inversion (bars 7–8). A set of this kind is said to be 'all-combinatorial', and it provides a rich network of relationships which the composer may utilize in associating serial forms so as to ensure a perpetual circulation of the chromatic total and to achieve, as here, a density of correspondence that does not depend on thematic relations.

Not only does the combinatorial property suggest which serial forms may be superposed; it also provides a clue for linear linking. In Example 6, for instance, each hand proceeds from one serial form to another in accordance with a combinatorial relationship: the second hexachord of P^4 forms an aggregate with the first of R^{10} (right hand, bars 2–3) and so on. There thus emerge what Babbitt refers to as 'secondary sets',[14] formed when one hexachord from a particular serial form is joined to a complementary hexachord from another. In this case the secondary sets are not emphasized, but in many later works they take on functional importance.

Example 6 also displays the use of non-pitch parameters to elucidate and mesh with the pitch organization according to Babbitt's stated principles. Four dynamic levels are associated with the four varieties of serial form – *mp* with the prime, *mf* with the retrograde, *f* with the inversion and *p* with the retrograde inversion – and these associations are retained throughout the development that follows (they are 'transposed' down by two degrees to ***pp, p, mp*** and ***ppp*** respectively in the eight bars which symmetrically close the piece). The organization of rhythm also proceeds in step with that of pitch. Babbitt chooses a basic set of 5–1–4–2, which may be interpreted in terms of duration (crotchet tied to semiquaver, semiquaver, crotchet, quaver) or may alternatively, since it sums to 12, be projected in the numbers of serial notes gathered together in bundles. The latter is the method adopted in Example 6, where the prime form of the rhythmic set occurs with the prime form of the pitch set (bars 1–2) and the rhythmic retrograde (2–4–1–5) with the pitch retrograde (right hand, bars 3–4, and left hand, bars 7–8). It may be difficult to accept the notion of rhythmic inversion, but in fact the process of intervallic inversion does provide a model for a rhythmic counterpart. If the pitches of a series are numbered according to their intervallic distances above C in semitones (e.g. C–D–A flat– . . . becomes 0–2–8– . . .) then it will be found that inversion involves complementing these numbers to 12 (C–B flat–E– . . . being equivalent to 12 [i.e. 0]–10–4– . . .). Thus, by a similar process of complementation, the set 5–1–4–2 may be inverted to yield 1–5–2–4, with a corresponding retrograde inversion of 4–2–5–1. As may be seen in Example 6, these are the rhythmic sets given to the inversion and retrograde inversion forms of the pitch set.

That eight bars of music may demonstrate so much organization is some measure of Babbitt's ability to make everything in his compositions serve a constructive function. A further central element in his technical repertory is to be found in the second of the Three Compositions for Piano: the use of 'derived sets'. Following the example of such works of Webern as the Concerto op. 24, he makes use of sets containing internal symmetries and derived from a parent by proliferation from a single fragment. Example 7*a* shows the form RI^{11} of the set of Composition I, a form whose first trichord can, by processes of retrograding, inversion and retrograde inversion, give rise to a derived set (Example 7*b*) which is presented in the right hand at the opening of Composition II (Example 7*c*). With derived sets the composer is thus able to explore systematically different harmonic areas contained within the original set: as Composition II proceeds it unfolds and develops derived sets obtained from each trichord of the parent series in turn.

Ex. 7

The techniques of the Three Compositions for Piano – those of rhythmic serialism, combinatoriality, secondary sets, derived sets and so on – are pursued in the Composition for Four Instruments (1948), the Composition for Twelve Instruments (1948) and the Composition for Viola and Piano (1950), each again with a title whose implications of 'abstractness and "formalism"' Babbitt has declared himself happy to accept.[15] The Composition for Twelve Instruments displays a rigorously serial application of the 'chromatic scale' of durations, which Babbitt would appear to have invented quite independently of Messiaen's *Turangalîla-symphonie*. His duration series is an arrangement of the values from one semiquaver to 12 (i.e. a dotted minim), and he transforms this series by the usual operations of transposition (i.e. increase of all values by the same unit, with the difference of a dotted minim regarded as the duration 'octave', so that minim plus minim, for instance, becomes crotchet), retrograding and inversion (i.e. complementation to the 'octave' value in an exactly similar manner to that adopted with the rhythmic set in the first of the Three Compositions for Piano). But the deployment of rhythmic serial forms is here, unusually for Babbitt, quite independent of the pitch organization; relation remains at the most basic level, in that the duration set is a 'translation' of the pitch set obtained by interpreting pitch-class numbers (C = 0, C sharp = 1, etc.) as duration values.

Example 8 shows a statement of the duration set in the Composition for Twelve Instruments (12–1–4–9–5–8–3–10–2–11–6–7 semiquavers, the durations often being completed by rests). Plainly this is not allied with a statement of the pitch set: there are, for instance, three appearances of A flat, including two in immediate succession. In fact the pitch organization of the first part of the work is based on a highly complex scheme of combinatorial relations

Ex. 8

among 12 serial forms, each permanently assigned to one of the instruments taking part, while the second part concerns itself with derived sets. Not only does the rhythmic organization make no use of derived sets, but it proceeds along its own much simpler combinatorial lines.[16] However, Babbitt was not long to remain content with rhythmic manipulations which were at loggerheads with pitch structures and which, in the case of the Composition for Twelve Instruments, also proved self-obscuring: there is, for instance, no way for the ear to disentangle two simultaneous or overlapping statements of different forms of the duration set, and the concept of a 'duration interval' is also somewhat problematic. During the next decade he was to develop new methods by which organizations of pitch and rhythm could be integrated without being, as in the first Composition for Piano, wholly imitative of each other.

OTHER 12-NOTE COMPOSERS IN AMERICA

As has already been remarked, Babbitt's early compositions came at a time when there was a rapid growth of interest in 12-note methods among composers in the U.S.A. Stravinsky began in *Orpheus* (1947) his gradual approach to serialism,[17] while Copland moved much more quickly in the same direction with his Piano Quartet (1950). Carter journeyed from neo-classicism to his dense atonal style along a path marked by the Piano Sonata (1945–6), the Cello Sonata (1948) and the First String Quartet (1951), and another Boulanger pupil, Roger Sessions, showed a not dissimilar development in such works as his Second String Quartet (1951) and Violin Sonata (1953), of which the latter was his first 12-note serial composition. Stefan Wolpe at the same time was gaining his clear though indirect motivic integration, atonal but not serial, in the *Enactments* for three pianos

(1950–53) and the Quartet for trumpet, tenor saxophone, percussion and piano (1950).

A closer comparison with Babbitt's development is suggested by that of George Perle, who, like Babbitt, had begun in 1939 to work his way towards a pre-compositional system of flexibility and range. Perle, however, found the most significant clues not in Schoenberg and Webern but in Berg and Bartók, and his 'twelve-tone modal system' codifies procedures of harmonic liaison which he discerned in their works. To quote his pupil Paul Lansky: 'Basically this system creates a hierarchy among the notes of the chromatic scale so that they are all referentially related to one or two pitches which then function as a tonic note or chord in tonality. The system similarly creates a hierarchy among intervals and finally among larger collections of notes, "chords". The main debt of his system to the 12-tone system lies in its use of an ordered set to structure its relations. This set, however, does not necessarily control linear successions in the same way that a 12-tone set does'.[18]

Perle's first compositions to use this system included his Third and Fourth String Quartets, which were exactly contemporary with Babbitt's Three Compositions for Piano. In subsequent works he has developed his system but not changed it fundamentally; he has also used serial methods on occasion, as well as a freer technique based on the procedures of serialism and 12-tone modality. Another of his innovations was that of 'metric modulation', by which changes of tempo are geared to changes of metre secured by re-grouping constant durations. This technique is more usually associated with the music of Blacher and especially Carter, but Perle's invention of it was apparently independent. Twelve-tone modality and metric modulation together are responsible for a precise yet fluid style well displayed in Perle's Fifth Quartet (1960, revised 1967), where the harmony, rich in 3rds, is controlled by the system in such a way that old chords are brought to hover in new relationships of impressive coherence, while metric modulation provides for a cogent handling of irregular beats.

Something more than a web of influence is suggested by the efforts of Babbitt, Perle and others in America in the late 1940s to find thoroughly systematic means of composition; it is tempting to see rather the action of a general will to construct on the basis of demonstrable principles. And the same will was to be observed at work in Europe, however different the kinds of music it stimulated.

REPERTORY

Babbitt: Three Compositions for Piano (1947–8, Boelke-Bomart).
—— Composition for Four Instruments [flute, clarinet, violin, cello] (1948, New Music). CRI 138.
—— Composition for Twelve Instruments [1.1.1.1–1.1.0.0–celesta, harp–1.0.1.1.1] (1948, Associated). Son Nova 1.
—— Composition for Viola and Piano (1950, Peters). CRI 138.
Cage: *Sonatas and Interludes* for prepared piano (1946–8, Peters). CRI 199, Decca HEAD 9.
—— String Quartet in Four Parts (1949–50, Peters). Columbia MS 4495, DGG 2530 735.
—— Concerto for prepared piano and orchestra (1950–51, Peters). Nonesuch H 71202.
Perle: String Quartet no. 3 (1947).
—— String Quartet no. 4 (1948).
—— String Quartet no. 5 (1960, revised 1967, Presser). Nonesuch H 71280.

3 Darmstadt/Paris, 1951–2

On 13 July 1951, in Los Angeles, Arnold Schoenberg died. As far as Boulez was concerned, he had already been displaced by Webern as the father of serial thought. His 'preclassical and classical forms' represented 'the most perfect *misdirection* that could have been offered in contemporary music',[1] and Webern alone had recognized the need to 'deduce the structure of a work from contrapuntal functions and from them alone'.[2] Given that Boulez draws attention in this context to Webern's Symphony op. 21, Quartet op. 22, Concerto op. 24, Piano Variations op. 27 and String Quartet op. 28, one may suppose that he had been particularly impressed by the close relation existing between the serial method, which implies repeated variation of the same shape, and the variation forms that Webern favoured: there is complete accord, in Boulez's terms, between the 'material' and the 'architecture'. In any event, the later instrumental works of Webern, so easily analysed as serial constructions, quickly became models for the European avant garde, though Boulez himself had a higher regard for the more hidden and supple forms of the Second Cantata op. 31.

At a time when performances of Webern were rare and often poor, so that the visual appearance of his scores carried more weight than the actual sound of his music, it was not difficult to regard him as an objective constructor of music artefacts. His fragile gestures could be shorn of their expressive load and viewed simply as struts in the musical engineering, while his continuing dependence on thematic working could be ignored in favour of his more obvious attention to motivic correspondence. Furthermore, the simplicity of his structures made it easy to join the ranks of 'post-Webernians', where to have become a 'post-Schoenbergian' might have been more hazardous and demanding. The elevation of Webern provided a clear blueprint for the future.

Exactly what that future might hold was suggested by Boulez in his notorious obituary 'Schönberg is Dead',[3] in which, after again roundly condemning the late master's defunct forms and other evidence of backsliding, he went on to propose that: 'Perhaps we could enlarge the field of twelve tone composition to include other intervals than the semitone: micro-intervals, irregular intervals, complex sounds'.[4] This was an area in which exploration had already begun. The mention of 'complex sounds' is a reference to the concept of 'aggregates' developed by Cage (though not, of course, used by him in a serial manner), while Boulez himself had applied serial procedures to quarter-tones in *Le visage nuptial* and had communicated his interest to Henri Pousseur, who reacted to his influence first with the Webernian *Trois chants sacrés* for soprano and string trio (1951) and then with *Prospections* for three pianos tuned at sixth-tone distances (1952). But the most pervasively influential thought was that which came next in Boulez's article: 'Perhaps', he wrote, 'the principle of the tone-row could be applied to the five elements of sound, viz., pitch, duration, tone-production, intensity, timbre'. Total serialism had become, if only for a short period, the most pressing necessity for composers of Boulez's generation, and it was in Darmstadt in July 1951, as Schoenberg lay dying on the other side of the Atlantic, that some of the crucial first steps were taken.

DARMSTADT RETROSPECT

The summer courses in composition at Darmstadt had been founded in 1946 by Wolfgang Steinecke, a young musicologist who recognized the need to acquaint his compatriots with the music and the ideas that had been under interdict during the Hitler years. At the first session the principal teacher was Fortner, then making his approach to serialism, and he brought with him his pupil Hans Werner Henze. During the next few years Henze was regularly at Darmstadt, where he was able to display his mastery of neo-classical gaiety and of the sweet-and-sour serialism preferred by Fortner, in which tonal materials are maintained in a serial milieu by adopting the technique of harmonic splitting, into tonal and complementary planes, opened up by Schoenberg in the third movement of his Suite op. 29. The works of Henze that were performed at Darmstadt between 1946 and 1950, including his first two symphonies and his attractive little cantata *Apollo et Hyacinthus,* established him as a composer who could adapt serialism to make music of crystalline poise or expressionist force, and for a time it seemed that his blend of the serial, the neo-classical and the Romantic might be more generally assumed as the consequence of the rediscovery of Schoenberg. The contemporary works of Bernd Alois Zimmermann, who also attended the Darmstadt courses at this time, show similar tendencies.

Hindemith's presence as leading figure in 1947 did little to disturb the current, nor did his replacement in 1948 by Leibowitz, whose recently published *Schönberg et son école*,[5] the first comprehensive study of the serial repertory in a language other than German, enshrined the Schoenbergian approach against which Boulez had reacted. It is hardly surprising that Boulez was not among the young French composers whom Leibowitz took with him to Darmstadt in the following years of 1949 and 1950, when works by Casanova, Martinet and Nigg were performed. In 1949 Messiaen was also present at Darmstadt, and it was there that he composed his *Mode de valeurs et d'intensités,* soon to have a powerful germinating effect on the younger generation at the summer courses.

But for the moment Darmstadt was dominated by the teaching of Leibowitz and the music of Schoenberg. Among the works introduced to Europe at Darmstadt were Schoenberg's *A Survivor from Warsaw* in 1950 and 'The Dance Around the Golden Calf' from *Moses und Aron* in 1951, both conducted by Hermann Scherchen. Scherchen also brought to Darmstadt in 1950 the two young Italians whom he had been instructing in 12-note methods, Luigi Nono and Bruno Maderna, and the former's *Variazioni canoniche* for orchestra, based on the series of *A Survivor from Warsaw,* was played. In 1951 Nono was again present, now joined by two younger men, Karel Goeyvaerts and Karlheinz Stockhausen. It was the meeting of these three, and their common enthusiasm for Messiaen's *Mode de valeurs,* that took the whole development of serial music in Europe into another phase.

DARMSTADT 1951

By the time Messiaen composed the *Mode de valeurs* his first Conservatoire pupils, those of the generation of Boulez and Nigg, had definitively established their allegiance to serialism. Speaking generally of his students, Messiaen has said that 'their questions and their attitude force me to investigations of which I would perhaps not have dreamed without them',[6] and nowhere is this more apparent than in the *Mode de valeurs*. He did not adopt serialism – as the title declares, the piece is, like all Messiaen's works, a modal composition – but he did supply something for which Boulez had been searching: the means for handling non-pitch parameters in a permutational manner analogous to that of pitch serialism.

As has been noted, Messiaen had introduced 'chromatic scales' of durations in his *Turangalîla-symphonie*, but it was not until 1949, in a section of *Cantéyodjayâ* and then in the whole of the *Mode de valeurs*, that he used such scales exclusively. In the preface to the *Mode de valeurs* he shows how the piece is composed with a pitch mode in three divisions, each of which is an ordering of the chromatic scale. Each division is also assigned a mode of 12 'chromatic' durations: from demisemiquaver to dotted crotchet in the first, from semiquaver to dotted minim in the second, and from quaver to dotted semibreve in the third. In addition, modes of seven dynamic levels and seven attacks are freely allotted, and each pitch keeps the same

Ex. 9

Modéré

duration, dynamic and attack throughout the piece. Example 9, from the opening of the work, indicates how the three divisions are used in the composition of a three-part counterpoint which continues all through the piece. Richard Toop has demonstrated that the piece tends to emphasize contiguous fragments of the modal divisions, but that in no sense is the organization serial: decisions about the ordering of the fragments are based much more on the wish to avoid octaves and other overt suggestions of tonality.[7]

In Messiaen's oeuvre the *Mode de valeurs* marked an extreme point of pre-compositional systematization. He has used modes of 'chromatic' durations in later works, notably the piano piece *Ile de feu II* (1950), the *Livre d'orgue* (1951), *La chouette hulotte* from the piano cycle *Catalogue d'oiseaux* (1956–8) and the orchestral *Chronochromie* (1960), but in all these cases there are other materials which counteract the purity of the schematic ordering, and new techniques to disturb the fixity of events. In *Ile de feu II* he introduced rhythmic 'interversion', which was to be more fully developed in the *Livre d'orgue*. A basic duration series of 12 values is permuted by taking members successively from the centre; this generates the first 'interversion', and the second is obtained from the first by applying the same process of exchange, as shown below:

Original	12	11	10	9	8	7	6	5	4	3	2	1
Interversion 1	6	7	5	8	4	9	3	10	2	11	1	12
Interversion 2	3	9	10	4	2	8	11	5	1	7	12	6

The process can be continued until one reaches the tenth interversion, which reproduces the original series. In *Ile de feu II* the complete cycle of interversions is used, with an interleaving of less highly organized episodes.

Ile de feu II and the *Mode de valeurs* were collected within the *Quatre études de rythme*, of which Messiaen made a commercial recording, and it was in this form that the *Mode de valeurs* returned to Darmstadt in 1951. The young Stockhausen was immediately attracted by what he called a 'fantastic music of the stars',[8] a kind of music which soon became known as 'pointillist': 'Because', Stockhausen has said, 'we hear only single notes, which might almost exist for themselves alone, in a mosaic of sound; they exist among others in configurations which no longer destine them to become components of shapes which intermix and fuse in the traditional way; rather they are points amongst others, existing for themselves in complete freedom, and formulated individually in considerable isolation from each other'.[9] The choice of the word 'mosaic' here is interesting, for on his return from Darmstadt to Cologne Stockhausen began work on a piece with the title 'Mosaik', scored for high voice and piano.[10] This project was to give rise to his *Kreuzspiel* for oboe, bass clarinet, piano and three percussionists (1951).

As the above quotation makes clear, Messiaen's *Mode de valeurs* had not only opened to Stockhausen the means for a serial organization of rhythm, dynamics and timbre but had also demonstrated the possibility of music in which all vestiges of theme or motif had been dissolved (though in fact the head fragments of Messiaen's three divisions do recur quite frequently in the piece). Disinclined, however, to accept Messiaen's intuitive methods of construction, Stockhausen still had to find formal procedures to govern the assembly of series, and here Goeyvaerts was able to help. Goeyvaerts had studied with Messiaen in 1947–8, but apparently he had no knowledge of the *Mode de valeurs* before coming to Darmstadt in 1951, when he brought with him his opus 1, the Sonata for two pianos (1950–51).[11] The pointillist writing of this score must therefore be attributed to the influence of earlier Messiaen works, and even more so to the study of Webern's Piano Variations that Goeyvaerts had made in 1949–50. The latter work, though it certainly cannot be claimed as an example of total serial organization,[12] proved to contain valuable pointers. Its second movement, for example, uses only three dynamic values and five varieties of rhythmic cell; from this it was not too large a step to Geoyvaerts's use of seven duration values, seven modes of attack and four dynamic levels in the middle two movements of his sonata (the outer two movements, planned to contrast with the rationality within, are counterpoints of irrational cells derived more directly from Messiaen).

But the more striking innovation of the Goeyvaerts sonata, certainly as far as Stockhausen was concerned, was its structural use of register, and this too had its roots in Webern's Piano Variations and in Messiaen (the 'Regard de l'onction terrible' from the *Vingt regards sur l'Enfant Jésus*). Example 10 shows a passage from the first movement of the Webern Piano Variations where palindromic perfection is distorted by the inversion of the two-note chords in the first and third figures and by registral displacement, the second figure moving up an octave and the first down two octaves. In the central movements of the Goeyvaerts sonata this technique is considerably

Ex. 10

developed. Initially a range of nearly five and a half octaves is available, gradually reducing to two and a half at the end of the second movement and then increasing again. Two pitches, A and D sharp, remain in the same registers throughout, but each time any other pitch recurs it is transposed up an octave, and if it goes over the registral ceiling it appears back at the bottom of the range. Goeyvaerts had thus introduced a formal process that did not, as in the early works of Boulez, depend even negatively on conventional models, nor, as in Messiaen's *Mode de valeurs,* on the composer's taste and judgment.

In retrospect it is perhaps surprising that Stockhausen should even have been interested in Goeyvaerts's compositional juggling, for little in his immediately preceding works suggests that he was ready ground for such sophisticated abstraction. Those early works, which include the *Drei Lieder* for contralto and small orchestra (1950) and the Sonatina for violin and piano (1951), show rather the predictable influences of Schoenberg, Berg, Bartók, Hindemith and jazz, admixed to form a style not so far from that of Henze at the time. The achievement of *Kreuzspiel* is therefore all the more remarkable, particularly since the work improves considerably on its models in Messiaen and Goeyvaerts.

The 'crossplay' of the title operates simultaneously on various different levels, affecting pitch classes, registers, durations, intensities and instrumentation.[13] Example 11 shows the opening of the first of the works's three main sections, enough to illustrate the first unfolding of the pitch series in the piano together with statements of 'chromatic' duration series in the piano, the tumbas and the tom-toms, all three measuring time in units of triplet semiquavers. The tumbas announce their series in repetitions of even values (2–3–4–5–6–12–1–7–8–9–10–11), while durations in the other two lines are measured from one attack to the next: the piano has the series 11–5–6–9–2–12–1–10–4–7–8–3 and the tom-toms

Ex. 11

2–8–7–4–11–1–12–3–9–6–5–10. Each of these series is subjected throughout the section to a cross-over process, and an exactly similar process is applied to the piano's pitch series. Example 12 shows the first six of the dozen 12-note statements contained in the section, with lines drawn to indicate the mechanisms of cross-over; the example also shows the register of each pitch, with '0' representing the lowest possible placement, '1' an octave above that, and so on. At the beginning of the section the pitch classes are evenly divided between the lowest possible register and the highest, and as the music proceeds they gradually exchange positions so that the six which had been at the top finish up at the bottom and vice versa, the registral movements being governed by the series 0–5–2–3–4–1–6 (this may be observed in Example 12). Furthermore, as the pitch classes traverse the middle of the pitch range, so they are taken over by the wind instruments: notes circled in Example 12 are played by the oboe or the bass clarinet and not by the piano. Thus around the centre of the section most notes are assigned to the wind (in the sixth serial statement the piano is left only with the two pitch classes remaining at registral extremities), while at each end the piano predominates.

In the second section the processes of registral and instrumental cross-over are turned inside-out, so that the music starts at the

Ex. 12

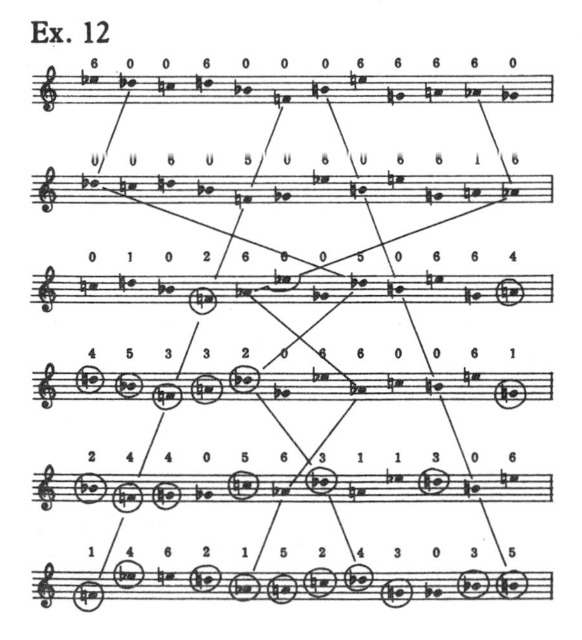

woodwind centre, moves out to the extremes of the keyboard, and then returns, though there is the complication of an additional process playing itself out in trichords in the piano. The third section combines the other two: piano and woodwind provide a retrograde of the convergent-divergent process of the first section, and the piano additionally has a retrograde of the divergent-convergent process of the second section. In the pure symmetry of this scheme, as well as in its development of the cross-over idea, *Kreuzspiel* reveals its debt to Goeyvaerts, while the influence of Messiaen's *Mode de valeurs* is evident in the piano writing and in the attachment, within a given section, of each pitch class to a particular duration (though there are structural exceptions to this rule, such as the progressively increasing duration of C in the second section). Yet the work affirms itself as Stockhausen's not only in its perfect digestion of its models but also in its intriguing introduction of discrepancies. The musical processes unfolding in the pitched instruments are disturbed when one of their attacks coincides with one in the percussion. Stockhausen was perhaps concerned that there should be some connection between the purely rhythmic rotations of the latter and the pitch-rhythmic rotations of the former. In any event, he was to attempt in many subsequent works to find some common ground between pitched and unpitched instruments.

Apart from these purposeful deviations, *Kreuzspiel* presents itself as a streamlined display of musical order. It draws from serialism an entirely new way of composing and of listening, in which the series becomes a source of rules by which individual notes, not thematic units, are ordered and changed. To be sure, there are repetitions of shape which give a hint of motivic working, but the music insists on alteration, and in particular on the exchanges of 'crossplay', as its principle.

At the same time the work is remarkable for its absorption of influences from jazz and from exotic musical traditions, an absorption which the passing of time has made to seem more usual but hardly less accomplished. The instrumentation is suggestive more of an African or an Asian ensemble than a European one, and the rhythmic style, bringing irregular accents within a context of uniform pulsation, sometimes nears jazz, though never so overtly as the boogie-woogie slow movement of the Violin Sonatina which Stockhausen had completed only a few months earlier. This uniform pulsation, which arises inevitably from the superimposition of serial rhythms constructed from 'chromatic' durations (and is, of course, emphasized by the tumbas in the first section), was something that Stockhausen soon became anxious to avoid, but in *Kreuzspiel* it makes an important contribution to the smooth flow of the musical processes.

In the last two months of 1951, immediately after the composition of *Kreuzspiel,* Stockhausen went on to apply similar principles of construction not to isolated points but to whole melodic and harmonic units; the result was *Formel* for an orchestra of 12 wind, 12 strings and pitched percussion (vibraphone doubling glockenspiel, celesta, harp and piano). This brought him a commission to write an orchestral piece for the 1952 Donaueschingen Festival, and with the promise of a fee he set off for Paris in January 1952, there to study with Messiaen.

PARIS, 1952

In Paris Stockhausen decided that *Formel* was too thematic, a cul-de-sac, and so he retained for Donaueschingen only the two movements which followed it, giving these the title *Spiel.* Here he returned to pointillist techniques and added to the *Formel* orchestra a large array of unpitched percussion instruments, used in the first movement to provide an enormous range of attacks for the isolated notes which gradually come together in melodies (in this process, as in *Formel,* the vibraphone has a guiding role), and in the second to generate clouds of resonance out of which sustained points appear as droplets of condensation. This second movement, proceeding at a slow tempo, brings to mind his contemporary statement that the new 'through-organised' music he was writing demanded a kind of 'meditative' listening: 'One stays in the music', he wrote, 'one needs nothing before or after in order to perceive the individual now (the individual sound)'.[14] This was a view that he was to emphasize again more than a decade later, in connection with his *Momente,* but it should not lead one to suppose that he had renounced his interest in musical processes.

In another work of the same period, the *Schlagquartett* for piano and six timpani (later revised for three players), there is a continuous process of exchange analogous to those operating in *Kreuzspiel* and *Formel.* Two melodic voices set out from opposite ends of the piano keyboard and are led through cross-overs to finish in exchanged positions. The timpani, tuned to a whole-tone scale displaced from the piano's pitch system by a quarter-tone, offer a 'contrary sound space' into which notes can disappear, so that register exchange is combined with exchange of sound worlds.[15] Perhaps the clue to the seeming contradiction between Stockhausen's preference for unified processes and his insistence on non-sequential listening is to be found in what Toop, on the basis of a reading of his letters to Goeyvaerts, has described as his wish 'to attempt a musical image of Divine Perfection'.[16] Certainly the works from his Paris period, which include the orchestral *Punkte,* his first four piano pieces, the *Etüde* in *musique concrète* and the beginnings of *Kontra-Punkte* for ten instruments, evince a desire to control all musical parameters in parallel schemes.

In this Stockhausen found a colleague in Boulez, who was working on the first book of his *Structures* for two pianos. Like Stockhausen, he had been struck by the possibilities for a serialization of all the parameters opened up by Messiaen's *Mode de valeurs,* but his response, given that he would have known of the piece shortly after its composition in 1949, was not so immediate. Only in 1951 did he embark on an essay in total serialism, *Structures Ia,* deriving his pitch series from the first division of Messiaen's pitch mode. Example 13

Ex. 13

shows the part for piano I in the opening section of the piece, where a form of the pitch series is combined with one of the 'chromatic' duration series using, as in the *Mode de valeurs* first division, the demisemiquaver as basic unit. As Ligeti has shown in his comprehensive analysis of *Structures Ia*,[17] the duration series is obtained from the pitch series by reading pitch classes as numbers of demisemiquavers. Boulez numbers the pitch classes of Example 13 from one to 12 (E flat = 1, D = 2, A = 3, etc.) and keeps the same number equivalences for each transposition; for example, the series beginning D–C sharp–A flat . . . is numbered 2–8–4. . . . These number sequences are not only converted into durations but also used to govern dynamic levels and modes of attack. The sequences are arranged vertically following the order in the original series of Example 13 (i.e. with the sequence beginning with 1 on top, then the sequence beginning with 2, and so on) to produce a 12-by-12 square of numbers (Example 14). From the inversion of the series, together with its transpositions, a second square is obtained, and the two squares are read diagonally to give sequences of dynamic levels and attacks, there being 'chromatic' scales of each. In the case of dynamics, for instance, 1 is interpreted as *pppp* and 12 as *ffff*.

Ex. 14

1	2	3	4	5	6	7	8	9	10	11	12
2	8	4	5	6	11	1	9	12	3	7	10
3	4	1	2	8	9	10	5	6	7	12	11
4	5	2	8	9	12	3	6	11	1	10	7
5	6	8	9	12	10	4	11	7	2	3	1
6	11	9	12	10	3	5	7	1	8	4	2
7	1	10	3	4	5	11	2	8	12	6	9
8	9	5	6	11	7	2	12	10	4	1	3
9	12	6	11	7	1	8	10	3	5	2	4
10	3	7	1	2	8	12	4	5	11	9	6
11	7	12	10	3	4	6	1	2	9	5	8
12	10	11	7	1	2	9	3	4	6	8	5

Structures Ia is quite simply a presentation of the 48 forms of the pitch series, each with a different form of the duration series (not its translation: the prime forms of the pitch series, for example, are assigned the retrograde inversions of the duration series, and so pitch classes are not, as in the *Mode de valeurs* and as a rule in each major section of *Kreuzspiel*, always assigned the same duration). Each serial statement is defined by its dynamic level and its mode of attack, the distribution of these being governed by the serial principle already mentioned, and the 48 forms are laid out in 14 sections, the latter being distinguished by the number of simultaneous serial lines (from one to six), by the registral space occupied, and by tempo. This sectional form owes something to the exposition from the Sonata for two pianos (1951) by Michel Fano, who had become a pupil of Messiaen the previous year, and whose work is in some measure the 'missing link' between the *Mode de valeurs* and *Structures Ia*[18] (despite this promising start Fano was soon to turn from abstract composition to working for the cinema). However, the Fano sonata continues with serial polyphonic developments employing rhythmic cells rather as Boulez had done in his Second Sonata and *Livre pour quatuor,* though at a lower temperature of change. *Structures Ia,* by contrast, retains its purity as a total serial construction, and was made in a conscious attempt to reach to the edge of automatism. As Boulez has recalled: 'I wanted to give the first *Structure* . . . the title of a painting by Klee, "At the limit of fertile land". This painting is mainly constructed on horizontal lines with a few oblique ones, so that it is very restricted in its invention. The first *Structure* was quite consciously composed in an analogous way. . . . I wanted to use the potential of a given material to find out how far automatism in musical relationships would go, with individual invention appearing only in some very simple forms of disposition – in the matter of densities, for example'.[19]

What Boulez here terms 'individual invention' – applied after the serial framework has, as it were, invented itself – is responsible for the shape of *Structures Ia,* established by a palindromic arrangement of tempos, an increasing and increasingly stable density, and a variation in the fixing of pitch classes to particular registers.[20] Boulez had used this last technique in the Second Sonata, though to very different effect. There the prominence of particular notes had given a sense of desperate insistence, whereas in *Structures Ia* the impression is of something more abstract, of what Ligeti aptly calls 'knots' in the serial web.

Thus by contrast with *Kreuzspiel,* where large-scale formal processes are founded on an extension of the permutational principle inherent in the serial manipulation, *Structures Ia* has a form dictated by decisions beyond its serial ideas. This does not imply any value judgment, but it does point to important ways in which Stockhausen's approach differed from Boulez's: 'His objective', Stockhausen was to remark, 'is the work, mine rather the working'.[21] Both composers were concerned to generalize the serial principle, but for Stockhausen this entailed deriving single, through-composed forms from the basic material (*Spiel* was to be his last work in distinct movements until the mid-1970s), whereas Boulez was anxious to establish the foundations of a musical language in which formal decisions might still be left to the composer's taste.

The work that followed *Structures Ia* was *Polyphonie X,* written for the 1951 Donaueschingen Festival and scored for an ensemble of 11 wind instruments and seven strings, all treated as soloists. Its title indicates that it was an essay in that 'cross polyphony', that diagonal thinking which had captured Boulez's imagination from the first. As in Stockhausen's independently conceived *Kreuzspiel* and *Formel*, the crossing involves exchanges of musical characteristics between ideas from one point in time to another, as well as a reciprocity between melodic and harmonic composition (this Boulez derived from Webern, and in particular from the Second Cantata). Beyond that, *Polyphonie X* was again an exercise in total serial control, though of a different kind from that essayed in *Structures Ia*. The rhythmic organization, proceeding from that of the Second Sonata and the *Livre pour quatuor*, does not use 'chromatic' duration series but rather quasi-serial transformations of cells: there are seven basic cells and seven ways of altering them. Instrumentation, too, is ordered along serial lines, the ensemble being divided at any time into, again, seven groups. To judge from accounts and a few published fragments,[22] all this required a neglect of instrumentalists' capacities and of sonorous appeal, and the work was soon withdrawn.

Moving forward from what he has himself described as the 'theoretical exaggeration'[23] of *Polyphonie X*, Boulez returned to *Structures* and composed the third piece of book one. Perhaps he had been most dissatisfied with the mechanical rhythms of *Structures Ia*, the tendency to even pulsation which has been noted also in *Kreuzspiel* as a result of 'chromatic' durational serialism, for the principal innovation of *Structures Ic* is the introduction of new rhythmic techniques – sequences in regular values and others obtained from diagonal readings of the number squares – which give the piece a much livelier rhythmic feel. The music is still a bald presentation of serial forms, but these can now be handled with freer changes of density and rhythmic character, and a tripartite form can be established on the basis of an increasingly irregular flow.

Structures Ib, the last piece of the set to be composed, is much the longest and most complex. It is also a piece of much greater significance in Boulez's output, if not in the history of serial music, than the exceptional *Structures Ia*. Boulez returns to his earlier subtlety of serial usage, not employing complete 12-note statements but using the series to generate 'a certain texture of intervals' in which the minor 2nd and its octave transpositions have pride of place. He returns also to the flexibility of motion he had achieved in the late 1940s, reintroducing grace notes, irrational values and, as in the slow movement of the Second Sonata, pauses to isolate interpo-

Ex. 15

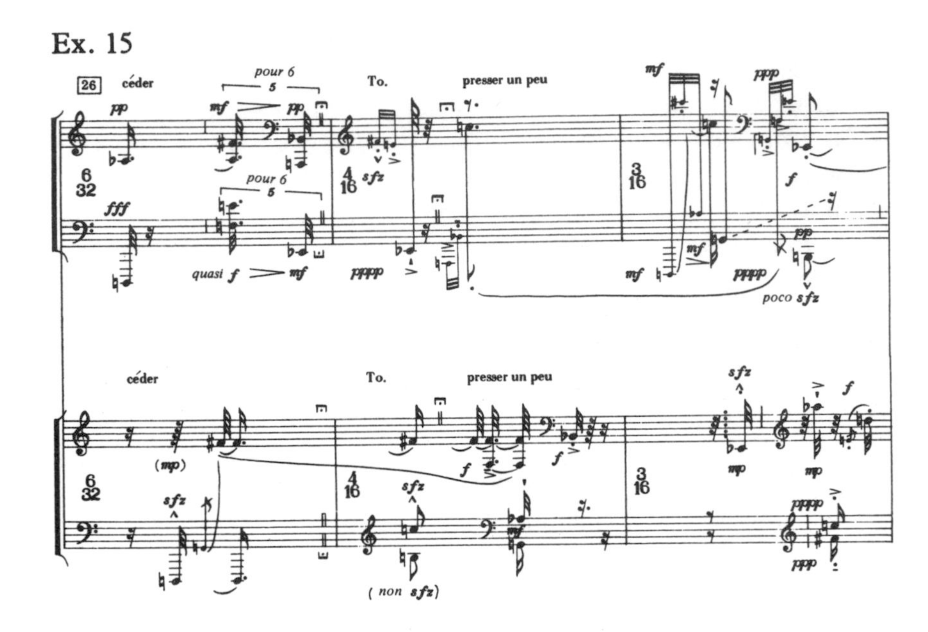

lated commentaries; Example 15, a not untypical passage, may suggest how much Boulez had resumed his former self within the discipline of total serialism. Formally, too, the piece takes up what had earlier been a characteristic method of balancing different kinds of musical motion. Short sections of two-part counterpoint in a strict fast tempo are alternated with longer and more convoluted passages allowing mobility within a slow tempo range (Example 15 illustrates the latter type). The contrasts of tempo are extreme, but there is a disparity between written and experienced tempo because the predominant note values also change widely. The opening 'Très rapide', for instance, sounds slower than the 'Lent' which follows it, because the prevailing crotchet, minim and semibreve values of the former are replaced by demisemiquavers. In a work of clear didactic intent, a work which was to help provide a blueprint for a new musical language, this may be taken as a dry demonstration of the interdependence of tempo and note value, though it can also be musically effective in a good performance.

The dualistic conception of *Structures Ib* is manifest not only in its converse time relationships and its two kinds of movement but also more generally in the interplay between, in Boulez's terms, technique and aesthetic. In *Structures Ia* he had been preoccupied with technique, to the extent that aesthetic qualities had had to be imposed secondarily. In *Structures Ib* he achieved a balance, taking the turbulent variety of his earlier music and, having passed through the experience of extreme compositional rigour, transforming it into creative virtuosity. By contrast, Stockhausen's works of the same period show no such dichotomy: the composer's aesthetic intention cannot be divorced from his technical aims, and the remaining dualisms of *Kreuzspiel*, its mutual exchanges and mirror forms, were soon to be eradicated in *Kontra-Punkte*.

Those various ways of generalizing serialism which Boulez had discovered in his *Structures*, in *Polyphonie X* and in the contemporary pair of *Etudes* in *musique concrète* were set out, though curiously without acknowledged reference to these works, in his article 'Eventuellement . . .',[24] which was published in a special issue of the *Revue Musicale* that came out in connection with a grand festival of contemporary art in Paris, 'L'oeuvre du XXe siècle' (Messiaen and Boulez played *Structures 1a* at one of the concerts). In this article Boulez insisted that 'every musician who has not felt – we do not say understood but indeed felt – the necessity of the serial language is USELESS'.[25] There could now be no mistaking the path forward.

But in Paris in 1952 there was another composer who stood apart from the urgent building of a totally serial language, who shared some of Boulez's premises but who worked with an unfashionable concern for musical statement in the grand manner: Jean Barraqué. He was also a pupil of Messiaen, and it was while under Messiaen's tutelage that he began his first acknowledged works, the Piano Sonata (1950–52) and *Séquence* for soprano and nine players (1950–54). The latter, completed before the sonata but thoroughly revised afterwards, shows at once the scale of Barraqué's thinking. Not only is it an unbroken movement of almost 20 minutes' duration, but the writing for both voice and ensemble has an ampleness quite without parallel in the contemporary works of Boulez or Stockhausen. And it is entirely characteristic of Barraqué that this ampleness should be so often and so unpredictably cut off, as if the music were striving for a Romantic rhetoric that the composer knows to be unattainable or else indefensible. The choice of poetic texts from Nietzsche, arranged by the composer for his purpose, makes it clear that the work's extraordinary blend of magnificence and impotence comes from a conviction that creative effort is at once irresistible and vain.

The Piano Sonata, again a single movement but twice as long as

Séquence, is also a work of density and desperation. It is apparent that Barraqué was impressed by Boulez's Second Sonata, which was published and first performed in the year when he began work on his own sonata: Example 16, from the opening, bears comparison with

Ex. 16

Example 2*a* from the Boulez work as an introductory statement of serial forms in rhythmic cells,[26] and Barraqué takes up Boulez's techniques of manipulating such cells. But where Boulez's rhythmic style tends either to obscure cellular shapes or to throw them against a steady pulse, Barraqué maintains an irregular momentum which allows cellular developments to be strong and cogent, and this is essential in a work where a compelling thrust is generated from the antagonisms among diverse tempos. Example 17 shows a typical passage in which the cells do not deny but rather establish, however uncertainly, a sense of progression, to which imitations of rhythmic or intervallic motif lend weight. Also noteworthy here is the registral locking of pitches, again a principle derived from the Boulez sonata, though here the fixing on a median range gives rise to a much more intense frustration.

The first part of the work is a quasi-sonata development of two kinds of music: a 'free' type, marked by a more virtuoso use of the keyboard, by the presence of quintuplet figures and by the absence of registral locking; and a 'strict' type in which register fixing goes along with a more sober musical growth (Example 17 comes, of course, from music of the latter type). The separate development and interpenetration of the two reaches a climax when the musical continuity is devastatingly interrupted by a sequence of progressively lengthening pauses. In the second part of the sonata the role of silence becomes ever larger as sections from the first part are brought back, reversed and greatly decelerated (the slow movement of Boulez's Second Sonata may have had an influence here). In the poetic but apt language of André Hodeir: 'Whole slabs of sound

Ex. 17

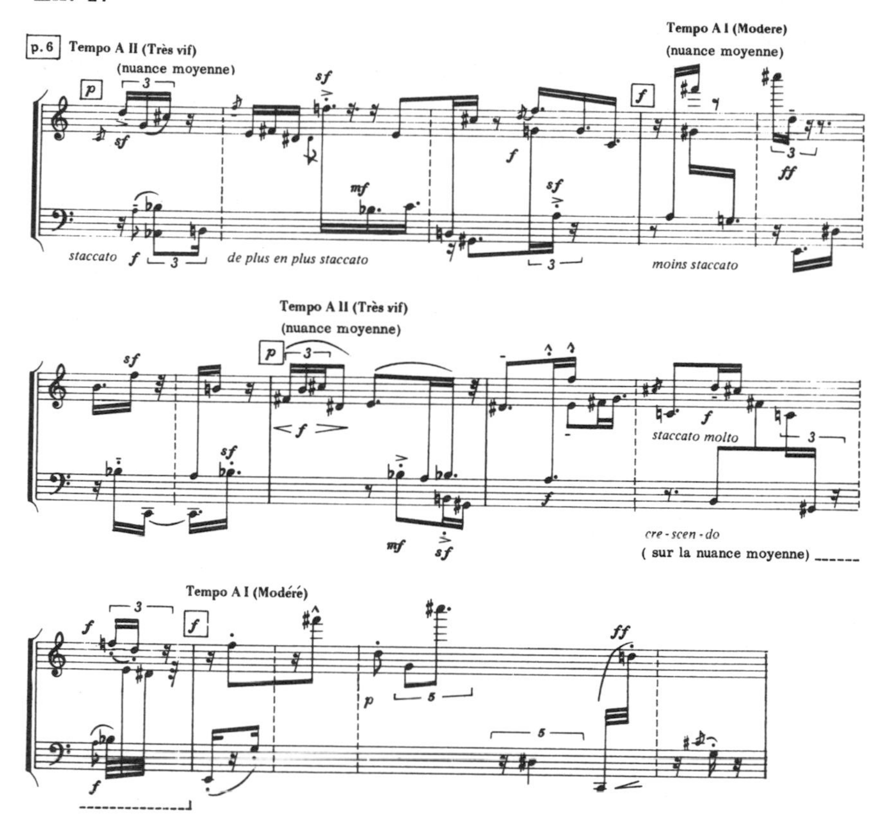

crumble and vanish in the silence which engulfs all. Only the 12 notes of the series remain, and these are plucked off, one by one'.[97] The sonata, while being a creative work of magisterial accomplishment, powerfully communicates its message of the futility of artistic effort, but in the climate of 1952 this was not a message that would be widely accepted.

DARMSTADT, 1952

When the avant garde reassembled at Darmstadt in the summer of 1952, Barraqué was not of the party, and indeed he was to play little part in the revolutions which were to emanate each year from the small German town. In that year of 1952 the courses were dominated no longer by Schoenberg but by Boulez and Stockhausen, with the première of *Kreuzspiel* and performances of Boulez's Second Sonata and tape *Etudes*. Among other new works were Maderna's *Musica su due dimensioni* for flute, cymbals and tape, which appears to have been the first piece to combine live with electronic resources, and Nono's *España en el corazon*, the first part of his *Epitaph auf Federico García Lorca*. The previous year, in his *Polifonica–monodia–ritmica* for five wind, piano and percussion, Nono had worked towards a serialization of duration and of percussion timbres; now he was proving that hermetic compositional devices need not stand in the way of an ecstatic lyricism which, in the Lorca epitaph, conveys by implication his impassioned socialist views (and it had surely not been by accident that he had chosen the series of Schoenberg's *A Survivor from Warsaw* as the basis for his *Variazioni canoniche* of 1950). Though usually associated with the human voice, as in the outer parts of the *Epitaph*, Nono's lyrical vehemence is equally powerful in the work's instrumental centrepiece, *Y su sangre ya viene cantando* for flute, strings and percussion, even if the movement does end with what Massimo Mila ungenerously but fairly describes as 'a slightly Hindemithian gigue'.[28] Unlike Nigg, Nono had found it possible, indeed necessary, to give expression to radical political views in a radical musical language. And, more generally, the avant garde had found at Darmstadt a home and a forum for the future development of that language.

REPERTORY

Barraqué: Piano Sonata (1950–52, Bruzzichelli). EMI EMSP 551, Unicorn UNS 263, Valois MB 952.

—— *Séquence* for soprano, violin, cello, piano, celesta, harp, vibraphone doubling xylophone and three percussionists (1950–54, Bruzzichelli). Valois MB 951, Véga C 30 A 180.

Boulez *Polyphonie X* for 18 instruments (1951, unpublished).

—— *Structures: premier livre* for two pianos (1951–2, Universal). Véga C 30 A 278, Vox 678 028, Wergo 60011.

Fano: Sonata for two pianos (1951, unpublished).

Goeyvaerts: Sonata for two pianos (1950–51, unpublished).

Henze: Symphony no. 1 (1947, revised 1963, Schott). DGG 139 203.

—— *Apollo et Hyacinthus* for contralto, flute, clarinet, bassoon, horn, harpsichord and string quartet (1949, Schott). L'Oiseau-Lyre DSLO 4.

—— Symphony no. 2 (1949, Schott). DGG 139 203.

Messiaen: *Cantéyodjayâ* for piano (1949, Universal). Argo ZRG 694, Véga C 30 A 139.

—— *Quatre études de rythme* for piano: 1 *Ile de feu I*, 2 *Mode de valeurs et d'intensités*, 3 *Neumes rythmiques*, 4 *Ile de feu II* (all 1949, Durand). Argo ZRG 694 (nos. 1, 3 and 4), Nonesuch H 71334, Columbia LFX 998–9.
—— *Messe de la pentecôte* for organ (1950, Leduc). Ducretet-Thomson DUC 6.
—— *Livre d'orgue* for organ (1951, Leduc). Ducretet-Thomson DUC 7.
Nono: *Variazioni canoniche* for orchestra (1950, unpublished).
—— *Polifonica–monodia–ritmica* for flute, two clarinets, alto saxophone, horn, piano and percussion (1951, Ars Viva). Time 8002.
—— *Epitaph auf Federico García Lorca:* 1 *España en el corazon* for soprano, baritone, chorus and ensemble (1952, Ars Viva), 2 *Y su sangre ya viene cantando* for flute, percussion, harp, celesta and string orchestra (1952, Ars Viva), 3 *Memento* for female speaker, speaking chorus, unison chorus and orchestra (1952–3, Ars Viva). RCA VICS 1313 (no. 2).
Pousseur: *Trois chants sacrés* for soprano and string trio (1951, Universal). Candide CE 31021, Vox STGBY 641.
—— *Prospections* for three pianos in sixth-tones (1952, unpublished).
Stockhausen: *Drei Lieder* for contralto and small orchestra (1950, Universal). DGG 2530 827.
—— Sonatina for violin and piano (1951, Universal). DGG 2530 827.
—— *Kreuzspiel* for oboe, bass clarinet, piano and three percussionists (1951, Universal). DGG 2530 443.
—— *Formel* for small orchestra (1951, Universal). DGG 2707 111
—— *Spiel* for orchestra (1952, Universal). DGG 2530 827.
—— *Schlagquartett* for piano and six timpani (1952, unpublished), revised as *Schlagtrio* (1974, Universal). DGG 2530 827.

4 New York, 1951–3

While his European colleagues were passing through the straits of total serialism in Darmstadt and Paris, Babbitt was developing the techniques he had introduced in his works of 1947–8. His compositions from the beginning of the 1950s, which include the August Stramm song cycle *Du* for soprano and piano (1951), marked further stages in the establishing of a genuine serial polyphony, where pitch relations, rhythms, instrumentation and contrapuntal layout all contribute to a coherent musical discourse. By contrast with such works as Boulez's *Structures* or Stockhausen's *Kreuzspiel,* which gain some of their dynamism from the shackling together of incompatible modes of organization, the contemporary works of Babbitt present themselves as essays towards a perfect community among the parameters, the composition becoming 'a multiple integrated set of determinate, particular relations among all its discernible components'.[1] As a teacher of composition at Princeton University, Babbitt was able to communicate to many younger composers his demanding standards of musical integration and continuity, but another group of musicians, gathering around Cage in New York, were taking very different attitudes.

CAGE AND THE ROAD TO SILENCE

The deceptive nature of the link between Cage and Boulez is nowhere more striking than in a comparison of the former's Concerto for prepared piano and chamber orchestra (1950–51) with the latter's first book of *Structures* (1951–2). Both composers made extensive use of number charts, but where Boulez saw them as an aid in total serial regulation, Cage took them as a means to attain non-intention. Both found themselves confronted by what Cage might have described as the complete dominion of 'Law' over 'Freedom', but where Boulez immediately attempted a new reconciliation, Cage was delighted by the possibility of removing personal creative wishes. 'I let the pianist express the opinion that music should be improvised or felt', he has said of the concerto's first movement, 'while the orchestra expressed only the chart, with no personal taste involved. In the second movement I made large concentric moves on the chart for both pianist and orchestra, with the idea of the pianist beginning to give up personal taste. The third movement had only one set of moves on the chart for both, and a lot of silences. . . . Until that time, my music had been based on the traditional idea that you had to say something. The charts gave me my first indication of the possibility of saying nothing'.[2]

The virtue, as opposed to the practicality, of saying nothing had been borne in upon Cage during the course of his studies of Zen philosophy with Daisetz T. Suzuki at Columbia University in the mid-1940s. Following his cultivation of quasi-oriental rhythms and timbres in many of his works since 1938 and his programmatic drawing on Indian thought in the *Sonatas and Interludes* and the String Quartet, he came now to take the more drastic step of raising the state of zero thought as his ideal, though that meant also denying all ideals. The need was for 'a musical composition the continuity of which is free of individual taste and memory (psychology) and also of the literature and "traditions" of the art'.[3] Though this statement suggests a similarity with Boulez's attitude in obliterating all received knowledge in *Structures Ia*, for Cage the aim was not to clear the decks for a new musical grammar but to dispense with audible structure and metaphorical connotation, to let sounds be just 'themselves'.

One of Cage's earliest and boldest attempts at purposeless music was his *Imaginary Landscape no. 4* for 12 radio receivers, first performed in the spring of 1951. In order to remove his own preferences from the composition he entrusted it to 'chance operations', using coin-tossing procedures derived from the ancient Chinese *I Ching*, of which an English edition had been published in New York the previous year.[4] Chance dictated the choices of wavelengths, durations and dynamic levels (expressed in terms of numbers on a volume control), all of which are notated with what is an ironic scrupulousness, given that the programmes received during a performance could not, of course, be foreseen. Thus the work is, in Cage's terms, not only 'indeterminate of composition', in that creative decisions are made by chance, but also 'indeterminate of performance', in that those decisions do little to prescribe what is heard.

In the autumn of the same year of 1951 Cage completed a big piano work, the four-volume *Music of Changes,* which is the *Art of Fugue* of chance operations. The music is still constructed of segments in fixed durational proportions, as in the *Sonatas and Interludes* and other earlier works, but changing tempos obscure the structural regularities. Moreover, the rhythm in small has no connection with the basic number sequence, for the strictly determined 'rhythmic structure' is merely the canvas for heterogeneous events placed upon it in accordance with the dictates of coin tosses and the *I Ching*.[5] Tempos, dynamic levels, durations, pitches and sound categories (single pitches, chords, complex linear events, noises and rests) were all chosen by chance to fill the space available, often with a degree of approximation, since the rhythmic notation is frequently inconsistent, and 'in such instances the performer is to apply his own discretion';[6] Example 18, from the opening of the first book, is typical.

Ex. 18

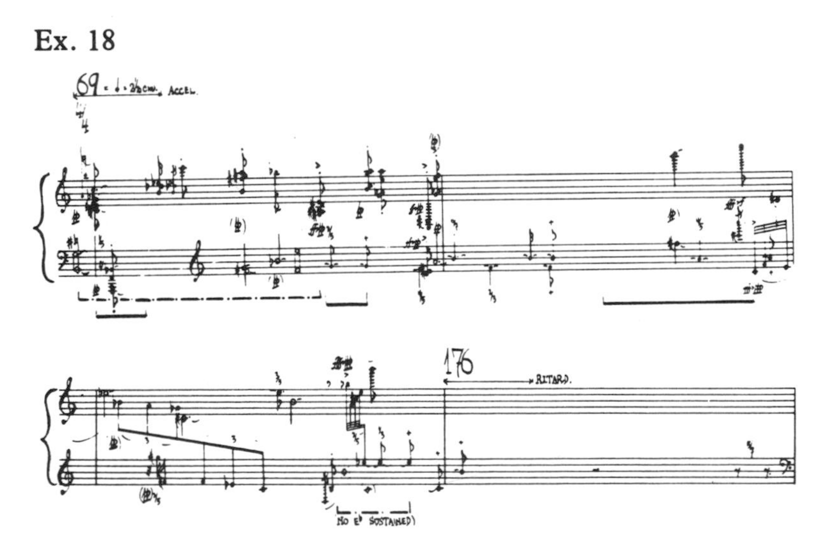

The *Music of Changes* might appear to embody the triumph of objective indeterminacy, particularly since its length, comparable with that of the Hammerklavier Sonata (or, indeed, the Second

Sonata of Boulez, with which it was bizarrely coupled at its first performance), would appear to suggest a breakthrough of some moment. However, despite all Cage's attempts to deprive the work of the benefit of his own inclinations, it is unmistakably his, and not only because nobody else would have embarked on the labour of chance-composing so lengthy a score. Its openness to an astonishing variety of sounds is characteristic, and so too is its cool unfolding, not troubled by passages of extreme activity or events of considerable complexity, for already in the String Quartet and the Concerto for prepared piano Cage had made the absence of rhetoric his own trademark.

He went on to apply *I Ching* methods to the electronic medium in *Imaginary Landscape no. 5* (1951–2) and *Williams Mix* (1952). Tape music was then in its infancy in the U.S.A.: Vladimir Ussachevsky, who taught at Columbia University, gave a demonstration of the new medium's potential in 1952, and he was soon joined in his endeavours by Otto Luening, with whom he created the pieces presented at the first concert of electronic music in America, given at the Museum of Modern Art in New York on 28 October 1953. Ussachevsky's *Sonic Contours*, composed like two of Schaeffer's early studies from piano recordings, and Luening's *Fantasy in Space*, which similarly extends the possibilities of the flute in unexpected ways, are representative of their efforts, which were eventually to lead to the foundation of the Columbia–Princeton Electronic Music Center in New York.

Cage differed from Ussachevsky and Luening in having no academic affiliation (he worked in the private studio of Louis and Bebe Barron, who were to be responsible in 1956 for the first electronic film music, that for *Forbidden Planet*); he differed from them also in his view of tape as a medium for collage rather than as a distorting mirror. Both *Imaginary Landscape no. 5* and *Williams Mix* provide details for the assembly of a tape, the former requiring any 42 source recordings, the latter bringing together broadly defined events in six categories: 'city sounds', 'country sounds', 'electronic sounds', 'manually produced sounds, including the literature of music', 'wind-produced sounds, including songs' and 'small sounds requiring amplification to be heard with the others.'[7] *Williams Mix* is thus, from the anarchist viewpoint which seems appropriate, a great advance on the *Music of Changes* in that the range of sounds allowed to be themselves is vastly extended (and with a typical kindly thought for 'small sounds'), though the rhythmic structure, presented as a daunting plan for splicing fragments into an eight-track recording, is still laid down.

Other works from the productive year of 1952 included the piano piece *Water Music,* which delicately allows space to the 'forbidden' sounds of octaves and other simple chords, and two works which initiated the series on which Cage was to be engaged for the next few years: Music for Piano 1, opening a cycle that would eventually extend to 84 pieces composed by chance operations, and *4′ 33″*, the first of several time-title works. But *4′ 33″* also stands at the end of a road, being one logical conclusion of Cage's quest to withdraw himself from his art and also a natural development from the yawning gulfs of the Concerto for prepared piano and the *Music of Changes:* it is silent. Though it has been claimed, reasonably enough, that *4′ 33″* consists not of silence but of the environmental sounds which an audience might otherwise ignore, and though the piece might be described as a prototype of music-theatre, in that the performer or performers (originally the work was intended for a pianist, but it has since been revised and made available to any forces) are asked to make it clear that a musical performance is in progress, these are incidental features. Cage's great achievement here, so far from creating an anonymous work, is to claim silence for his own. If one is not listening to anything else, and maybe even if one is, then one is listening to Cage.

THE CAGE GROUP

Morton Feldman has spoken of Cage's work as granting 'permission' for him and others to carry out their own experiments,[8] but it is perhaps equally the case that Cage was encouraged in his rapid evolution of 1951–2 by the support of the fellow artists with whom he was associated at the time. In David Tudor he found a pianist of sufficient stamina and control to tackle the Boulez sonatas he had brought back from Paris and to make the *Music of Changes* conceivable. In Jasper Johns and Robert Rauschenberg he found painters with similar concerns for the small currency of experience. And in Morton Feldman, Earle Brown and Christian Wolff he found younger composers to join him in trying to release music from intention, for although their paths were soon to diverge, they worked with many common aims at the beginning of the 1950s, and each of them was permanently marked by what was then achieved. Cage could remark with a certain pride of ownership that 'as contemporary music goes on changing in the way that I'm changing it what will be done is to more and more completely liberate sounds from abstract ideas about them and more and more exactly to let them be physically uniquely themselves',[9] for his views were being echoed in the statements and the compositions of his three colleagues. But their methods differed, and that was crucial, for as in Cage's work, the particular choice of method irrevocably branded each piece with the personality of its author, so that one is faced, paradoxically, with several quite distinctive kinds of anarchy.

Wolff tried to free himself from 'the direct and peremptory consequences of intention and effect'[10] by grossly simplifying the materials he used in his fully notated pieces. His Duo for Violins (1950) employs just three pitches within the minimal chromatic range of minor 2nd, and 'Serenade' for flute, clarinet and violin (1951), whose opening is shown in Example 19, has again only three

Ex. 19

pitches, this time forming two interlocking perfect 5ths. Having restricted his options, in the choice of durations as well as of pitches, Wolff paces around his tiny cell in a manner that excludes logical consequence: the choices exerted appear to be wholly arbitrary. Less extreme examples of this minimal style include *For Prepared Piano* (1951) and *Nine* for instrumental nonet (1951).

Feldman at this time was taking the almost opposite tack of disclaiming choice by allowing performers a great deal of freedom in the choice of pitches. His *Projections* and *Intersections*, two series dating from 1950–53, are 'graph' compositions in which events are rudimentarily notated on time squares, as in Example 20, which shows the opening of *Projection II*. Here he typically specifies only

Ex. 20

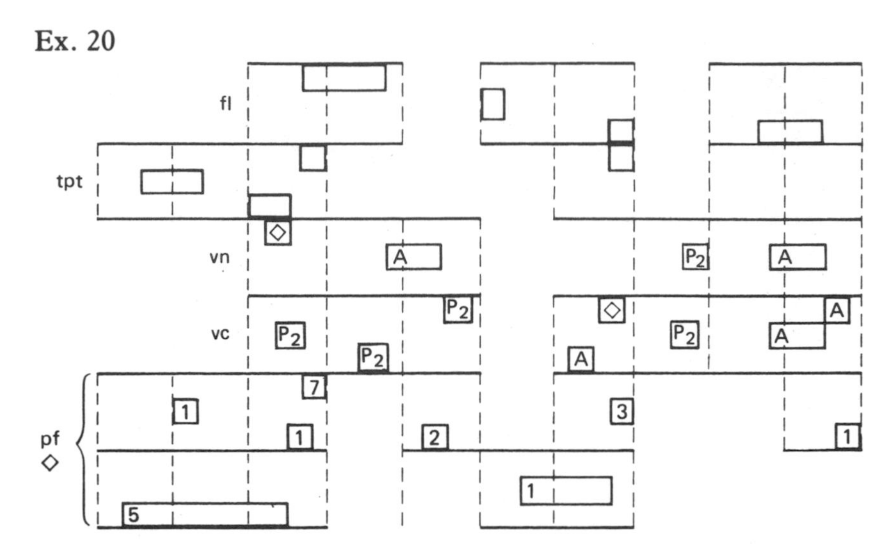

the register, the number of simultaneous sounds, the instrument and mode of production, the tempo and the duration: the music must begin with a five-note chord in the extreme bass of the piano, overlaid by a middle-range trumpet note, a note in the middle treble of the piano, a low trumpet note and a high violin harmonic, and so on. Feldman has spoken of his pieces as being distinguished by their 'weights'; each one is, as it were, a ground primed with a particular hue, characterized by the instrumentation, the density of events and the speed of their unfolding. Most usually, throughout Feldman's output, the density is low, the speed slow and the dynamic level soft, though the piano *Intersection III* has a rapidity of event exceeded only by the unrealized and probably unrealizable *Intersection* for tape.[11]

In other works of the same period, such as the cycle of *Extensions* or the *Structures* for string quartet, Feldman used conventional notation, which allowed him to achieve purposelessness by having delicate figures repeated over and over again. But the approach is essentially the same: as Cage has pointed out, 'Feldman's conventionally notated music is himself playing his graph music'.[12] And whether the score is in symbols or in squares, the performer is faced with a similarly high ideal of purity. 'I have yet to hear', the composer has said, 'an easy harmonic played beautifully and without vibrato with a slow bow on the cello. I have yet to hear a trombone player come in without too much attack, and hold it at the same level. . . . That's why these instruments are not dead for me: because as yet they have not served my function.'[13]

Feldman has also spoken of his work as 'paralleling a historical precedent in the visual arts',[14] but it is in the music of Brown that such parallels are clearest. Stimulated by 'the integral but unpredictable "floating" variations of a Calder mobile and the contextual rightness of Pollock's spontaneity and directness in relation to the material and his particular image of the work',[15] he created such compositions as the Music for Violin, Cello and Piano (1952) from units whose assembly was merely 'one static version of compositionally mobile elements'.[16] True mobility was to come in *Twenty-five Pages* (1953), where the sheets provided may be used in any order and by any number of pianists up to 25, so that there is no limit to the horizontal combinations and vertical superpositions of the composed material.

In *Twenty-five Pages* Brown employed the 'time notation', or prescription of duration by the length of a straight line on the staff instead of by a symbol, which he had introduced in the collection *Folio* (1952–3), a set of seven pieces exploring a whole range of indeterminate procedures. The piano piece *October 1952*, for instance, has no rests but only blank spaces separating the notes, the performer being free to set his own tempo, while *1953*, also for piano, uses 'time notation' (also known as 'proportional notation' or 'time-space notation') for the sounds as well. Another approach is taken in *November 1952*, written on a staff of 50 lines, where the conventional note symbols scattered over the page may be performed by an instrument or ensemble and may, in effect, be interpreted in virtually any way whatever (though when called upon to assist at performances Brown has shown himself to have definite notions of what is permissible).[17] *December 1952*, reproduced in Example 21, takes the obvious next step of casting off all links with traditional notation: it is at once the earliest, the most enigmatic and the most elegant of graphic scores.

There is an extraordinary coincidence in the fact that Cage, Wolff, Feldman and Brown should have been investigating the far reaches of indeterminacy in New York at the very time when, on the other side of the Atlantic, Boulez and Stockhausen were attempting total serial control. Some have argued that the gulf is illusory, since, to quote Pousseur, the effect of the procedures of *Structures Ia* is 'to guarantee a *permanent renewal*, and an absolute degree of unpredict-

Ex. 21

ability'.[18] But *Structures Ia* is a very special case. Boulez obliterated all traces of the past in order that he might be himself; Cage did so in order that sounds might become themselves: the difference is that between art and anarchy. And when Boulez made his first trip to New York, in the autumn of 1952, he became convinced that Cage was on a very different path from his own. The correspondence between the two came to an end, and the wider influence of American indeterminacy on the European avant garde was to be delayed until 1958, when Cage arrived in the citadel of serialism at Darmstadt.

REPERTORY

Babbitt: *Du* for soprano and piano (1951, Boelke-Bomart). Son Nova 1.
Brown: Music for Violin, Cello and Piano (1952, Universal). Time 8007.
—— *Folio:* 1 *October 1952* for piano, 2 *November 1952* for any instruments, 3 *December 1952* for any instruments, 4 *MM-87* for piano, 5 *MM-135 March 1953* for piano, 6 *Music for 'Trio for Dancers'* for piano and/or other instruments, 7 *1953* for piano (all 1952 or 1953, Associated). EMI C 165 28954–7.
—— *Twenty-five pages* for up to 25 pianos (1953, unpublished).

Cage: *Imaginary Landscape no. 4* for 12 radio receivers (1951, Peters).
——*Music of Changes* for piano (1951, Peters).
——*Imaginary Landscape no. 5* for tape (1951–2, Peters).
——*Music for Piano 1* (1952, Peters).
——*Water Music* for piano (1952, Peters).
——*Williams Mix* for tape (1952, Peters). Avakian.
——*4′ 33″* for undetermined forces (1952, Peters).
Feldman: *Projection I* for piano (1950, Peters), *II* for flute, trumpet, violin, cello and piano (1951, Peters), *III* for two pianos (1951, Peters), *IV* for violin and piano (1951, Peters), *V* for three flutes, trumpet, three cellos and two pianos (1951, Peters).
——*Extensions I* for violin and piano (1951, Peters), *III* for piano (1952, Peters), *IV* for three pianos (1952–3, Peters).
——*Intersection* [unnumbered] for tape (1951, unpublished), *I* for large orchestra (1951, Peters), *II* for piano (1951, Peters), *III* for piano (1953, Peters), *IV* for cello (1953, Peters).
——*Structures* for string quartet (1951, Peters).
Wolff: Duo for Violins (1950, Peters).
——*For Prepared Piano* (1951, New Music).
——*Nine* for flute, clarinet, horn, trumpet, trombone, celesta, piano and two cellos (1951, Peters).
—— Serenade for flute, clarinet and violin (1951, unpublished).

5 Cologne, 1953–4

One major problem with the application of serialism to all the parameters had been the lack in the other domains of anything corresponding to the uniform scale of pitch or to the principle of octave equivalence. Boulez in 'Eventuellement . . .' had suggested that the involvement of tempo might provide answers in the field of rhythm: one could define 12 durations reproducing the frequency ratios of the chromatic scale (for example, the major triad would have its durational equivalent in the collection of, say, crotchet, crotchet plus quaver, and dotted crotchet), and then these basic durations could be 'transposed' by changing the tempo, a doubling of speed being equivalent to octave transposition.[1] But clearly this is still an arbitrary system, since there is no true comparison, either in psycho-acoustical or in formal mathematical terms, between change of tempo and pitch transposition. Most important, the system offers no durational counterpart to the interval: a major 3rd is always a major 3rd, but Boulez's duration intervals (if such a concept has any meaning) would vary from one 'transpositional level' to another. As has been noted, Babbitt had worked out more sophisticated approaches to the serialization of rhythm, but as yet his work was little known in Europe.

If rhythmic serialism was fraught with difficulties, then the serialization of timbre presented still more intractable problems. It was reasonable enough to establish a scale of attacks in piano music, as Boulez had done in the first book of *Structures*, but there was no obvious way in which to apply serial rules to such unquantified phenomena as the sounds of orchestral instruments. To use a 12-piece ensemble, as Babbitt had done in his Composition for Twelve Instruments, offered only very partial and limited solutions;

so too did the grouping schemes adopted by Boulez in *Polyphonie X* and by Stockhausen in *Formel*. Effective serialization of this parameter demanded an ordering of related timbres, and electronic means alone held the possibility of timbre synthesis (which Stockhausen had first attempted in *Spiel*) and hence of the establishment of a timbre repertory amenable to serial manipulation. Furthermore, the use of tape would make it considerably easier to realize durations with precision, since one needed only to cut a recording to the desired length. It is not surprising, therefore, that many of the young serial composers of the early 1950s were quickly attracted to the new medium.

FROM 'MUSIQUE CONCRÈTE' TO 'ELEKTRONISCHE MUSIK'

The twin advantages of the electronic medium, in terms of defining rhythms and timbres, drew Messiaen and several of his pupils to Schaeffer's studio in 1952. Messiaen there produced his 15-minute *Timbres-durées,* an unusually substantial composition for the period, and short studies were realized by Boulez, Stockhausen and Barraqué, all of whom brought to the new domain their current concerns with serialism. Something of the excitement of the adventure springs from the pages of Schaeffer's essay 'L'objet musical', published in the special issue of the *Revue musicale*[2] which also contained Boulez's 'Eventuellement . . .'. Following up earlier suggestions of his own, and almost certainly influenced by the group of young collaborators he had acquired, Schaeffer proposes serial manipulations of sound objects which could be transformed in quite precise ways; he even theorizes about procedures which were to engage Stockhausen's attention throughout the next decade, such as the conversion of a complex event into a single sound, or the treatment of duration as a variable with the same capacity for complex relationships as pitch.

For the moment, however, it was the use of electronic techniques to generate serial structures of pitch, rhythm, timbre and volume that excited most interest. In his *Etude sur un son* Boulez elaborated scales of timbre from a single percussion sound, and his *Etude sur sept sons* is based on the same techniques applied to a richer source material. Both pieces contrast markedly in their seriousness of purpose with the productions of the regular *musique concrète* composers, but the equipment was not sufficiently advanced for Boulez to be able to realize his distinctions with clarity, and the studies have a quite untypically inert sound. Boulez emerged from the studio totally disenchanted with its facilities and personnel,[3] and with a suspicion of electronic music which appears to have lasted until the early 1970s.

Stockhausen, by contrast, recognized from the first that the regulation of timbre had to come not from the transforming techniques of *musique concrète* but from sound synthesis,[4] and that fuelled his consistent interest in the medium. The work of Helmholtz and Fourier had shown that any sound could be analysed as a particular collection of pure frequencies, or sine tones, so called because their wave forms follow the smooth undulation of sine curves. Stockhausen had practical experience of this in Paris when he analysed hundreds of instrumental sounds, and it seemed reasonable to suppose that the process could be reversed, that timbres could be synthesized from the simultaneous playing of a chosen group of sine tones. It would thus be possible to create a repertory of artificial timbres related in defined ways and therefore suited to serial composition. This Stockhausen tried, working with a sine-wave generator at the postal headquarters in Paris, but practical difficulties kept him from producing a composition with this technique. Instead, in December 1952, he turned to the use of the initial moments from prepared piano sounds in his first electronic piece, the *Etüde.*[5]

The following spring he returned to Cologne, where Herbert Eimert and Robert Beyer had begun experiments in electronic music at the radio station. There he found the equipment which enabled him to create the first sine-tone composition, his *Studie I* (1953), in which each sound is constructed from up to six pure frequencies taken from a table based on the proportions 48 : 20 : 25 : 15⅝ : 37½ : 30, that sequence being derived from the frequency ratios in the interval succession of falling minor 10th (12 : 5), rising major 3rd (4 : 5), falling minor 6th (8 : 5), rising minor 10th (5 : 12), falling major 3rd (5 : 4). For example, the first sound of the piece contains the frequencies 1920 Hz, 800 Hz, 1000 Hz and 625 Hz, which, it will be observed, express the relations among the first four members of the proportion sequence. And the same sequence governs the rhythmic construction, so that, for example, the first sound occupies 1920 mm of tape (at a speed of 762 mm per second), the second 800 mm. Other six-unit series, made up of the whole numbers from one to six, determine the number of sine tones packaged into each sound, the intensities of the components, the dynamic curve applied to the sound and the durations of pauses.[6] Nothing could better illustrate Stockhausen's will to achieve a perfect image of unity.

However, the sine tones obstinately failed to gel into the hoped-for new timbres, and so in his next electronic composition, *Studie II* (1954), he tried a different technique.[7] The piece is again based on an artificial frequency gamut, this time a simpler one of 81 frequencies each related to the next by the ratio $1{:}\sqrt[25]{5}$ (approximately 1:1.07); this is an octave-less scale with a constant interval between adjacent frequencies of slightly more than a semitone. From the scale Stockhausen draws 193 'note mixtures', each containing five sine tones, and these constitute the work's repertory of sounds. But instead of simply superposing the sine tones, as he had in *Studie I*, Stockhausen spliced together each group of five, played the recording in resonant space, and then recorded the reverberation of the mixture. This brought more fusion than had the earlier procedure, but again the work's success in generating unified timbres is modest.

Even so, Stockhausen's failure to achieve a full realization of his aims in the *Studien* does not mean that the pieces are without value, for, as so often, he was able to snatch musical worth from the jaws of technical defeat. Unlike most contemporary essays in *musique concrète*, these studies ask to be heard as works of music and not to be savoured for their evocative resonances. *Studie I* offers a pure structure in sound, the sine tones creating a surface of ringing chimes and deeper thuds, and the work's intricacy, together with its duration of nearly ten minutes, calling for a contemplative approach. *Studie II*, by contrast, is brief and dynamic, its scintillating bundles of frequencies leaping about the novel pitch framework: Example 22, taken from the published score (this was the first electronic work to appear in print), may give some impression of the piece at its most excited. Here the blocks in the upper part show the frequencies used in each note mixture; the numbers indicate durations in centimetres of tape, and the jagged lower part shows the dynamic envelopes imposed on the mixtures.

Stockhausen's work at the Cologne studio encouraged the development there of an atmosphere conducive to serious investigation of the problems of sound synthesis and of serial electronic composition. The term 'Elektronische Musik' was coined to distinguish work carried out at Cologne from the *musique concrète* of Paris, and the ground was prepared for a mutual antipathy which

Ex. 22

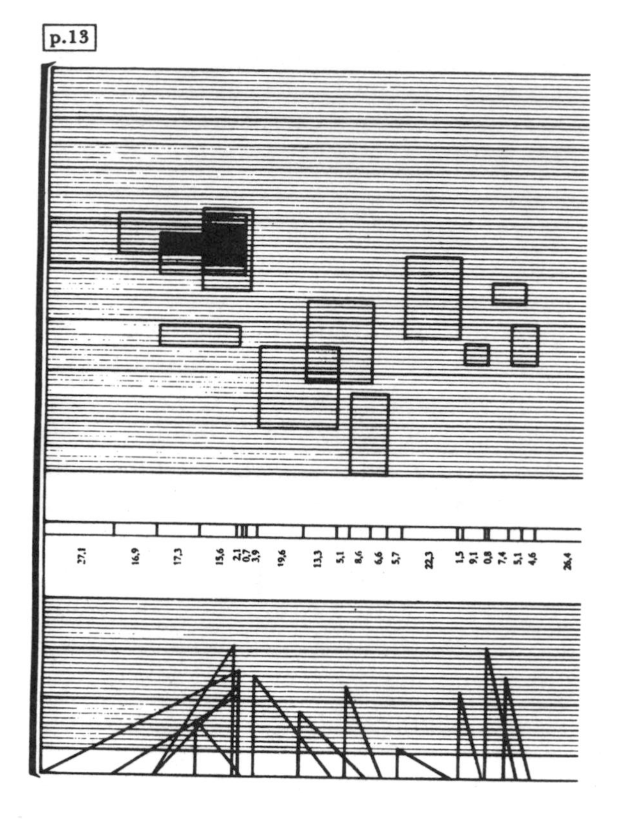

lasted for some years, the Cologne composers favouring sound synthesis from purely electronic resources while their Parisian counterparts continued to exploit recordings of natural sounds. For young serial composers throughout Europe, however, there was no question as to which camp claimed their loyalty. Stockhausen and Eimert, the latter accepting his younger colleague's principles in his works of this period, were joined for more or less brief periods by others who shared Eimert's vision of a 'real musical control of Nature'[8] based on the sine tone as the fundamental particle of the art. On 19 October 1954 the Cologne radio station broadcast a selection of works that had been produced there, including pieces by Stockhausen, Eimert, Goeyvaerts (*Composition no. 5 aux sons purs,* 1953) and Pousseur (*Seismogramme,* 1954). There were only seven compositions, lasting in all for less than half an hour, but they held decisive importance as the prototypes of pure electronic music.

FROM POINTS TO GROUPS

The pursuit of timbre synthesis in the electronic medium left Stockhausen free in his instrumental music to go after other goals. *Punkte* (1952), unperformed in its original version,[9] had apparently convinced him that pointillist composition had its limitations: technical limitations in that it was impossible to place timbre on an equal footing with pitch, duration and intensity when working with standard instruments, and aesthetic limitations in that highly divided textures worked to restrict both the nature and the perception of those formal processes in which he was interested. In the 1960s he revised the work for a larger orchestra, though still confining himself to pitched instruments, and converted most of the original points into melodic lines, chords and swarms of sound. More immediately he presented a creative criticism of the earlier score in *Kontra-Punkte* for ten instruments (1952–3), whose title is to be understood as signifying 'Against-Points' and 'Against-*Punkte*' as well as 'Counter-Points'. The work is also a demonstration that through total serialism there had arrived the means to create unified musical processes of great range.[10] It was the first composition in which Stockhausen matched his characteristic intellectual élan with perfection of achievement, and he properly gave it the distinction 'Nr. 1' in his catalogue of works. Published in 1953 and recorded in 1956, it brought its composer to that position of enormous influence which he has retained ever since.

For simple evidence of long-term planning in *Kontra-Punkte* one need look only to its very beginning and its very end (Example 23). The first six notes, heard in a partly overlapping linear statement, are converted into a piano chord which has been pushed up by two octaves; also noteworthy is the levelling out of timbre (from five instruments to one), volume (from five levels to one) and duration (from six values to one), evidence of a process of reducing diversity which unfolds throughout the work. As the music proceeds, so the instruments drop out one by one, the six 'families' of the opening – flute/bassoon, clarinet/bass clarinet, trumpet/trombone, piano, harp and violin/cello – giving place to the single timbre of the piano. At the same time the ranges of dynamic level and rhythmic value are curtailed, and the point texture of the opening gives place to two-part counterpoint.

Furthermore, the work exhibits a more or less progressive change

Ex. 23

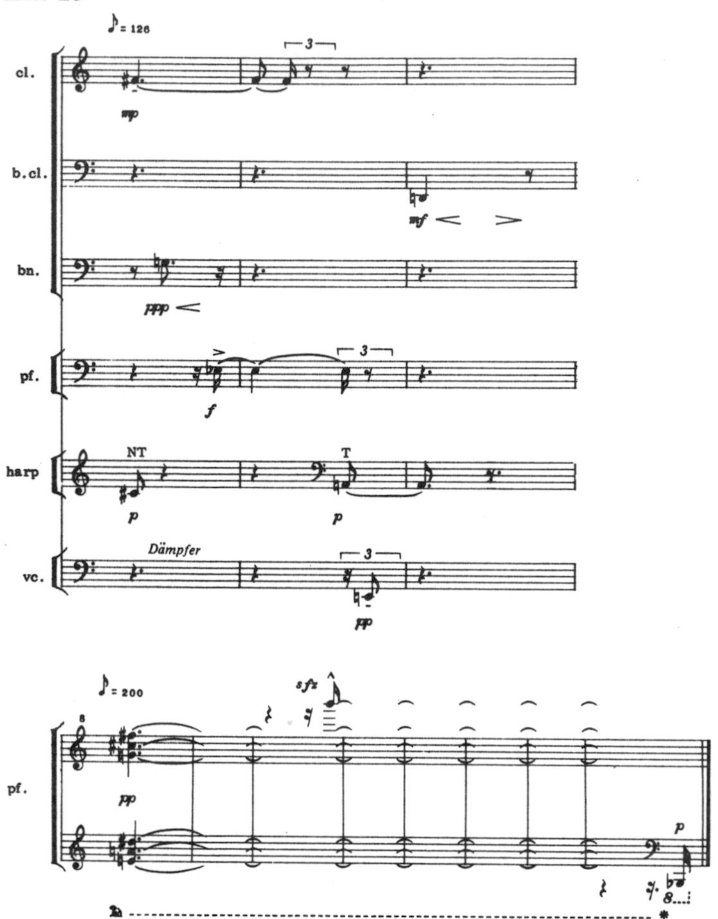

in style from pointillism to what Stockhausen has termed 'group composition', a 'group' being a collection of notes (it may be a chord, a melodic line, a rapid burst or a more complex event) to which the composer in some way gives an identity. Example 24 shows a typical example of group counterpoint from the piece and suggests how Stockhausen achieves the compelling small-scale continuity of *Kontra-Punkte*. The groups define more or less distinct harmonic fields whose antagonisms are resolved in the large piano group at the end of the example: here one finds references in bar 345 to the preceding harp group, in bar 346 to the clarinet group, and in bar 347 to the piano's own *sforzato* chord and group, while in the extreme bass there is a varied transposition of the flute group. Such working with allusive harmonic connections, which runs throughout the work, was to have a determining influence on Boulez among others, and it provided the European avant garde with a very powerful and versatile technical resource. Equally typical of *Kontra-Punkte*, and certainly equally central to its impressiveness, is the virtuoso flair of the scoring, suggesting a joy in creative discovery which has remained a feature of Stockhausen's best music.

Kontra-Punkte thus offers a novel combination of bold gesture, particularly in the writing for piano, with the most complex devices of the composer's serial working, these to be observed not only in the

Ex. 24

intervallic connections exemplified in Example 24 but also in the use of serial durations (the familiar 'chromatic' scale of values and also divisions of the bar, which always has the length of a dotted crotchet, into up to 12 equal parts), the fastidious placing of volume markings, and the beginnings of a serially inspired tempo structure.[11] If Webern's Concerto op. 24 may be discerned as a distant model, then its precise tactics have been replaced by a creative strategy of great flexibility and strength, where, as in *Studie I* and other works of this period, a fixed system of proportions governs the profusion of ideas presented. Stockhausen's own description is picturesque and exact: 'not the same shapes in a changing light. Rather this: different shapes in the same, all-pervading light'.[12]

Contemporary with *Kontra-Punkte* and *Studie I* are the Piano Pieces I-IV, the first set in a projected cycle of 21. The scope of the cycle was probably determined by the arithmetical series 1–2–3–4–5–6, which is almost an obsession in Stockhausen's music of this period (see the above discussion of *Studie I*), but so far he has published only sets of four (I–IV), six (V–X) and one (XI). Piece III was written first and is so short that it can be quoted complete (Example 25).

The organization of pitch here is not easy to analyse: Robin Maconie[13] suggests that it is based on three overlapping four-note segments of the chromatic scale (D–F, F–G sharp, G sharp–B), whereas Dieter Schnebel[14] and Jonathan Harvey[15] both see the five-note set of bar 1 as the structural determinant, but neither approach is entirely satisfactory. It is somewhat tempting to see here, alternatively, the operation of the Fibonacci series 3–5–8–13–21–34–55, which is undoubtedly important to the construction of much of Stockhausen's later music: there are 55 notes, 34 different pitches, and a total pitch range, traversed at a stroke

Ex. 25

between the last two notes, of 50 (= 3 + 5 + 8 + 13 + 21) semitones. Furthermore, intervals of three, eight or 13 semitones often appear at significant junctures; examples include the chordal minor 3rds in bars 7, 10 and 13.

However this may be, the rhythmic structure lies relatively open to investigation. As Maconie demonstrates,[16] the music may be regarded as made up of linear six-note groups (e.g. bar 1, bar 2, or bars 13–16) and wholly or partly harmonic trichords (e.g. bars 3–4, bar 5, or bar 6). At first separated, these are brought together from bar 8 to bar 13; then the piece ends as it began, in monody. Both the linear and the chordal elements are based on two varieties of rhythmic cell, one consisting of a note with a pause and two even values (e.g. the first half of bar 1, the last three quavers of bar 2, or the whole of bar 13), the other made up of three unequal durations, usually in a simple ratio (e.g. the first two quavers of bar 2, where the proportions are 1 : 3 : 2, or the whole of bar 5, where they are 6 : 3 : 2).

One may be justified in viewing the temporal ordering of this piece as more important than its pitch organization, for Stockhausen has said that in Piano Pieces I–IV he was concerned with 'imparting a new way of feeling time in music, in which the infinitely subtle "irrational" shadings and impulses and fluctuations of a good performer often produce what one wants better than any centimetre gauge'.[17] It should not be supposed from this statement that the player is at liberty to add 'irrational' deviations to the notation, for the composer is surely at pains in these sketches of structured time to prescribe relationships as exactly as possible: Piece I, notorious for the complexity of its rhythmic notation, poses many more problems of counting than does Piece III.[18] The 'shadings and impulses and fluctuations' are all built in; the pianist, however, has the power to project them in a manner that the studio composer may find it difficult to emulate, and this is the true distinction.

But if Stockhausen was coming to recognize a fundamental difference between electronic and performed music – a dualism that was to be transcended in his next electronic works, *Gesang der Jünglinge* and *Kontakte* – one need look no further than to the seventh bar of Piano Piece III to find him transferring into the instrumental world an electronic phenomenon, that of time reversal. Instead of following the common practice of successively building up a chord, as in bar 5, he progressively releases one, and there are many more complex instances of this in Piece II. Such moments suggest that Stockhausen was trying out ideas that had newly stimulated him in Schaeffer's studio, rather as Piece IV, in Maconie's just view,[19] shows him leaning over Boulez's shoulder at the worktable of *Structures*.

But this was to be one of the last occasions on which it is possible to detect a direct influence on Stockhausen: from this period onwards he was to gain his stimulation in the first place from the new systems of organization which he drew from his generalized approach to serialism. 'We are all', he wrote at this time, 'more or less treading on ice, and as long as this is the case, the organizational systems being put forward represent guidelines to prevent the composer from faltering. And one has to face the fact that there are as many systems as there are grains of sand, systems that can be dreamed up and set in motion as easily as clockwork. Their number is probably infinite, but certainly only a very few of them are acceptable systems, compatible with their means of expression, and applicable without self-contradiction to all the dimensions of music. Of these, still fewer are so perfectly prefigured that they yield beautiful and interesting music.'[20] It was to be Stockhausen's task to find these 'perfectly prefigured' systems, and to find a new one for each new work of the next decade.

REPERTORY

Barraqué: *Etude* on tape (1953, unpublished). Barclay 89005.
Boulez: *Etude sur un son* on tape (1951–2, unpublished).
—— *Etude sur sept sons* on tape (1951–2, unpublished). Barclay 89005.
Eimert: *Glockenspiel* on tape (1953, unpublished). DGG LP 16132.
—— *Etüde über Tongemische* on tape (1953–4, unpublished). DGG LP 16132.
Goeyvaerts: *Composition no. 5 aux sons purs* on tape (1953, unpublished).
Messiaen: *Timbres-durées* on tape (1952, unpublished).
Pousseur: *Seismogramme I-II* on tape (1954, unpublished).
Stockhausen: *Etüde* on tape (1952, unpublished).
—— *Punkte* for small orchestra (1952, unpublished), revised for large orchestra (1962, further revised in 1964 and 1966, all three versions Universal). DGG 2530 641 (1966 version).
—— *Kontra-Punkte* for flute, clarinet, bass clarinet, bassoon, trumpet, trombone, piano, harp, violin and cello (1952–3, Universal). DGG 2530 443, RCA VICS 1239, Véga C 30 A 66.
—— Piano Pieces I–IV (1952–3, Universal). CBS 72591–2.
—— *Elektronische Studie I* on tape (1953, unpublished), *II* on tape (1954, Universal). DGG LP 16133 (both pieces).

6 The Avant-garde Achievement, 1954–8

The mid-1950s brought confirmation of Stockhausen and Boulez as the leaders of a movement whose musical innovations were proving their power and their influence. The studio period was over, and the young composers of the European avant garde were producing works of great ambition and of public intention, such as Boulez's *Le marteau sans maître* or Stockhausen's *Gruppen* and *Gesang der Jünglinge*. Among the other composers who had taken part in the total serial effort, Pousseur and Nono both wrote several of their finest works during this period, and new composers arrived to join the original group, men such as Luciano Berio and Mauricio Kagel. Student musicians from all over Europe regularly repaired to Darmstadt each summer to learn the latest thinking from Stockhausen, Boulez and the rest. Festivals at Donaueschingen, Hamburg and elsewhere continued to give a platform to the newest music, and the avant garde began to produce its own conductors, first Maderna and later Boulez.

Boulez was responsible in 1954 for the foundation of a concert series in Paris, the Domaine Musical, which offered stimulating programmes of premières mixed with 20th-century classics and 'works of reference'; Stockhausen's *Zeitmasze*, Nono's *Incontri*, Berio's *Serenata I* and Messiaen's *Oiseaux exotiques* were among the works introduced there during only the first three seasons. Many of the Domaine's discoveries, including all of the works cited, were recorded by the firm of Véga, while the publishing house of Universal Edition embarked on a policy of fostering the avant garde, so that by 1958 their list included the works of Stockhausen, Boulez, Berio, Kagel and many others. Universal also brought out the journal *Die Reihe*, of which the first number (1955) was devoted to electronic music, and which served as a forum for a rare mixture of optimistic analyses of Webern, half-digested mathematics or acoustics, apparently deliberate obfuscations and genuinely significant contributions to musical thought. The pathways of communication were being opened, and the musical achievements of the avant garde were beginning to impinge on a wider world.

SERIAL STRUCTURING

Although the European avant garde held by the mid-fifties a position of much greater authority than had been the case at the start of the decade, there was no firm agreement as to how to proceed after the experience of total serialism; and although the impression might have been one of monolithic unity, the seeds of later divisions were already present. Boulez in his 1954 article 'Recherches maintenant'[1] chided his colleagues, and indeed his former self, for galloping too readily and too thoughtlessly towards the illusory goal of total organization: 'One soon sees', he wrote, 'that composition and organisation cannot be confused for fear of maniac inanity'.[2] He went on to propose the possibility of 'a dialectic surfacing at every instant of the composition between a rigorous global organisation and a momentary structure subject to free choice'.[3] It is implicit that the 'rigorous global organisation' was to be assured by the application of standard serial transformations and new methods of derivation to units of pitch, rhythm, timbre and dynamic level. The composer would thus find himself faced with a vast field of possibilities, among which he could direct himself by an alert marriage of intellect and instinct. Here Boulez suggested that the late works of Debussy might provide even more useful indications than those of Webern, and it was to Debussyan allusiveness rather than to Webernian symmetry that he appealed in *Le marteau sans maître*.

In this essay Boulez also points the way towards the aleatory principles that were to occupy the avant garde later in the decade. He speculates about the possibility of a composition existing as a set of 'formants', each linked to the organizational bases of the work as the formants of a timbre are linked to the fundamental, and yet each quite independent. This suggestion, testifying to the importance to Boulez and his colleagues of acoustical studies (however much misunderstood on occasion), was to be realized in his Third Piano Sonata, whose formal procedures are astonishingly predicted in the following passage: 'Let us reclaim for music the right to parentheses and italics . . .; a notion of discontinuous time achieved thanks to structures which will become entangled instead of remaining partitioned and insulated; finally a sort of development in which the closed circle is not the only imaginable solution. We want a musical work to be something other than a succession of compartments which must be visited unremittingly one after the other; instead let us try to think of it as a domain in which, as it were, one might choose one's own direction.'[4]

This labyrinthine conception, though manifested more obviously in the Third Piano Sonata, is already present in *Le marteau sans maître*, as indeed it had been in the Second Piano Sonata; for Boulez, after *Structures Ia*, had quickly returned to his view of serialism as a means of proliferation, as a source of techniques to create music in which relationships could be made more or less distinct, more or less veiled by transformation, temporal distance, complexity of texture or speed of unfolding. The apparatus of total serialism remains in *Le marteau* – the dynamic levels which change almost from note to note, the arithmetical durations – but as a serial construction the work is to a very large degree impenetrable. The techniques are so various and versatile that a pitch series can give rise to almost any configuration, and the composer is perhaps justified in his view that a complete analysis is impossible.

Among Boulez's colleagues, only Barraqué at this time shared a somewhat similar approach to the serial method. Berio, in his *Chamber Music* for mezzo-soprano and three players (1953), preferred a straightforward serial technique close to that of his teacher Dallapiccola, and his *Nones* for orchestra (1954) is quite clearly based on a 13-note series, the repetition of one pitch class assisting in the creation of a structure that slowly oscillates between complex harmonies and the simple sound of octaves.[5] Since the series also emphasizes major and minor 3rds, Berio is able to give his work a much smoother harmonic consistency than would have been countenanced by most of his confrères, though there is no attempt at accommodation to the structural methods of tonality, as in Henze, for example. These early compositions also display a characteristic delight in the human voice and in orchestral sonorities of an almost physical allure. Despite the bleak tone of *Nones* there is an enjoyment of the material which is also to be found in the first works composed by Berio and Maderna at the electronic studio they founded in Milan in 1955, a studio which offered composers some haven from the warring factions of Paris and Cologne. Pieces such as Berio's *Perspectives* (1956) and *Momenti* (1957) or Maderna's *Continuo* (1958) proved that the new medium could be used with spontaneity, ease and flamboyance. The two Italians were even prepared to compose serial pieces of a divertimento character, expressing some continuity with the neo-classicism of a Malipiero or a Casella: Berio's *Serenata I* and Maderna's *Serenata* (1954, revised in 1957) convey, not least in their choice of title, a note of friendly criticism of the seriousness with which musical 'research' was being conducted at Darmstadt.

Much closer to the enthroned Webern were the works composed at this time by Pousseur and Zimmermann. Example 26, from the

Ex. 26

latter's *Perspektiven* for two pianos (1955), suggests how far composers were prepared to go in imitating and developing the ideas of their chosen master. Obviously stimulated by the geometric perfection of the second movement of Webern's Piano Variations, the passage is an almost perfect palindrome in which pitches, rhythmic cells, dynamic levels, modes of attack and pedallings are all turned backwards after the D in the sixth bar.[6] However, the composer also succeeds in giving his mirrored motifs Stravinskyan life as sprightly dancers in what he described as an 'imaginary ballet', using a favourite metaphor.

Pousseur was taking a rather different path from Webern, evolving means of harmonic organization based on his analyses of the latter's atonal works as well as the serial compositions,[7] and founded too on a taste he shared with his model for 7ths and minor 9ths: 'indistinct octaves', as he calls them. His *Quintette à la mémoire d'Anton Webern* (1955), scored for the distinctly Second Viennese ensemble of clarinet, bass clarinet, violin, cello and piano, employs the series of Webern's op. 22, but the intervals are filled in with the intervening chromatic notes to provide for a harmony rich in 'indistinct octaves';[8] and in his next work, the book of *Exercices* for piano (1956), he used a scheme of harmonic ordering without reference to a series.[9] Example 27, which shows the opening of the 'Impromptu'

Ex. 27

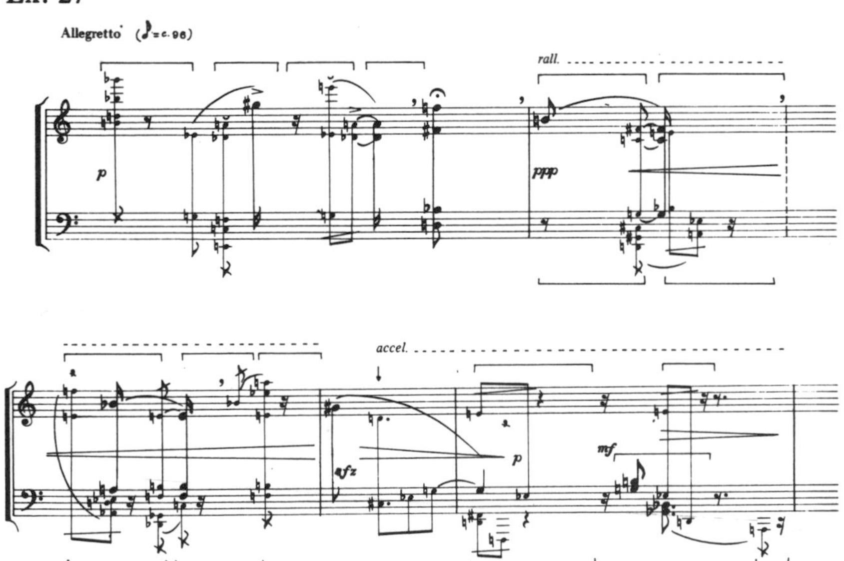

from the book, gives some indication of the compositional method at its simplest. The piece is based on 'harmonic fields' containing one or more of the whole-tone intervals less than an octave (minor 2nd, major 3rd, tritone, minor 6th, minor 7th) together with one or more pitches forming intervals of a major 7th or a minor 9th with the pitches of the whole-tone intervals. For instance, the fundamental interval in the first bar of the example is the minor 6th (D–B flat and B flat–G flat in the first chord, etc.), always with chromatic additions or postscripts. Pousseur thus provides himself with an elegant technique through which chords may be made to echo and shadow one another as one harmonic field merges into the next; the contained looseness of the music's feel is enhanced by the interaction, influenced no doubt by Stockhausen's Piano Pieces V–X (1954–5), between strict rhythm and interferences introduced by grace notes and commas, both of these taking time from the value with which they are joined by a square bracket.

As Ligeti pointed out in his article 'Metamorphoses of Musical Form',[10] the original conventions of serialism, and even those of the total serialism of 1951–2, have been so far adapted in the immediately subsequent works of Pousseur, Stockhausen, Boulez and others that to describe those works as 'serial compositions' is almost meaningless. At best, only the basic principles – those of establishing an order within a defined set of elements which is fixed for the composition, and of transforming that set according to determined rules – remain.

The European approach to serialism proved a disappointment to Babbitt, who has recalled how, after his hopes had been aroused by news of seemingly similar endeavours to his own taking place on the other side of the Atlantic, he discovered that his presumed comrades' 'music and technical writings eventually revealed so very different an attitude towards the means, and even so very different means, that the apparent agreement with regard to end lost its entire significance. . . . Mathematics – or, more correctly, arithmetic – is used, not as a means of characterizing or discovering general systematic, pre-compositional relationships, but as a compositional device. . . . The alleged "total organization" is achieved by applying dissimilar, essentially unrelated criteria of organization to each of the components, criteria often derived from outside the system, so that – for example – rhythm is independent of and thus separable from the pitch structure; this is described and justified as a "polyphony" of components, though polyphony is customarily understood to involve, among other things, a principle of organized simultaneity'.[11]

Babbitt's distress, not unmixed with a certain amount of self-congratulation, is occasioned by little more than the fact that his European colleagues did not share his view of what constituted 'general systematic, pre-compositional relationships'; the criticism may be ill-founded, but it does point up the great distance that separated serial composers in America from those in Europe. Examination of the music makes the point still more clearly. By contrast with the vague and convoluted serial workings of such pieces as *Kontra-Punkte*, *Le marteau sans maître* or *Grüppen*, Babbitt's contemporary Second String Quartet is a model of lucid serial organization. The quartet is based on an all-interval series which is introduced interval by interval, as it were, with each new arrival initiating a development of the interval repertory acquired thus far, each development being argued in terms of derived sets. Important landmarks in the continuous argument are firmly underlined: Babbitt calls upon harmonic octaves at the points where new intervals are brought into play, brings in a rare solo line when the first hexachord has been completed (bar 114) and has the first serial statement begun by all four instruments in unison (bars 266–8). Example 28 may suggest the assurance with which Babbitt engineers his serial polyphony. The example begins with the ending (bar 18) of a short passage based on the first two intervals of the series, the minor 3rd and the minor 6th, then continues with a derived set based on the next interval, the perfect 4th (bars 19–23), followed by the start of a development of this interval in combination with its predecessor. Serial structuring of this thoroughness was certainly not to be found among the works of European contemporaries.

MUSIC AND LANGUAGE

In an article[12] in the sixth issue of *Die Reihe* Stockhausen gave analytical sketches of three works, one by each member of the triumvirate of the European avant garde in the early 1950s: his own *Gesang der Jünglinge*, Boulez's *Le marteau sans maître* and Nono's *Il canto sospeso*, all of them completed in 1955–6. The article had the title 'Music and Speech', and its main point was to show how the three composers had, in different ways, made words, and the comprehensibility of words, compositional variables. In 1951–2, when the precise definition of musical parameters had been all-important, language

Ex. 28

had seemed too impure a medium, a recalcitrant mode of expression which offered no obvious scope for serial organization: only Nono had been unable to resist his Italian impulse to song and his urgent need to give vent to his political ideals and sympathies. But now serial and electronic techniques had been developed to a state of sufficient range for attempts to be made at an integration of words into music.

Of course, for composers who, like Henze, had been little touched by the charms of total serialism, the problem of containing language was by no means so acute. His closest approach to a strict serial formulation of the musical parameters had come in his Second String Quartet (1952), and soon after completing this rather uncharacteristic score he had moved to Italy, where he appears to have felt himself freed to develop an eclectic style in which serialism has rather less part to play in long-term planning than do diatonic progressions veiled and acidulated by chromaticism and bitonality. He also chose to cultivate more orthodox forms and genres, and he differed markedly from his contemporaries in composing so abundantly: his first five years in Italy produced two full-length operas, the rich and magical fantasy *König Hirsch* (1952–5) and *Der Prinz von Homburg* (1958), as well as a number of orchestral and smaller vocal works. He was still rubbing shoulders with Stockhausen, Boulez, Nono and Pousseur in the fourth issue of *Die Reihe*,[13] and he retained for the moment an association with Darmstadt; he even contributed the *Concerto per il Marigny* (1956) for Boulez's Domaine Musical. But all the time he was moving into realms of romantic lyricism far removed from the Darmstadt ethos. *Der Prinz von Homburg*, though based on a military play by Kleist, reflects a burgeoning enthusiasm for early 19th-century Italian opera, and the contemporary *Kammermusik 1958* for tenor, guitar and octet, setting verse by Hölderlin, is most typical in expressing the northerner's dream of an antique, sunlit Mediterranean world.

Henze's compromises with the 19th century could hold little appeal for Boulez, who was concerned with returns only to his own expressive territory. In 1953, beginning his first new work with the techniques he had developed beyond total serialism, he turned, as he had in 1946, to the poetry of René Char. But the three poems he chose came from an earlier collection, *Le marteau sans maître*, where the verse is very much more concise, its obscure images hammered into a few lines, and the tone less personal. In both respects the poems suited Boulez's aim, which was not so much to set them to music as to use them as the essence of elaborate musical forms. His new approach to language, subtle and analytic, gave rise to a sequence of essays, of which the central ideas are contained in the following paragraph:

Structure: one of the key words of our time. It seems to me that if there must be a connection between poetry and music, then it is to this notion of structure that one will appeal if one is to be as effective as possible; and here I include everything from basic formal structures to vaster structures of definition. If I choose a poem in order to make it something other than the starting-point for an ornamentation of arabesques woven around the text, if I choose a poem to make it my music's source of irrigation and thus to create an amalgam such that the poem becomes 'centre and absence' of the

> sounding whole, then I cannot limit myself only to expressive relationships between the two entities; rather I am faced with a web of connections, including expressive relationships but also covering all the mechanisms of the poem, from its pure sound to its intellectual organisation.[14]

It is perhaps naïve to assume that earlier composers of vocal music had not been excited by aspects of 'pure sound' and 'intellectual organisation' in the texts they chose to set, but in consciously applying himself to those aspects Boulez was doing something new, though he was by no means alone. Berio's delight in verbal sounds is evident right from *Chamber Music,* which dates from the year before his meeting with Maderna, Pousseur and Stockhausen drew him into the Darmstadt circle, and which shows in its monotone second song a great number of patterns of timbre or rhythm suggested by the poem. As far as 'intellectual organisation' is concerned, Babbitt's 'Spelt from Sybil's Leaves', from his Two Sonnets for baritone and instrumental trio (1955), exhibits a neat parallel between the rhyme scheme and the serial forms employed. Boulez was also to develop musical reflections of sonnet forms in his later works based on poems by Mallarmé, but in *Le marteau sans maître* the correspondences between poetic and musical structures lie for the most part hidden, though some indications will be given below.

Only four of the nine movements of *Le marteau sans maître* are vocal, the others being little instrumental glosses which obliquely recall or prefigure the poetic announcement with which they are associated. 'L'artisanat furieux', sung in movement III, has a prelude (I) and a postlude (VII); 'Bourreaux de solitude' (VI) has three commentaries (II, IV, VIII); and 'Bel édifice et les pressentiments' (V) has a 'double', or variation (IX). The interweaving of the three cycles resembles that in Messiaen's *Turangalîla-symphonie,* but Boulez keeps up a sophisticated play between distinguishing and confusing his cycles, their separateness or similarity depending on features of vocal style, rhythm, texture and instrumentation.

It is to its instrumentation that *Le marteau sans maître* owes many of its strengths and qualities, even though Boulez's ensemble has been endlessly imitated. The work is scored for contralto voice, alto flute, viola, guitar, vibraphone, xylorimba and unpitched percussion instruments (one player), a grouping which provides for a wide variety of colours and yet which emphasizes fragile or resonant sounds in the middle-high register. It is also a formation derived from that of *Pierrot lunaire,* acknowledged as ancestor in the voice–flute duet which is the third movement, though the weighting of percussion suggests more exotic models: according to Boulez, the vibraphone relates to the Balinese gamelan, the xylorimba to the music of black Africa and the guitar to the Japanese koto,[15] all exposing the temperamental affinities which he was later to acknowledge.[16] There is, however, little surface exoticism as in, for example, the *Turangalîla-symphonie;* rather the work creates its own integrated sound universe and may thus be regarded as a pioneering essay in that 'music of the whole world' which Stockhausen was to take as an ideal.[17] This unity is the result partly of Boulez's refusal of exotic flavour in matters of harmony and rhythm, and partly of the connections drawn between the chosen timbres. As the composer has explained, the voice connects with the alto flute as an instrument of breath, the alto flute with the viola as a sustaining instrument, the viola (pizzicato) with the guitar as a plucked string instrument, the guitar with the vibraphone as a resonator, and the vibraphone with the xylorimba as an instrument to be struck.[18] The unpitched percussion he leaves out of account as 'marginal', though in fact the xylorimba's high noise content establishes some rapport. More important, however, are the liaisons at the other end of the scale, enabling the alto flute to serve as a substitute for the voice, dramatically so in the final movement, and thus to effect a subsuming of language into music.

Boulez's derivation of music from words on a smaller scale can be demonstrated with reference to the 'L'artisanat furieux' cycle. Example 29 shows the opening of the vocal movement, which throughout is marked by an ornate vocal manner and a tangential relationship between the two parts. The initial flute solo, beginning with a characteristically Boulezian flourish, offers only vague hints of the vocal entry which follows (the falling F–F sharp of bar 3, for instance, is perhaps to be heard as herald of the C–C sharp drop in bar 6), but then the instrument, flutter-tonguing, announces a 12-note series which is an almost exact retrograde of the contralto's on 'du clou'.

Both the prelude and the postlude to 'L'artisanat furieux' take place at double speed: they are, as it were, harmonics of the song. Both allude to the vocal movement also in their counterpointing of two parts which now and then close together, though this basic conception is very often concealed by lacing a line through different

Ex. 29

instruments in quick succession or by splitting a part into two. Example 30 shows an unusually simple passage, the opening section of 'Avant: "L'artisanat furieux" ', which Boulez's solid rectangles invite one to dissect. It is clear that the music is in two parts, flute and vibraphone being set against guitar and viola, and that each part has five segments. These segments relate to one another diagonally, so that the section may be regarded as another example of that 'cross polyphony' dear to Boulez. Not only that, the five segments of each part refer more or less directly to the first five words of the vocal setting: the alto flute's final G sharp–F sharp, for instance, both parallels the E–D at 'bord' and echoes the guitar's opening F sharp–G sharp. A few moments' examination of the two examples

Ex. 30

will reveal numerous other correspondences, both of rhythmic cell and intervallic motif.

Such allusive connections, which are entirely characteristic of the work, were made possible by the rapidly proliferating serial techniques which for Boulez opened up countless possibilities of continuation and linkage at any point.[19] The means naturally entailed an organizing intelligence of commanding power, but they also, being so flexible, made possible the pursuit of the irrational; and Boulez increasingly saw it as his task to seize the indefinable by means of the most sharply defined techniques. 'More and more', he wrote at this time, 'I find that in order to create effectively one has to consider delirium and, yes, organise it.'[20] *Le marteau sans maître* is organized delirium in that it fixes and transports the violent surreal instants of its text; it also marks Boulez's advance into that 'universe in perpetual expansion' which for him was serial thought.[21]

As the earlier works of the two composers have already suggested, Stockhausen's understanding of serialism was fundamentally different from Boulez's. For Boulez, serial manipulations provided a vast range of related patterns of pitches, durations, intensities and timbres, the elements in a musical discourse which, though bounded by the series in the long term, offered immense scope for momentary decisions. For Stockhausen, the serial principle suggested ways of mediating between extremes: the 'basic conception' of *Gesang der Jünglinge,* he wrote, was 'to arrange everything separate into as smooth a continuum as possible, and then to extricate the diversities from this continuum and compose with them'.[22] In the specific case of this work, his first vocal composition since the student pieces of 1950–1, the obvious extremes to be considered first were those of sounds and words, of pure acoustic events and linguistic units. The way to mediate between the two, to establish 'scales of degrees of comprehensibility', was suggested by what Stockhausen had learned as a student of phonetics and information theory under Werner Meyer-Eppler at the University of Bonn. Since vowel sounds are distinguished, whoever is speaking, by characteristic 'formants' (emphasized bands of frequencies), it ought to be possible to create by electronic means synthetic vowels, so that pure electronic music could begin to function as language.[23] Working from the other end, the whole repertory of tape transformations was available to alter spoken or sung material so that it more or less lost its verbal meaning and could be heard simply as sound.

Thanks to these techniques Stockhausen was able to create in *Gesang der Jünglinge* a more complete union of music and language than had ever been achieved before: the synthesized electronic sounds follow analogous principles of construction to those which operate in vocal sounds, and the recorded voice, that of a boy treble, is made to infiltrate the electronic world. Nothing on either side, therefore, is quite foreign to the other, though one's natural inclination to seek a message in vocal sound may create some imbalance. Stockhausen does his best to reduce this inclination by using a text with which he could reasonably expect a church-going, German-speaking audience to be familiar: the canticle *Benedicite omnia opera,* in German 'Preiset den Herrn, ihr Werke alle des Herrn', which appears in the Apocrypha as sung by the three young Jews in Nebuchadnezzar's furnace (hence the title). Since the text is known, the listener may be prepared to attend to different degrees of comprehensibility in a moderately relaxed manner, not feeling the need to grasp at the fragments in order to gather information, and so the composer can range freely from plain syllabic song to virtuoso electronic gestures by way of the more or less meaningless intermediates of synthetic choral singing (the sense obscured by the density of superimpositions of the soloist on himself), singing heard as if from a great distance, words scrambled by tape editing, electronic sounds mimicking phonemes, and so on.

In using natural sound material together with electronically synthesized sounds, Stockhausen achieved another mediation, between the *musique concrète* of Paris and the *Elektronische Musik* of Cologne, and so demonstrated that the rivalry between the two was unnecessary and unhelpful to the further development of the medium. His use of the voice in tape music was to have a wide influence, notably on Luciano Berio, whose *Thema – omaggio a Joyce* (1958) transforms a passage from *Ulysses* to produce a stream of comprehended and half-comprehended utterance, though with a physical, sensuous handling of the female voice which connects more with the vocal writing in the composer's concert works, such as *Chamber Music,* than with the flame-like purity of *Gesang der Jünglinge.* Stockhausen's work also stimulated somewhat similar enterprises in Cologne, where Krenek arrived to compose his most ambitious electronic work, the Pentecost oratorio *Spiritus intelligentiae, sanctus* (1956), and where Eimert used techniques of textual disintegration in *Zu Ehren von Igor Stravinsky* (1957) and several later pieces.

Equally influential was Stockhausen's introduction of a spatial dimension into electronic music. *Gesang der Jünglinge* was originally prepared for five tape channels, later reduced to four, and its ebullience is greatly enhanced by antiphonal effects. Stockhausen himself was to apply in many later works the discoveries he had made in the treatment of language and of space (the latter was already claiming his attention in *Gruppen*); yet perhaps the most deeply significant lesson of *Gesang der Jünglinge* was that there existed musical aspects, particularly concerning degrees of likeness between unlike phenomena, which could not be quantified, and which therefore demanded something other than the precise pre-compositional schemes of total serialism for their effective use. 'More than ever before', he wrote, 'we have to listen, every day of our lives. We draw conclusions by making tests on ourselves. Whether they are valid for others only our music can show.'[24] And increasingly he was to be led to allow room for empirical judgments, whether made by himself or left to his performers.

Nono's *Il canto sospeso* exhibits a more robust route through total serialism than those of the subtle Boulez or the mediating Stockhausen, and it is much more immediate in its approach to language, certainly not shunning those 'expressive relationships' of which Boulez was suspicious. Stockhausen detected in the cantata something like his own technique of composition with degrees of comprehensibility, but in a footnote to his analysis[25] he was bound to admit that this was a projection of his own concerns, even though Nono undoubtedly contrasts movements where the words can be understood (e.g. the fifth, for tenor and orchestra) with others in which the sense is almost totally confounded by his serial mechanics. He adopts this latter course, Stockhausen interestingly suggests,[26] when the texts, which are all taken from the farewell letters of condemned political prisoners, are such as to shame musical interpretation.

Example 31 shows the opening of the second movement, for unaccompanied chorus, where the meaning of the text – 'I am dying for a world which will shine with such a strong light and with such beauty that my sacrifice is nothing . . .' – is obscured by the division of four contrapuntal lines across the eight-part chorus. As so often, Nono erects a rigorous structure to contain the ecstatic intensity of his music: the parts move in units of quintuplet semiquavers (second bass in bar 2, first soprano in bar 3, etc.), semiquavers (first soprano

Ex. 31

in bars 1 and 2, first tenor in bar 3, etc.), quaver triplets (second soprano in bar 1, first bass in bars 2–5, etc.) and quavers (second alto in bars 1–3, first tenor in bars 3–5, etc.). In each time layer the durations are obtained by multiplying the unit by a member of the Fibonacci series 1–2–3–5–8–13, and all four lines are drawn together in the pitch organization, which simply repeats one of Nono's favoured all-interval, wedge-shaped series, A–B flat–A flat–B–G–C–F sharp–C sharp–F–D–E–D sharp, without inversion, reversal or transposition. There is also a quite separate quasi-serial organization of dynamic levels. And yet, despite the use of techniques so elementary and incompatible, the overwhelming effect is one of passionate commitment and strength, for in no way do Nono's compositional subterfuges conceal his sympathetic response to the text.

A further, quite different approach to the conjunction of music and language is to be found in Kagel's *Anagrama* (1955–8), arguably the most musically ambitious work by a composer who was increasingly to be drawn to theatrical exercises in cultural criticism. Kagel arrived in Cologne from his native Buenos Aires in 1957, and though he had already shown an interest in the newest musical developments (the tape *Musica para la torre* dates from 1952), he was evidently impressed by Stockhausen's work on verbal–musical synthesis in *Gesang der Jünglinge*. The four vocal soloists and the chorus of *Anagrama* treat the text, in four languages, as phonetic rather than meaningful material, and bring a wide variety of means of utterance to bear upon it, including whispering, singing, shouting and so on; Example 32 is characteristic of a work that played a key role in

Ex. 32

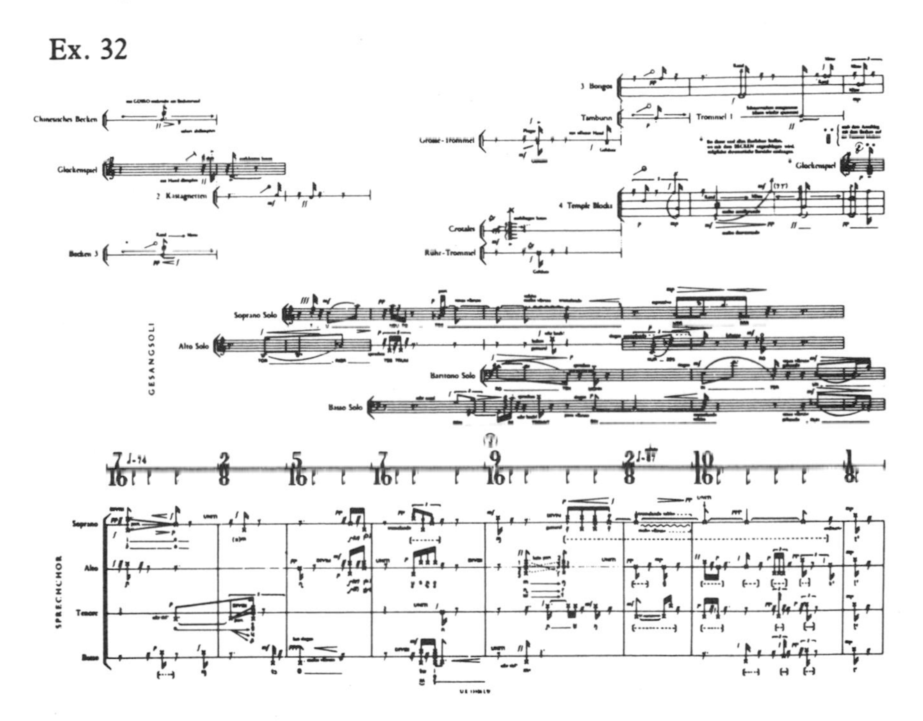

opening up new vocal and choral resources which were to be exploited by many composers in the next decade. The instrumental material, for a varied ensemble of 11 players, similarly abounds in new performance techniques, without doing much to elucidate the hermetic scheme by which pitches are made to correspond with phonemes of the texts.

. . . HOW TIME PASSES . . .

'Music consists of order-relationships in time.' That opening statement from Stockhausen's 1957 essay '. . . how time passes . . .'[27] contains the essence of the new thinking on musical time which he had developed under the influence of Meyer-Eppler and which was of fundamental importance in his works of 1954–7, fruitful years which saw the composition not only of *Gesang der Jünglinge* but also of Piano Pieces V–X (VI, IX and X were later revised), *Zeitmasze* for five woodwind and *Gruppen* for three orchestras.

Work in the electronic studio on his *Studien* had brought Stockhausen to the realization that pitch and duration are aspects of a single phenomenon, that of vibration: a vibration of, say, 32 Hz will be perceived as a pitched note, whereas one of 4 Hz will be heard as a regular rhythm, and somewhere in between the one will merge into the other. It seemed illogical, therefore, to build a total serial organization on different rules of ordering applied to the two parameters, and for the works of 1954–7 Stockhausen introduced a variety of techniques for handling rhythmic aspects by analogy with pitch aspects. The 'chromatic' duration scale that Messiaen had used in his *Mode de valeurs et d'intensités* was inadequate because, as an additive series, it had no correspondence with the logarithmic relationships of the pitch scale; moreover, it led to contradictions and inconsistencies, in that long durations gained unwarranted importance and superimpositions of series obscured the carefully devised organization, leading instead, as has been noted, to a uniform pulsation.

Composers had, of course, already been troubled by this problem and found different ways to circumvent it. In *Le marteau sans maître* Boulez had developed his techniques of transformation to such a stage that he could range from strongly pulsed music to plastic counterpoint propelled by irregular beats or to completely ametrical movement. Stockhausen himself had added equal bar-divisions to 'chromatic' durations in *Kontra-Punkte* and Piano Pieces I-IV, but now he preferred to take his cue from the nature of his material, from the nature of sound. In the first place he replaced the additive duration scale by a logarithmic scale of 12 tempos, a true counterpart of the chromatic pitch scale and one which can be 'transposed' by changing the rhythmic unit (e.g. a change from crotchet units to semibreve units, and therefore a deceleration by a factor of four, is equivalent to a downward transposition by two octaves). Within this system, the obverse of that proposed earlier by Boulez,[28] a rise of a perfect 12th would have its analogue in a change of tempo by a factor of 3/2 (the frequency ratio of a perfect 5th) coupled with a halving of the rhythmic unit. It is thus possible for the composer to construct a rhythmic succession which exactly parallels any melodic succession. Moreover, he has available also a counterpart of timbre, in that 'partials' may be added in any number and proportion. Example 33 shows the first group from *Gruppen* (exhibiting, very evidently, an expansion of the group technique of *Kontra-Punkte*) in which the 'fundamental' minim duration (violas) is combined with 'overtones' of crotchets (cellos), triplet crotchets (harp), quavers (wooden drums) and so on up to the '10th harmonic' (flute and alto flute). In this way each group of the work is composed as the analogue of a particular pitch in a particular octave with a particular timbre: as Jonathan Harvey has shown, the whole rhythmic structure is the vast expansion of a serial melodic thread.[29]

This equivalence leads naturally to the novel layout of the work, for if different 'fundamentals' are to be overlaid, then there has to be a way of maintaining different tempos simultaneously, and if each 'fundamental' is to have a rich overtone spectrum, then there has to be a generous supply of instruments: hence *Gruppen* for three orchestras, each with its own conductor. But having re-invented orchestral antiphony for the sober needs of his structural scheme, Stockhausen was characteristically drawn to take advantage of the spectacular opportunities afforded by the widespread distribution of three ensembles, notably in the splendidly sonorous climax where a brass chord is hurled from one orchestra to another. Moreover, in this first published orchestral work he was able to pursue his preference for relatively small, highly variegated formations, a preference alredy shown in the *Drei Lieder, Formel, Spiel* and *Punkte*. Each orchestra is made up of three dozen players, about half of them are strings, the rest being constituted equally from the woodwind, brass and percussion (both pitched and unpitched). If *Gruppen* began as an essay in articulating a new conception of rhythmic organization, it soon became also a virtuoso exercise in orchestration, teeming with richly figured textures.

Its innovatory exuberance was bound to impress the composers with whom Stockhausen was associated. Nono wrote for four ensembles and developed his impasto orchestral style in his *Com-*

Ex. 33

posizione per orchestra no. 2: Diario polacco (1958), while his compatriot Berio divided the orchestra into five groups for his *Allelujah II* (1956–7), which, like his earlier *Nones*, moves between poles of simplicity and complication, the former represented by a returning B flat on solo flute. Pousseur's *Rimes pour différentes sources sonores* (1958–9) and Boulez's *Poésie pour pouvoir* (1958) both develop the orchestral finesse of *Gruppen* in combination with material on tape, and the latter's *Doubles* (1957–8), later revised as *Figures–Doubles–Prismes,* has the orchestra seated on a conventional platform but considerably rearranged in order to allow numerous small groups to be distinguished.

In the U.S.A., however, the orchestral redisposition of *Gruppen* excited less interest, nor was Stockhausen's derivation of rhythmic structures from acoustic phenomena to be accepted.[30] Though Babbitt was also dissatisfied with the 'chromatic' duration scale, which he had used in his Composition for Twelve Instruments, his quarrel was not based on the incongruity of employing additive measures of duration with logarithmic measures of pitch; instead he was troubled by formal incompatibilities between the serial systems used for the two parameters. His search for means of achieving a polyphony in which the rhythmic organization might mesh with, though not necessarily reduplicate, the pitch organization led to his introduction of the notion of 'time points'[31] and to his use of time-point sets in most of his works from 1957 onwards (the earliest pieces in which this system is adopted would appear to be *Partitions* for piano and *All Set* for jazz ensemble, both dating from that year).

The time point of a musical event is a measure of its position within the bar: thus if the time signature is ¾ and the unit of measurement is the semiquaver, a note attacked on the first beat may be said to occur at time point zero, a note attacked a semiquaver later is at time point one, and so on. Example 34 shows a time-point set which is,

Ex. 34

following Babbitt's practice, an ordering of 12 different values. The advantage of the time-point system, as far as consistency with the pitch-class system is concerned, is that it includes an analogue of interval: whereas the 'interval between two durations' is a concept of doubtful meaning, the interval between two time points is a duration. Moreover, there is now a rhythmic counterpart of the octave in the bar: the equivalent of transposing a pitch by one or more octaves is delaying a time point by one or more bars, and so the composer is provided with considerable scope for choice in rhythmic composition. The corollary is that, if the time points are to be heard to create structures, then the metre must be apparent, and performances of Babbitt's music may sometimes lead one to the conclusion that – leaving aside the question of whether the ear can be trained to respond to serial operations on time-point groupings – musicians have an awesome task in projecting the densely packed information of his scores (see, for instance, Example 44 on p. 156). That the time-point system is not at all inconsistent with music of surface rhythmic appeal and wit is proved by the punningly tilted *All Set,* the intermediacy of 'combinatorial' being, as always in Babbitt's music, understood. During the next decade, however, he was to produce most of his major works in the electronic studio, where the rhythmic precision demanded by his system could be realized with relative ease.

STATISTICS

Although serialism of some kind was claiming the interest of most younger composers in the mid-1950s, there were dissenting voices. Iannis Xenakis, in his article 'La crise de la musique serielle',[32] attacked the new serial music in terms rather similar to those adopted by Pousseur[33] and other members of the European avant garde themselves. 'Linear polyphony', he wrote, with implicit reference to such works as Boulez's *Structures,* 'destroys itself by its very complexity; what one hears is in reality nothing but a mass of notes in various registers.' The answer was to grapple directly with these statistical phenomena by introducing 'the notion of probability, which implies in this particular case, combinatory calculus'.

An architect by training and inclination, though also a pupil of Messiaen, Xenakis set himself to the development of 'stochastic music' in which sound masses were to be composed and transformed according to laws obtained from the mathematics of probability, and especially from the stochastic laws which mathematicians had devised to describe phenomena that can be defined globally but not in detail (Xenakis gives as examples 'the collision of hail or rain with hard surfaces, or the song of cicadas in a summer field').[34] Musical interpretation of such laws allowed Xenakis to generate, for example, massive curves of overlaid string glissandos in *Metastaseis* for orchestra (1953–4), his first acknowledged composition and the last to include fragments of serial motivic working, or highly differentiated and alive textures in his next piece, the orchestral *Pithoprakta* (1955–6). But Xenakis's methods must give one cause for extreme doubt that the sophistication of his mathematics is expressed in his music, which is not to say that his works fail to impress as bold panoramas of sound.

It would, however, be misleading to suggest that an awareness of statistical phenomena in the composition, performance and perception of music could help only in the handling of sound masses, for Stockhausen at the same time was demonstrating otherwise. Again the starting-point was his work with Meyer-Eppler and his discovery of basic truths about sound. Among these was the fact that one could define the formant spectrum of a complex sound without being sure just which frequencies would be present at any particular instant: the example quoted from *Gruppen* shows the expression of this statistical distribution of frequencies (in their rhythmic embodiments), some present throughout, others making only an occasional contribution. In works for smaller formations, the quintet of *Zeitmasze* and the soloist of the Piano Pieces V–X, Stockhausen was able to allow statistical uncertainties of musical flow.

Writing these compositions after a period of intensive work in the electronic studio, he was determined to take advantage of musical possibilities peculiar to live performance, among which, most notably, is a freedom of rhythmic interpretation. Experience with *Kontra-Punkte* and the first group of piano pieces had perhaps indicated that notated durations, however scrupulously marked, did not define timings precisely but served rather as mean values for the approximations of performers. In *Zeitmasze* and the second set of piano pieces this imprecision is made structurally functional, in that the rates of musical unfolding (and in *Zeitmasze* the temporal relationships among the five parts) are dependent less on notational prescription than on the limitations of performance technique. *Zeitmasze* is thus an elastic play of five time-strands, each of which mixes passages in strict tempo with others whose speeds are determined by, for example, the players' capacities to play as fast as possible or as slowly as possible within one breath, with a fluid variability in the need for synchronization. Each of the piano pieces combines fixed rhythms with elements whose rhythmic characters depend on the performer's dexterity; each also brings together determined pitch structures and others which contradict these or which contribute only a generalized effect. The massive clusters and cluster-glissandos of Piece X are among the most striking of these statistical phenomena, or super-groups, where the character of the whole matters much more than the detailed contents. But in this respect the work is no more than a representative member of a set which throughout reveals new pianistic techniques and sonorities: Piece VII, for instance, beautifully exploits the resonance effects obtained when strings are freed by silent depression of the keys.

Notwithstanding the qualities of sound and shapeliness shown by the piano pieces, *Zeitmasze* is Stockhausen's most ambitious essay in integrating metronomic definition with free tempo and fixed metre with ametrical scatterings of notes. At the same time, like some of the piano pieces, it mixes points and groups in what the composer calls 'collective form'.[35] Example 35 gives some indication of this, and also of the work's counterpointing of different time layers as well as its profusion of imitations of interval and contour (compare, for example, the cor anglais and clarinet lines). Clearly such music poses great problems of coordination, yet the relative independence of the parts gives players scope to bring out the bounding energy in Stockhausen's ideas. No work could better illustrate the self-confidence of the European avant garde at this point, nor the exhilaration they felt in fresh discovery.

THE OLDER GENERATION

By the mid-1950s the achievements of composers then in their 20s or early 30s were beginning to have an effect on those of an earlier generation. Though Stravinsky set out on his personal road to serialism before any such influence could have been possible, his Movements for piano and orchestra (1958–9) plainly reflect, both in their instrumentation and in their unusual rhythmic complexity, his admiration for *Kontra-Punkte*. Meanwhile his contemporary, Varèse, had joined with his younger colleagues still more decisively by becoming a composer of electronic music, though this had also been a dream of his own since the time of World War I.

Varèse's first work to employ electronic resources was *Déserts* (1949–54), which offers opportunity for reflection on the differences between the new medium and the old, since the 'organized sound' on tape is interpolated into a composition for an orchestra of wind

Ex. 35

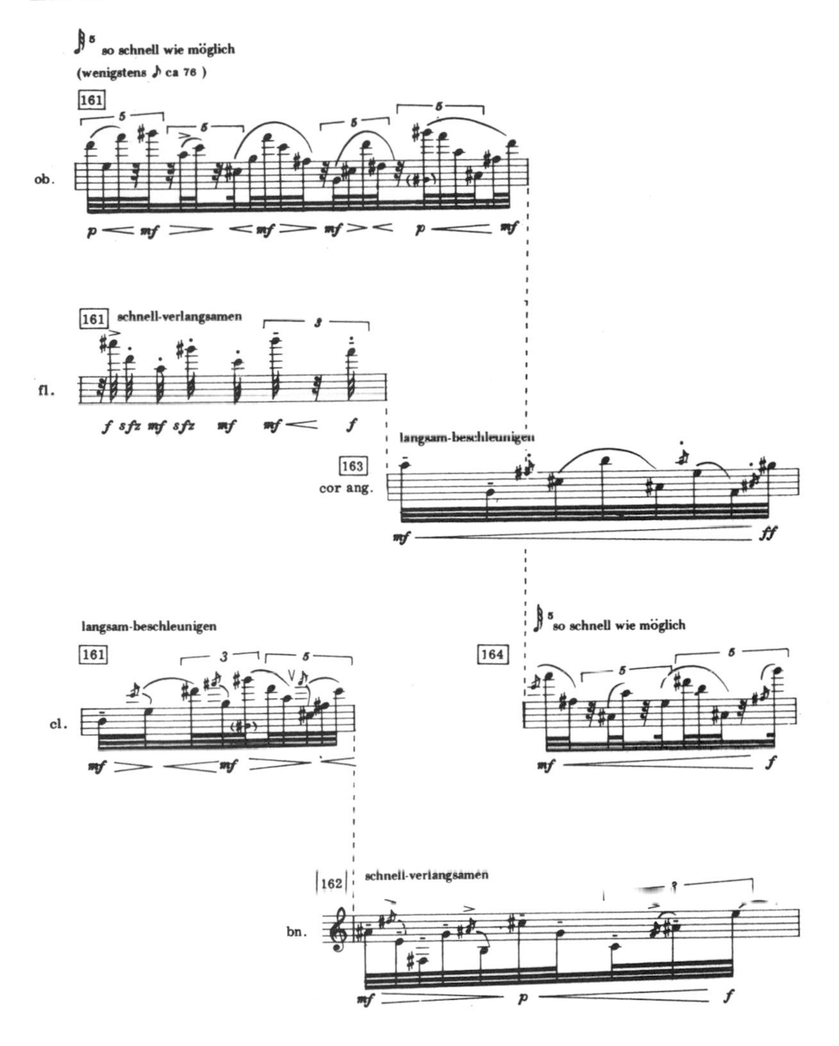

instruments, piano and percussion. Babbitt has justly drawn attention to the subtlety with which Varèse assembles timbres from his ensemble,[36] and indeed much of the scoring suggests an almost Webernian feeling for timbre-melody which was quite new to Varèse's music, the instruments being used to vary the colours of the sustained pitches which serve as points of arrival and reference in the athematic development.[37] By contrast, the three tape inserts are crude and often ill defined, perhaps reflecting the poverty of the facilities in the Paris studio where Varèse worked on his material, perhaps limited rather by an old man's natural difficulty in adapting to new modes of composition.

But the latter suggestion is immediately contradicted by the *Poème électronique* for tape alone (1957–8), in which Varèse used a variety of sound sources: electronically generated melodies, wedges of distorted organ sound (a potent image which occurs also in *Déserts*), industrial noises and fragments from a recording of his own *Etude pour 'Espace'*. Only a bold imaginative drive could weld together material so diverse and so rich in expressive resonance to make a piece lasting for no more than eight minutes. In its destined auditorium, a futuristic pavilion designed by Le Corbusier (with the help of his assistant Xenakis) for the 1958 World Exhibition at Brussels, and given the spatial effects that could be obtained from batteries of loudspeakers on the interior walls, the effect of the *Poème* must have been overwhelming.

Among those present to witness it were many of the leading younger composers, pictured at the time in a much published photograph.[38] Stockhausen is there, and so too are Kagel and Berio, Maderna and Pousseur, Brown and Schaeffer, all in jovial mood; the relaxed comradeship of the group is unmistakable. But they are presiding over the supine body of John Cage, and it was his influence that was to rear up and rout whatever unity they had supposed themselves to have.

REPERTORY

Babbitt: String Quartet no. 2 (1954, Associated). Nonesuch H 71280.
—— Two Sonnets for baritone, clarinet, viola and cello (1955, Peters).
—— *All Set* for jazz ensemble (1957, Associated). Nonesuch H 71303.
—— *Partitions* for piano (1957, Lawson). CRI 288.
Berio: *Chamber Music* for mezzo-soprano, clarinet, cello and harp (1953, Suvini Zerboni). Philips 6500 631.
—— *Nones* for orchestra (1954, Suvini Zerboni). RCA RL 11674.
—— *Perspectives* on tape (1956, unpublished). Compagnia Generale del Disco ESZ 3.
—— *Allelujah II* for orchestra (1956–7, Suvini Zerboni). RCA RL 11674.
—— *Momenti* on tape (1957, unpublished). Limelight LS 86047, Philips 836 897 DSY, Philips 835 485 AY.

——*Serenata I* for flute and 14 players (1957, Suvini Zerboni). RCA VICS 1313, Véga C30 A139.
—— *Thema – omaggio a Joyce* on tape (1958, unpublished). Philips 836 897 DSY, Philips 835 485 AY, Turnabout TV 34177.
Boulez: *Le marteau sans maître* for contralto, alto flute, viola, guitar, vibraphone, xylorimba and percussion (1953–5, revised 1957, Universal). Adès 16003, CBS 73213, Harmonia Mundi HMS 30682, Philips 1488, Véga C25 A67.
—— *Doubles* for orchestra (1957–8, unpublished), expanded as *Figures–Doubles–Prismes* (1963–8, unpublished).
—— *Poésie pour pouvoir* for orchestra and tape (1958, unpublished).
Eimert: *Zu Ehren von Igor Stravinsky* on tape (1957, unpublished). Wergo 60006.
Henze: *König Hirsch,* opera (1952–5, Schott), revised as *Il re cervo oder Die Irrfahrten der Wahrheit* (1962, Schott).
—— *Concerto per il Marigny* for piano and seven players (1956, Schott). Véga C30 A65.
—— *Kammermusik 1958* for tenor, guitar and eight players (1958, Schott). L'Oiseau-Lyre DSLO 5.
—— *Der Prinz von Homburg,* opera (1958, Schott).
Kagel: *Musica para la torre* on tape (1952, unpublished).
—— String Sextet (1953, revised 1957, Universal). Véga C30 A 278.
—— *Anagrama* for four singers, speaking chorus and 11 players (1955–8, Universal).
Krenek: *Pfingstoratorium – Spiritus intelligentiae, sanctus* on tape (1956, unpublished). DGG LP 16134.
Maderna: *Serenata* for 11 players (1954), revised as *Serenata no. 2* (1957, Suvini Zerboni). Time 8002 (revised version).
—— *Continuo* on tape (1958, unpublished). Limelight LS 86047, Philips 835 485 AY.
Messiaen: *Oiseaux exotiques* for piano, 11 wind and seven percussion (1955, Universal). Véga C30 A65.
Nono: *Incontri* for 24 players (1955, Ars Viva). Véga C30 A66.
—— *Il canto sospeso* for three singers, chorus and orchestra (1956, Ars Viva).
—— *Composizione per orchestra no. 2: Diario polacco* (1958, Ars Viva).
Pousseur: *Symphonies à quinze solistes* (1954–5, Universal).
—— *Quintette à la mémoire d'Anton Webern* for clarinet, bass clarinet, violin, cello and piano (1955, Universal).
—— *Exercices* for piano (1956, Universal).
—— *Rimes pour différentes sources sonores* for orchestra and tape (1958–9, Suvini Zerboni). RCA VICS 1239.
Stockhausen: Piano Pieces V–X (1954–5; VI, IX and X revised 1961; all

Universal). CBS 72591–2 (complete), Philips 6500 101 (IX), Véga C30 A278 (VI), Vox STGBY 637 (VIII), Wergo 60010 (X).
—— *Zeitmasze* for flute, oboe, cor anglais, clarinet and bassoon (1955–6, Universal). DGG 2530 443, Véga C30 A139.
—— *Gruppen* for three orchestras (1955–7, Universal). DGG 137 002.
—— *Gesang der Jünglinge* on tape (1955–6, unpublished). DGG LP 16133, DGG 138 811.
Stravinsky: Movements for piano and orchestra (1958–9, Boosey). CBS 72007.
Varèse: *Déserts* for small orchestra and tape (1949–54, Colfrank). Columbia MS 6362, CRI 268, EMI C 061 10875.
—— *Poème électronique* on tape (1957–8, unpublished). Columbia MS 6146.
Xenakis: *Metastaseis* for orchestra (1953–4, Boosey).
—— *Pithoprakta* for orchestra (1955–6, Boosey). Nonesuch H 71201.
Zimmermann: *Perspektiven* for two pianos (1955, Schott).

7 Chance and Choice

In retrospect it is less surprising that Cage should have had a great influence on the European avant garde than that the impact of his work should have been delayed. The reason may perhaps be found in Boulez's antipathy towards Cage's indeterminacy, following a period of warm mutual regard, so that it was not until 1954, when Cage returned to Europe for a concert tour with Tudor, that his music came to the notice of European composers. Stockhausen was then impressed by the new piano sonorities revealed by Cage and Feldman, and also by their new approach to musical time, rhythms being defined in performance, not on paper: the Piano Pieces V–X implicitly acknowledge the debt in their dedication to Tudor. But not until 1956, when he composed the next piece in the cycle, did Stockhausen allow more than the moderate relaxation of *Zeitmasze*, composing a piece in which separate fragments are to be joined in any order; and only after Cage and Tudor had paid another visit to Europe, in 1958, did the innovations of the American vanguard gain a wide following. The ground had been prepared in the previous year, when Maderna had discussed Cage's work at Darmstadt and when *Die Reihe* had published, between Stockhausen's '. . . how time passes . . .' and Pousseur's elucidation of the current state of his technique, a short piece by Cage describing the 'compositional process' involved in creating his Music for Piano 21–52 (1955) by means of chance operations.[1] Nevertheless, the real turning-point came with Cage's personal appearance in 1958.

MOBILE FORM

Before Cage's arrival, however, the European vogue for mobile form had already been initiated by Stockhausen's Piano Piece XI and

Boulez's Third Piano Sonata (1956–7). The Stockhausen piece was the first European composition to give the performer the freedom to alter the form within a movement: 19 'groups' are disposed on a large sheet of paper, and the player 'begins with whichever group he sees first'.[2] He next 'casts another random glance to find another of the groups' and continues in that manner until a group has been reached for the third time; the piece then ends. The order of the groups is thus entirely free, but Stockhausen manages to link them into what he may have seen as a Markov chain, 'a sequence of mutually dependent symbols',[3] since at the end of each group he gives a 'registration' of the tempo, dynamic level and mode of touch to be used for the next, whichever that is.

Though the mobile form of Piano Piece XI suggests comparison with earlier works by Brown (and, indeed, with the earliest example of 20th-century indeterminacy, Cowell's 'Mosaic' Quartet of 1934), in concept it has much closer links with Stockhausen's own immediately preceding compositions, both in the use of a notion from information theory and in the creation of a musical form as the analogue of a sound (see *Gruppen*). 'Piano Piece XI', he has said, 'is nothing but a sound in which certain partials, components, are behaving statistically. . . . As soon as I compose a noise . . . then the wave structure of this sound is aleatoric. If I make a whole piece similar to the ways in which this sound is organised, then naturally the individual components of this piece could also be exchanged, permutated, without changing its basic quality.'[4]

Boulez was mistrustful of his colleague's new departure, finding in it 'a new sort of automatism, one which, for all its apparent opening the gates to freedom, has only really let in an element of risk that seems to me absolutely inimical to the integrity of the work'.[5] For him the need was not to introduce chance but to limit its field of action, and that need had been made urgent by his own experience, as he made clear in his article 'Aléa', a key document in the aesthetics of chance: 'Despairingly one tries to dominate one's own material by an arduous, sustained, vigilant effort, and despairingly chance persists, slips in through a thousand unstoppable loopholes. "And it's fine that way!" Nevertheless, wouldn't the composer's ultimate ruse be to *absorb* this chance?'[6]

Chance is to be absorbed, Boulez goes on to suggest, in musical structures that depend on a degree of flexibility, perhaps in tempo: there were already examples of such structures in his own music

(*Structures Ib, Le marteau sans maître*) and in that of Stockhausen (*Zeitmasze,* Piano Pieces V–X). Chance can also be accommodated, he proposes, in musical forms which are mobile, and this possibility he explored most deeply in his Third Piano Sonata, which is perhaps a creative criticism of Stockhausen's Piano Piece XI and certainly a complement to it. Characteristically, Boulez does not arrive at a musical structure by seeking parallels between form and timbre, but from serial necessity and an eagerness to transpose a literary influence, that of Mallarmé. The sonata is mobile on the largest scale in that there are eight possible ways of ordering the five movements, or 'formants' as Boulez calls them, following the nomenclature of his earlier theoretical speculations.[7] He has also suggested that there might be 'développants', other movements 'strikingly distinct but none the less related by their structure to the initial formants'.[8] However, so far from growing in this way, the work has remained a torso, with only two complete formants, *Trope* and *Constellation-Miroir,* in print. Each of these manifests the literary sources of the composer's ideas: *Trope* has a 'Texte' which is the subject of a 'Parenthèse', a 'Commentaire' and a 'Glose', while *Constellation-Miroir* is laid out in sprinklings of fragments which can be linked in alternative routes, thus recalling the appearance of Mallarmé's *Un coup de dès.*

The structural link between the formants is at the level of the basic series, which in *Trope* is considered as a succession of four units suggesting cyclical concatenations of serial forms (Example 36)[9] and also containing the germ of the mobile form of the whole formant. Two of the serial units, *b* and *d,* together have the same content as a transposition of *a* down a minor 3rd; the foreign group *c,* a symmetrical pairing of minor 3rds, is a 'trope' which interrupts the larger symmetry. Like the serial units, the four sections of the formant can be cyclically permuted (the piece is spirally bound to facilitate this), and the piece also takes up the idea of 'troping', in that the music abounds in commentaries interpolated into or superimposed upon the basic structural skeleton. This is a formal principle which Boulez had employed in the slow movement of the Second Sonata and in *Structures Ib,* as has been noted, but in *Trope* there is the additional refinement of a distinction between obligatory and optional glosses. Example 37, from the opening of 'Parenthèse', shows one of the latter inserted into a straightforward serial chain which is that of Example 36.

Ex. 36

Ex. 37

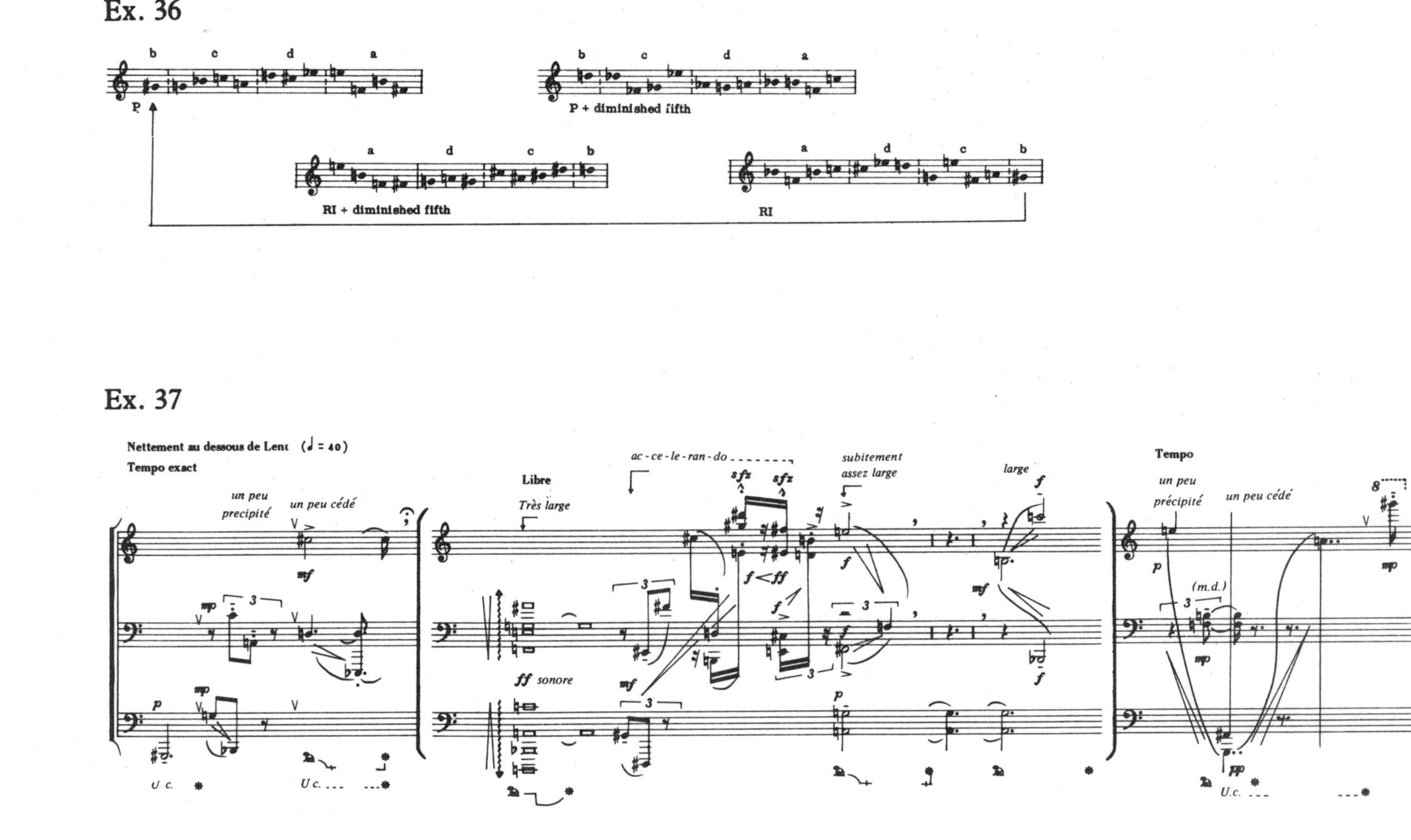

b
c
d
a
P
P + diminished fifth
RI + diminished fifth
RI
Nettement au dessous de Lent (♩ = 40)
Tempo exact
un peu
precipité
un peu cédé
mf
mp
3
p
U c.
Libre
Très large
ac - ce - le - ran - do
sfz
sfz
f < ff
f
subitement
assez large
large
ff sonore
Tempo
un peu
précipité
un peu cédé
8
(m.d.)
pp
U.c.

It is not difficult to see how, in terms of its serial units, registral placings and rhythmic cells, the parenthetic material comments on what has gone before: compare, for example, the accelerando run of *c* units in the parenthesis with the preceding *c* group at 'un peu précipité', or the parenthetic *d* groups with that in the main text, or the registral fixing of the A–G minor 7th. In this short extract, as in *Trope* as a whole, it is possible to observe the ways in which Boulez utilizes networks of correspondences – rhythmic, intervallic, dynamic and timbral – to develop and connect his ideas. The only exceptional feature of Example 37 is the obviousness of the demarcation between a strict framework of serial unfolding and its vast possibilities for extension, a contrast emphasized by oppositions of tempo, rhythmic variety and textural density, and further pointed by such details as the sensed 'correction' when the second obligatory passage repeats an E–F fall just heard in the free material.

Constellation-Miroir, planned as the central sun around which the sonata's other formants revolve, is considerably more complex in form, though again shaped by contrasts of texture between its 'points' (single-note structures) and 'blocs' (massive chords and arpeggios): the formant begins with a brief mixture of the types and then alternates three sections of 'points' with two of 'blocs'. This large-scale organization is fixed, but within each section numerous orderings are available, so that the player 'must direct himself through a tight network of routes' as he confronts what Boulez has likened to a map of an unknown city.[10] Unforeseen and subtle connections infiltrate the paths, and these give the formant its feeling of labyrinthine openness, though hardly less important are the fluidities of movement (a controlled rubato is generally demanded), and the wide variety of sounds obtained from scrupulously marked pedallings as well as from resonance effects, so that the visual distinction of the score, printed in red for 'blocs' and green for 'points', is matched by its tonal appeal.

The Third Piano Sonata is related to Boulez's next major undertaking, *Pli selon pli,* a 'portrait of Mallarmé' for soprano and orchestra (1957–62),[11] rather as the first book of *Structures* is related to *Le marteau sans maître:* in both cases the keyboard works are essentially explorations of compositional technique (hence in both the comparatively unsecretive exhibition of serial derivations) while the vocal compositions exploit the poetic implications and discoveries of their predecessors. But though it owes much to the sonata, *Pli selon pli* is by no means so open in form. Instead the five movements, if all are played, must be placed in a symmetrical sequence, beginning and ending with pieces for full orchestra (*Don* and *Tombeau* respectively) and reaching inwards to one for soprano with nine-piece percussion ensemble (*Improvisation sur Mallarmé II*). The formal choices which are permitted – in the ordering of orchestral blocks at the end of *Don*, for instance, or in the selection from alternative materials in *Improvisation sur Mallarmé III* – are much restricted by comparison with those in the sonata; *Pli selon pli* owes its elasticity more to variable tempos and to the superimposition of orchestral streams flowing at different rates, as in *Gruppen*. Of course, from the point of view of a composer concerned with measuring the limits of chance, it would be hazardous to repeat in orchestral music the multiple routings of the Third Sonata. That might be possible with a duo, as Boulez and Pousseur showed in their respective works for two pianos, the second book of *Structures* (1956–61) and *Mobile* (1956–8), but it soon became impractical with larger ensembles.

In any event, being formed on texts, and on a particular arrangement of texts, *Pli selon pli* is bound to be more directed in form. The poems chosen for the outer movements are 'Don du poème' and 'Tombeau' (the homage to Verlaine), one of Mallarmé's earliest non-juvenile poems and one of his last. These movements represent, therefore, the birth and the death of the poet, but they stand too for the nature of artistic creation, at once a genesis of expressive value and an extinction of creative impulse. 'Don du poème' is further the celebration of a literary birth, in that the poem contains some foretaste in imagery and metre of the *Hérodïade*, and Boulez's *Don* similarly looks forward to the remainder of *Pli selon pli*. After a dedicatory setting of the opening line, the text disappears (becomes 'central and absent', to recall Boulez's terminology) and the music goes into a state of nascence, of suspended chords, through which prefigurings of the other four movements are drawn to the fore in reverse order and then lost. *Tombeau* is also largely an orchestral piece, with the voice entering this time only at the end, there to be extinguished by a *sforzato* chord which links with the opening crack of *Don* in a typically Mallarméan assimilation of birth to death.

The first two *Improvisations sur Mallarmé* allow the poem to be present as well as central, and so the transposition of text into music is more readily observed.[12] As in *Le marteau sans maître*, the operation takes place simultaneously on levels of imagery and deeper structure, the former represented by, for example, the ornate vocal melismas for the undulating lace curtain of 'Une dentelle s'abolit' (Example 38) or the use of registral fixing (see again Example 38) and a scintillating, resonant instrumentation to correspond with metaphors of coldness, transparency, whiteness and reflection in both poems. Verbal structures find expression in changes of vocal style to mark formal divisions (four of the five poems of *Pli selon pli* are sonnets), in the deployment of different compositional principles to distinguish masculine from feminine endings, and in musical eightnesses for octasyllabic lines. All this is very far from Cage's abandonment to chance, and indeed Boulez's containment of free-

Ex. 38

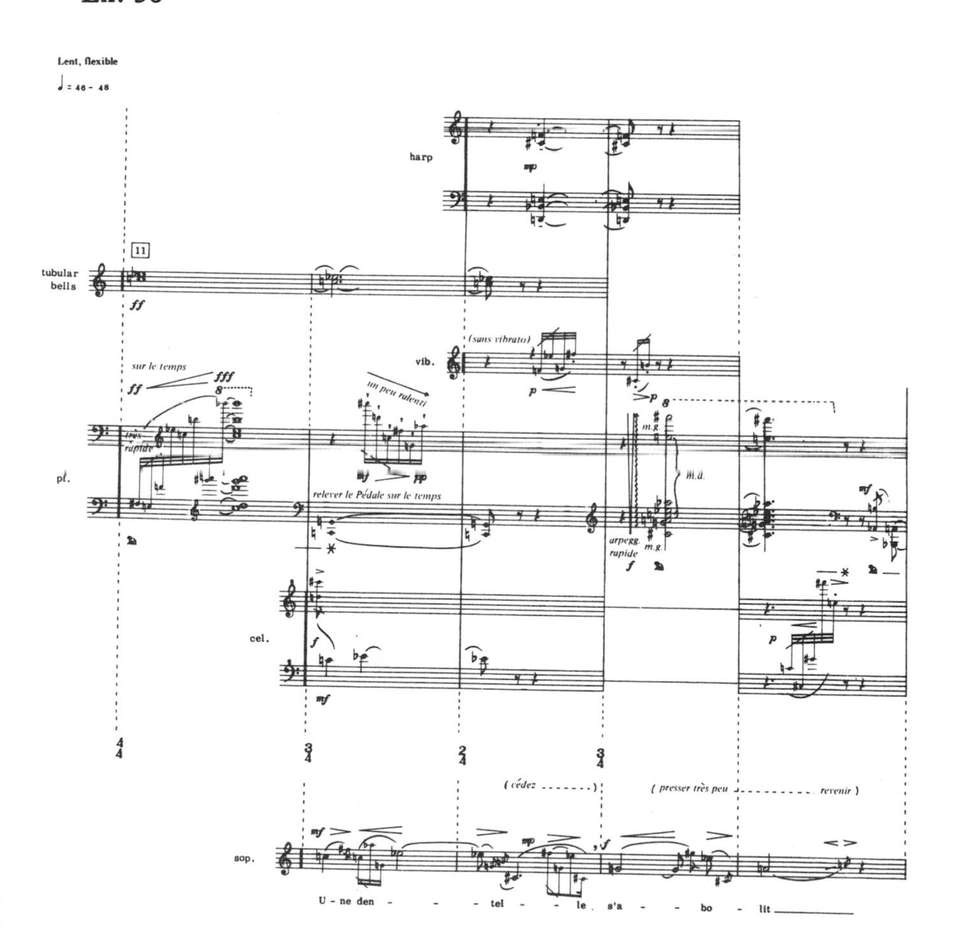

dom in the Third Sonata, the second book of *Structures* and *Pli selon pli* allows room for the unpredictable, the vague and the flexible while ensuring that these indeterminacies arise strictly within the bounds of an artistic discipline.

THE AMERICAN CONTRIBUTION

Cage's opposing viewpoint is implicit in such statements as this, a very characteristic anecdote from his lecture 'Indeterminacy': 'Down in Greensboro, North Carolina, David Tudor and I gave an interesting program. We played five pieces . . . that have in common indeterminacy of performance. . . . I pointed out to the audience that one is accustomed to thinking of a piece of music as an object suitable for understanding and subsequent evaluation, but that here the situation was quite other. . . . I said that since the sounds were just sounds this gave people hearing them the chance to be people, centred within themselves where they actually are, not off artificially in the distance as they are accustomed to be, trying to figure out what is being said by some artist by means of sounds. Finally I said that the purpose of this purposeless music would be achieved if people learned to listen; that when they listened they might discover that they preferred the sounds of everyday life to the ones they would presently hear in the musical program; that that was alright as far as I was concerned'.[13]

It is perhaps paradoxical, therefore, that at this time Cage should have been producing new works in some numbers, unless one holds to the view that the message of meaninglessness and anarchic freedom needs to be stated many times and in many different ways. Typical of this period, though unusual in its encyclopaedic survey of indeterminate notations, is the *Concert for Piano and Orchestra* (1957–8), providing a solo part which can be played in any order with any omissions, together with 13 similarly libertarian instrumental parts. The work may furthermore be performed simultaneously with others from the same phase in Cage's output: the comic and virtuoso *Aria,* which calls for contrasting kinds of vocal deportment, or the *Solos for Voice,* or *Fontana Mix*, which may be realized on tape. This last is not an electronic composition but rather a game-kit to be used in the manufacture of a tape piece: the score is a set of transparent sheets inscribed with lines and dots.

Cage worked on his own realization of *Fontana Mix,* as a flux of the most diverse sounds and recordings, at the electronic studio in Milan, where he also produced two works for solo performance on television, *Sounds of Venice* and *Water Walk* (both 1959). These audio-visual entertainments introduced an explicit theatrical dimension to Cage's work, though they had been preceded in 1952 by his participation in the prototypes of what later came to be known as 'happenings' (events involving several performers in unstructured activities). Theatre, thus broadly interpreted, now began to be identified with music in Cage's view, and in 1960 he created two works in which dramatic anarchy is at least as important as musical purposelessness: the *Theatre Piece*, an inchoate spectacle for up to eight performers, and *Cartridge Music*.

Leaving aside the earlier pieces which Cage had intended for broadcasting, *Cartridge Music* is the earliest example of live electronic music, requiring several players to generate sounds by inserting objects into gramophone cartridges or by acting upon pieces of furniture to which contact microphones have been attached. The aim was not only 'to make electronic music live' but also 'to bring about a situation in which any determination made by a performer would not necessarily be realizable. When, for instance, one of the performers changes a volume control, lowering it nearly to zero, the other performer's action, if it is affected by that particular amplification system, is inaudible. I had been concerned with composition which was indeterminate of its performance; but, in this instance, performance is made, so to say, indeterminate of itself'.[14]

For someone with Cage's desire to eliminate all traces of dictatorship by the artist, this must clearly be regarded as some kind of breakthrough, but by now his extreme abstention from responsibility was not shared by those who had been his close colleagues at the beginning of the decade. Brown declared his distance from Cage in denying that his work was 'intended to be "free" of art, choice, responsibility, beauty, form, content or anything' and insisting on the virtue of choice, though of choice 'within an intentionally ambiguous environment'.[15] His works of this period, such as the two sets of *Available Forms* for orchestra (1961–2), usually provide more or less conventionally notated materials which permit choices of formal sequence, tempo and so on; the attitude is that of a relaxed Boulez.

Feldman meanwhile, having abandoned his graph scoring, developed a new technique for specifying sounds while allowing them to flower in their own time. In his Piece for Four Pianos (1957) he provided each player with the same part, made up of exquisitely placed chords, and then instructed them to choose their own durations for each chord within an agreed tempo, producing 'a series of reverberations from an identical sound source'.[16] Subsequent works, including the *Durations* series (1960–61) and *For Franz Kline* (1962), employ more varied ensembles and give each instrument a different part while removing the requirement for a common tempo, so that lines drift to their conclusions one by one.

Wolff, by contrast, was anxious to encourage interaction among groups of instrumentalists. His *Duo for Pianists II* (1958) is exacting in its demands that the performers should use their freedom in quite precise ways: each part gives rudimentary coded information for the choice of notes to be played within a given time span, and the two players have to be alert to cues from each other.[17] A composition, Wolff has said, 'must make possible the freedom and dignity of the performers. It should have in it a persistent capacity to surprise (even the performers themselves and the composer)'.[18] In later works, such as *In Between Pieces* for three players (1963), he was to pursue this ideal by removing the precise definitions of the *Duo for Pianists II* in order to focus attention, his own and that of his musicians, on a keen response to what is heard.

INDETERMINATE NOTATION

At Darmstadt in 1959, the year after Cage's visit, it became clear that the introduction of chance into composition would have much more far-reaching effects than it had been allowed in the mobile forms of Stockhausen and Boulez. A course in 'music and graphics' included a performance of Cage's *Concert* and also brought forward works by European composers who had been stimulated by American innovations in notation and by Tudor's style of playing, among them Kagel's *Transición II* for pianist, percussionist and tapes (1958–9), Sylvano Bussotti's *Five Piano Pieces for David Tudor* (1959) and Stockhausen's *Zyklus* for percussionist (1959). There was also a lecture by Stockhausen,[19] in which he spoke of a 'music for reading' made conceivable by the 'emancipation of the graphic from the acoustic element' which he noted in the scores of Cage and Bussotti. As if to demonstrate that emancipation, Cage had in the previous year given an exhibition of his scores as graphic art, when the art critic of the *New York Times* had found in them 'a delicate sense of design . . . that transcends the purely technical matter of setting down music'.[29]

The transcendence of this 'purely technical matter' is also to be observed in the scores of Bussotti, which exhibit a creative draughtsmanship not hitherto associated with the business of composing. In his case, however, the extravagant appearance of the music would appear to serve a function in exciting not only the reader's imagination but also that flamboyant behaviour he expects of his performers. Example 39 a section from his *Per tre sul piano*

Ex. 39

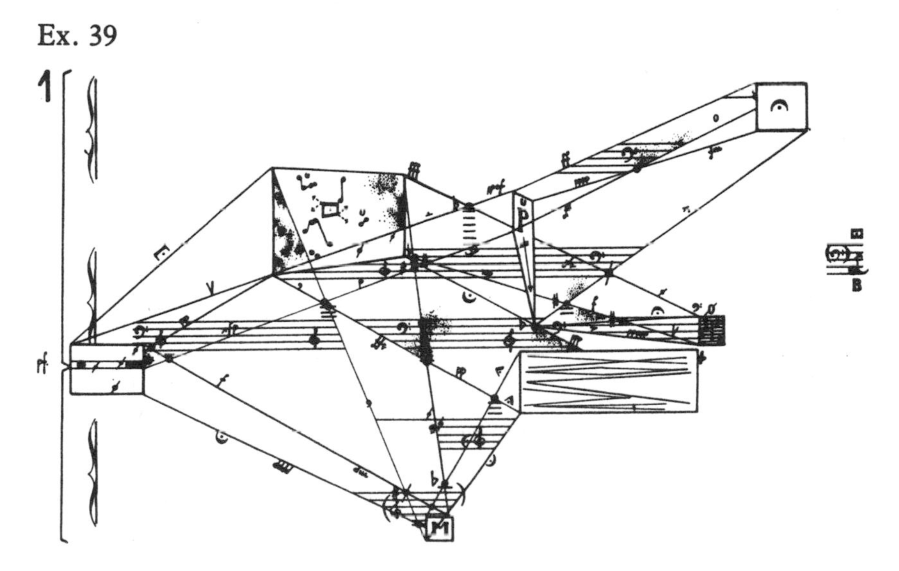

(1959), is typical. In this piece, for three players at one piano, 'the instrument becomes a prone body, alternately caressed, cajoled and assaulted by its suitors',[21] and the notation is not unhelpful in suggesting a properly erotic manner of performance. A prefatory note to the published score of Bussotti's *Sette fogli,* of which *Per tre sul piano* is one, states that the composer had originally planned an explanatory apparatus, but that, during the decade which passed between composition and publication, the works had established their own performing tradition. The enigmas of such notations as those of Example 38, therefore, are to be unravelled in the light of that tradition.

Bussotti's glorification of the decadent and sensual is even more explicit in his *Pièces de chair II* (1958–60), a cycle of homosexual love poems set for various combinations of piano, voices and instruments, and available in various versions. Even when there is no text, as in the arrangements published as *Five Piano Pieces for David Tudor* (1959) and *Pour clavier* (1961), the physicality of this music is unmistakable, and Bussotti's view of musical performance as a theatrical display of eroticism can no more be ignored in his other instrumental works of the period, among which the *Fragmentations* for one player on two harps (1962) are significantly dedicated to Sade and Artaud.

Such a casting of the instrumentalist as seducer or rapist was made possible by what Tudor had achieved in his performance of Cage's music, exploring the whole body of the piano for the sounds it can produce and so extending earlier work by Cowell and Cage himself. Kagel was also influenced by this, as well as by Cage's calligraphy, but instead of pressing player and instrument into a physical relationship, as Bussotti was doing, he preferred to regard with a certain ironic detachment the incongruity between complex notations and impure results. In its outlandish sophistication, its rotatable discs and movable slides, the score of *Transición II* proceeds from such a work as Boulez's Third Sonata, while its intention to fuse 'in one single declension' the musical present (heard in performance) with the past (returning on tape) and the future ('pre-experienced' by means of tapes made beforehand) suggests a Stockhausen-like will to integrate temporal strata.[22] And yet a performance of the work can hardly fail to seem an absurd spectacle in which two musicians, operating on a piano, undertake meticulous actions in the service of musical aims which remain obscure, and in that most important respect *Transición II* may be taken as a caricature of avant-garde endeavour.

In subsequent works Kagel developed what came to be known as 'instrumental theatre' in a more overtly comic and critical manner. Often he shows also, as he had in *Anagrama* and *Transición II*, an interest in neglected possibilities of sound: *Sonant* (1960), scored for the unusual ensemble of guitar, harp, double bass and drums, suggests the influence of Feldman in its unsynchronized parts and its absorption with extremes of quiet, but the players' bashfulness also has a theatrical import quite alien to Feldman's music, and Kagel went still further in taking the then unusual step of requiring his musicians to speak. Also from this period is *Sur scène* for bass, mime, speaker and three keyboard players (1958–60), a work whose fundamental idea was 'to create a spectacle out of elements borrowed from traditional musical life: instrumental playing, exercises which precede performance (Scales, vocalises, etc.), the commentaries of a musicologist. . . . Music becomes a character on stage, which represents the reversal of the situation in opera, lyric theatre or dramatic music generally'.[23]

Any conjunction with theatre had been specifically avoided by most young European composers in the 1950s, for no dramatic addition could be controlled with precision or made to serve the appreciation of music which demanded clearly focused listening to multiple aspects of sound. But now that the dam of determinacy had been thoroughly demolished by Cage, music-theatre could become an alluring medium. Even Stockhausen was encouraged to follow *Sur scène* with his *Originale* (1961), which also takes up the use of recordings to combine musical tenses as in *Transición II*. However, this was for some years an isolated venture, and the work has only very rarely been revived. The more important fruits of Stockhausen's second encounter with Cage and Tudor are to be found in *Zyklus* and in the trio *Refrain* (also 1959), of which the former proves him as much a master of graphic invention as Cage, Bussotti or Kagel, with the important difference that here the new signs are always strictly functional. They are made necessary by Stockhausen's choice of sounds which cannot be completely defined by conventional notation (the marimba and the vibraphone, the two precisely pitched members of the instrumentarium, are used only in glissandos) and by his ranging from determined events to others which are prescribed only as statistical distributions on a particular instrument in a given time.

Characteristically, Stockhausen establishes a scale of nine degrees of aleatory freedom within an event, and the work is, like Piano Piece X, an attempt at allowing the ordered to co-exist with the disordered. It also has links with Piano Piece XI as the magnified image of single sound, in this case a complex vibration in which nine constituents (or different instruments) followed staggered cycles of growth and decay, the performer turning through a circle within his battery of instruments. The circle may be started at any point, and the score is, like Boulez's *Trope,* spirally bound to make this feasible. This cyclical structure also arises from Stockhausen's determination here to combine 'the predominantly static open form of Piano Piece XI' with 'the idea of a dynamic, closed form: the result is a circular, "curvi-linear" form'.[24] The need to complete the cycle gives *Zyklus* the goal-directed dynamism which had been absent from the piano piece, but at the same time the player has the opportunity to introduce optional elements provided and to interpret signs with more or less latitude without the formal shape being threatened.

The tranquil *Refrain,* so different in character from the virtuoso test piece which *Zyklus* was designed to be, shares with it the aim of accommodating chance within a determined framework. Returning to a favourite technique, Stockhausen assembles sounds from his complement of piano, celesta and vibraphone, using additional percussion instruments and vocal enunciations by the players to affect attacks and resonances. Example 40 shows one system from

Ex. 40

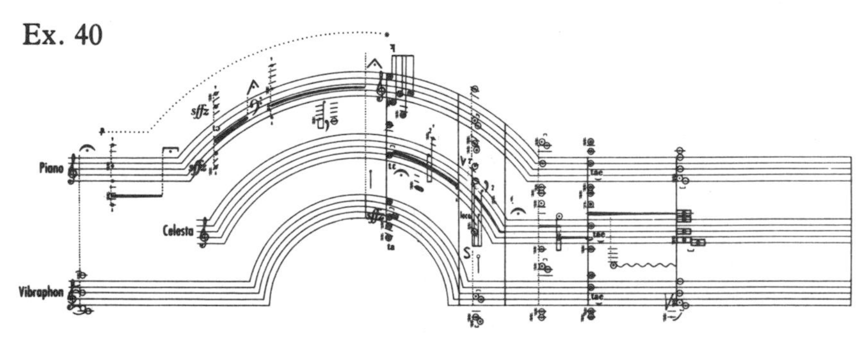

the single-page score; the shape is no notational quirk but a real necessity, since the 'refrain' that gives the work its title is printed on a transparent strip which can be swivelled at the centre, so that its material can be made to overlay any section of the fixed systems. Thus the meditative resonances and figurations of Example 40 and the other fixed material, suggestive of oriental music in both instrumentation (see Boulez's *Improvisations sur Mallarmé I–II,* whose exotic borrowings have been acknowledged by the composer)[25] and time scale, are repeatedly and unpredictably disturbed by glissandos, clusters, trills and so on, all more physical and dynamic in feel.

Mediation between the determinate and the indeterminate, variously essayed in works by Boulez and Stockhausen from this period, is also a concern in Berio's *Circles* for female voice, harp and two percussion (1960). Berio had earlier, in his *Sequenza I* for flute (1958), introduced proportional rhythmic notation in the manner of Brown, and in *Tempi concertati* for flute, violin, two pianos and ensemble (1958–9) he had provided a masterly exercise in the integration of different kinds of musical movement, incorporating a development from fixed to proportionally notated rhythms, and including also some degree of choice in the interpretation of the flute part. *Circles* extends the controlled openness of *Tempi concertati* to the composer's favoured mode of vocal expression, and forms a link with *Chamber Music* and *Thema – omaggio a Joyce* in the close relationship fostered between voice and instrument, word and sound.

Berio uses three poems by Cummings, repeating two of them to form a palindromic form of the type *ABCB'A'*. Since the poems are, in the order *A–C*, of increasingly dislocated syntax, the work describes an arc from words as information to words as sound and back again, and the same movement is shown in the musical transition between extremes of rhythmic definition (conventional symbols in *A*, *B*, *A'* and *B'*, but proportional notation in *C*) and precision of instrumental pitch (harp alone in *A*, free mixture of pitched and unpitched instruments in *C*, harp and mostly pitched percussion in *A'*). Example 41 is a passage from the central section which shows the typical *C* qualities as well as the work's general response, on both vocal and instrumental planes, to the sound and sense of the words: examples include the hi-hat and suspended cymbal strokes which connect with the 's' sounds in the voice, or the drum rolls which take their cue from the text, or, most obviously, the outburst at the word 'collide'. The percussion notation here owes something to *Zyklus*, with which the work shares the combination of circular with directed form, though Berio fixes a starting-point. Circular features have already been mentioned; the direction comes in the vocal treatment. The ornamented lyricism of the first poem is progressively stripped as the work proceeds to its centre, with a change to syllabic singing in *B* and the introduction of speech and rounded Italian forms of Sprechgesang in *C* (see Example 41, where the rectangular note heads indicate approximate pitch and the open ones speech). But then, instead of recovering its expressive *fioriture*, the voice is drawn more and more within the musical ambit of the instruments in *B'* and *A'*, and this integration is dramatized by having the soloist move to positions nearer the ensemble.

Berio's use of different vocal styles to articulate a form – a technique made possible by the artistry of his then wife Cathy Berberian, whose mimic agility Cage had exploited in his *Aria* – appears again in *Epifanie* for female voice and orchestra (1959–61, revised 1965), his only essay in Boulezian formal mobility. The score

Ex. 41

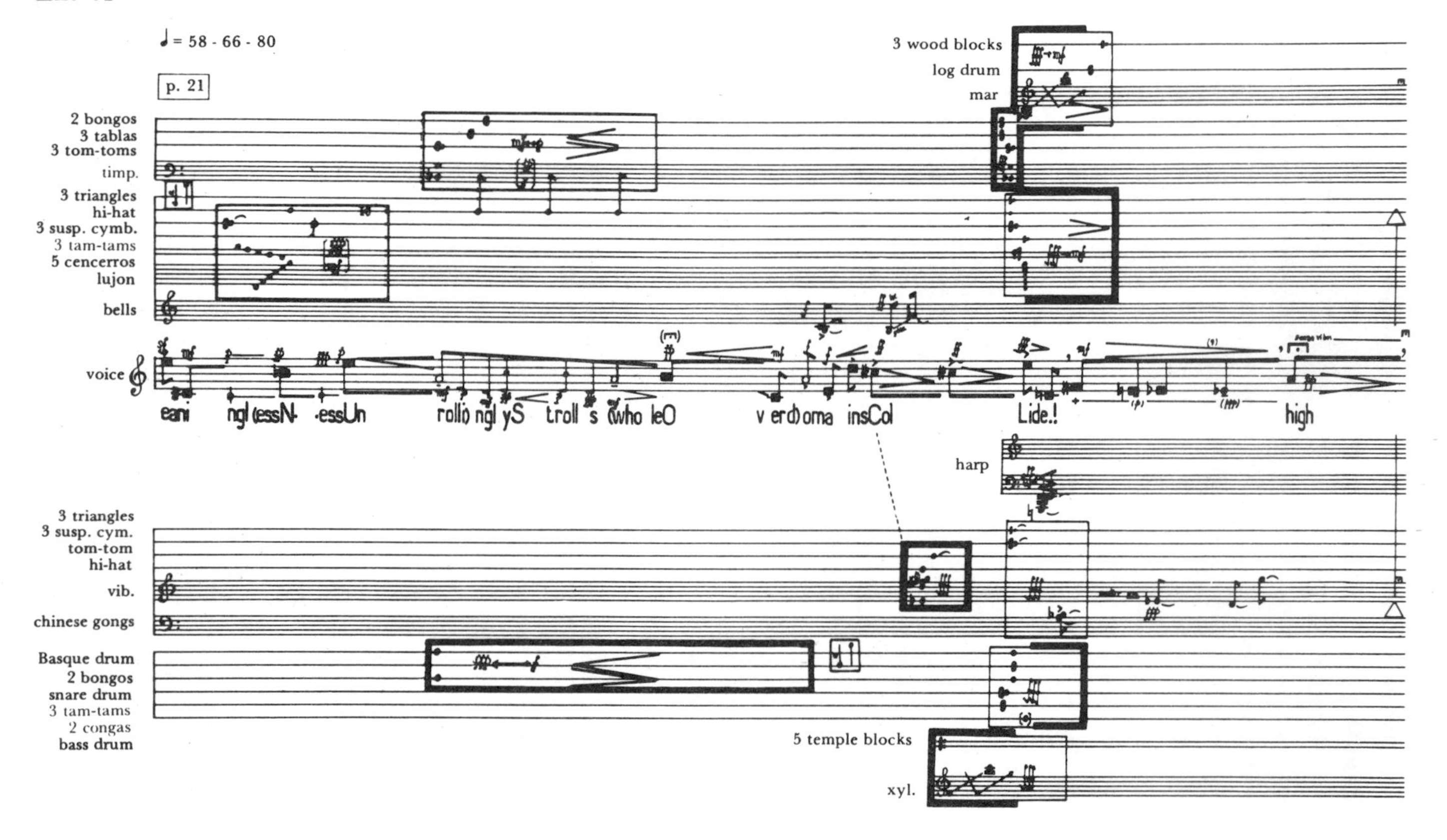
♩ = 58 - 66 - 80
p. 21
2 bongos
3 tablas
3 tom-toms
timp.
3 triangles
hi-hat
3 susp. cymb.
3 tam-tams
5 cencerros
lujon
bells
voice
eani ngl(essN- -essUn rolli) ngl yS troll s (who leO v erd)oma insCol Lide.! high
3 wood blocks
log drum
mar
harp
3 triangles
3 susp. cym.
tom-tom
hi-hat
vib.
chinese gongs
Basque drum
2 bongos
snare drum
3 tam-tams
2 congas
bass drum
5 temple blocks
xyl.

comprises seven orchestral pieces, which can be played separately as *Quaderni,* and five vocal items to texts by various European writers in the original languages, all 12 sections to be arranged in one of several permitted sequences. But as distinct from the case of Boulez's *Pli selon pli* or even his Third Sonata, rearrangement of the segments can grossly alter the work's meaning. 'The chosen order', Berio notes, 'will emphasize the apparent heterogeneity of the texts or their dialectical unity.'[26] In his recording it is the latter which comes to the fore, with 'a gradual passage from a lyric transfiguration of reality (Proust, Machado, Joyce) to a disenchanted acknowledgement of things (Simon)'[27] and finally to Brecht's warning that words should not be allowed to seduce us from deeds.

GAMES, SOME WITH COMPUTERS

Mobile musical forms, with their rules and alternative routes, almost inevitably have to some extent the appearance of games, but usually only the performers have access to the board. If the audience is to share in some of the secrets, then the rules of play must in some manner be exhibited, as they are in Pousseur's *Répons* for seven instruments and actor (1960, revised 1965). Pousseur, who had composed his *Mobile* and his tape piece *Scambi* in aleatory forms, here presents the musicians with 'a set of rules of play and with musical material which permits them to respond, with a certain margin of improvisation, to all the situations into which the game puts them'.[28] The game is not a competitive match but rather a means of generating a musical form in which musicians can, within limits, use their own initiatives in deciding how to fulfil the roles they are at different times assigned, those of 'conductor', 'soloist', 'duo player' and so on; the work has the same democratic intention as the contemporary pieces of Wolff. But Pousseur found, not surprisingly, that the rules remained obscure to the audience, and so the work took on an esoteric character which he had wished to avoid. The 1965 version, prepared in collaboration with Michel Butor, adds an actor to the original septet and makes the musical masque more intelligible.

Two orchestral games devised by Xenakis, *Stratégie* (1962) and *Duel* (1958–9), lack the possibilities for collective invention dear to Pousseur and are indeed competitions in which, the composer remarks with unashamed élitism, 'there exists a gain and a loss, a victory and a defeat, which may be expressed by a moral or material reward such as a prize, medal or cup for one side, and a penalty for the other'.[29] Each score provides a set of 'sonic constructions' for each of two conductors, who win points according to which 'construction' they choose as rejoinder to the opponent's last move. There is no aesthetic connection whatever between the 'constructions' and the game, any more than there is between ivory and the rules of chess, and it may be felt that the game holds less compulsion for the audience than for the warring maestros.

Xenakis's musical games came about not so much through the influence of his colleagues' aleatory works as through his own interest in the mathematics of probability: game theory was bound to catch his attention along with the stochastic formulae he was using at the same period in a number of pieces composed with the aid of a computer. These use the computer not to generate sounds but rather to undertake the calculations required by Xenakis's compositional method: after he has defined his 'sonic entities', their mode of relation in time and the general formal process of the composition, the determination of events can safely be left to mechanical computation, and then the computer output can be translated into a musical score.[30] This was the procedure adopted in such pieces as *ST/4* for string quartet (1956–62), *ST/10* for ensemble (1956–62) and *ST/48* for orchestra (1959–62), the prefix in each case indicating that these are stochastic works and the numeral showing the number of instruments employed. Composition here is limited to the setting of ground rules, and it is therefore not surprising that the difficulty and complexity of these scores should be quite out of proportion to their density of musical thought, nor that Xenakis's achievement should be the greater in those pieces in which he could work directly with his material, notably in the subtly related textures of *Orient-occident* on tape (1959–60) or the bold effects of another electronic work, *Diamorphoses* (1957).

Another computer composition of this period, and one which gained some notoriety as the first piece of music thus produced, was the *Illiac Suite* for string quartet (1957), programmed at the University of Illinois by Lejaren Hiller and Leonard Isaacson. In this case again the computer's decisions were hedged in by rules and instructions,[31] but the way was open to an abdication from aesthetic choice no less complete than that of Cage. Before long Hiller and Cage would even be collaborating on a work, *HPSCHD* (1967–9), the indeterminacy of automatism joining hands with the indeterminacy of chance.

REPERTORY

Berio: *Sequenza I* for flute (1958, Suvini Zerboni). Adès 16005, Mainstream 5014, Nonesuch HB 73028, Wergo 319, Wergo 60021, Wergo 60052.
—— *Tempi concertati* for flute, violin, two pianos and 21 players (1958–9, Universal). Adès 16001, Adès 16012, Philips 836 897 DSY.
—— *Circles* for female voice, harp and two percussion (1960, Universal). Candide CE 31027, Mainstream 5005, Wergo 60021.
—— *Epifanie* for female voice and orchestra (1959–61, revised 1965, Universal). RCA LSC 3189, RCA SB 6850.
Boulez: Piano Sonata no. 3: 1 *Antiphonie*, 2 *Trope*, 3 *Constellation/Constellation-Miroir*, 4 *Strophe*, 5 *Séquence* (1956–7, Universal, 1 [fragment *Sigle*], 2 and 3 [*Miroir* version] only). CBS 72871, Guilde Internationale du Disque SMS 2590 (both nos. 2 and 3 only).
—— *Structures: deuxième livre* for two pianos (1956–61, Universal). Wergo 60011.
—— *Pli selon pli:* 1 *Don* for soprano and orchestra (1962, Universal); 2 *Improvisation sur Mallarmé I: Le vierge, le vivace et le bel aujourd'hui* for soprano and seven percussion (1957, Universal), version for soprano and small orchestra (1962, Universal); 3 *Improvisation sur Mallarmé II: Une dentelle s'abolit* for soprano and nine percussion (1957, Universal); 4 *Improvisation sur Mallarmé III: A la nue accablante tu* for soprano and small orchestra (1959, unpublished); 5 *Tombeau* for soprano and orchestra (1959–62, Universal). CBS 72770 (complete); Qualiton SLPX 1130 8 (nos. 2–3); Candide CE 31021, Vox STGBY 611 (no. 3).
Brown: *Available Forms I* for 18 players (1961, Associated), *II* for orchestra (1962, Associated).
Bussotti: *Sette fogli:* 1 *Couple* for flute and piano, 2 *Coeur* for percussion, 3 *Per tre sul piano,* 4 *Lettura di Braibanti* for voice, 5 *Mobile-stabile* for guitars, voice and piano, 6 *Manifesto per Kalinowski* for chamber orchestra, 7 *Sensitivo* for string instrument (all 1959, Universal). Columbia MS 7139 (no. 2), EMI EMSP 551 (no. 3).
—— *Pièces de chair II* for piano, voices and instruments (1958–60, Ricordi), extracts collected as *Five Piano Pieces for David Tudor* (1959, Ricordi), others arranged as *Pour clavier* for piano (1961, Ricordi). EMI EMSP 551 *(Pour clavier).*
—— *Fragmentations* for harpist (1962, Bruzzichelli).
Cage: *Concert for Piano and Orchestra* (1957–8, Peters). EMI C 165 28954–7.

——*Aria* for voice (1958, Peters). Mainstream 5005, Time 8000 (both with *Fontana Mix).*
——*Fontana Mix* for tape or other resources (1958, Peters). Turnabout TV 34046, see also above.
——*Sounds of Venice* for solo television performance (1959, unpublished).
——*Water Walk* for solo television performance (1959, Peters).
——*Cartridge Music* for amplified sounds (1960, Peters). DGG 137 009 (with other works), Time 8009.
——*Theatre Piece* for up to eight performers (1960, Peters).
Feldman: Piece for Four Pianos (1957, Peters).
——*Durations I* for alto flute and piano trio (1960, Peters), *II* for cello and piano (1960, Peters), *III* for violin, tuba and piano (1961, Peters), *IV* for violin, cello and vibraphone (1961, Peters), *V* for violin, cello, horn, vibraphone, harp and piano doubling celesta (1961, Peters). Time 8007 (complete).
——*For Franz Kline* for soprano, violin, cello, horn, piano and chimes (1962, Peters). EMI C 165 28954–7.
Hiller and Isaacson: *Illiac Suite* for string quartet (1957, Presser).
Kagel: *Transición II* for pianist, percussionist and tapes (1958–9, Universal). Mainstream 5003, Time 8001.
——*Sur scène* for bass, mime, speaker and three keyboard players (1958–60, Peters).
——*Sonant* for guitar, harp, double bass and drums (1960, Peters).
Pousseur: *Scambi* on tape (1957, unpublished). Limelight LS 86048, Philips 835 486 AY.
——*Mobile* for two pianos (1956–8, Suvini Zerboni). Véga C30 A278.
——*Répons* for actor, flute, harp, two pianos, percussion, violin and cello (1960, revised 1965, Suvini Zerboni).
Stockhausen: Piano Piece XI (1956, Universal). CBS 72591–2, Philips 6500 101.
——*Zyklus* for percussion (1959, Universal). CBS Sony SONC 16012 J, Columbia MS 7139, Erato STU 70603, Mainstream 5003, Time 8001, Wergo 60010.
——*Refrain* for piano, vibraphone and celesta, all doubling small percussion (1959, Universal). Mainstream 5003, Time 8001, Vox STGBY 638.
Wolff: *Duo for Pianists II* (1958, Peters).
——*In Between Pieces* for three players (1963, Peters). EMI C 165 28954–7.
Xenakis: *Diamorphoses* on tape (1957, unpublished). Erato STU 70530, Nonesuch H 71246.
——*Duel* for two orchestras (1958–9, Boosey).

——*ST/4* for string quartet (1956–62, Boosey). EMI CVT 2086.
——*ST/10* for clarinet, bass clarinet, two horns, harp, percussion and string quartet (1956–62, Boosey). EMI C 061 10011.
——*ST/48* for orchestra (1959–62, Boosey).
——*Orient-occident* on tape (1959–60, unpublished). Erato STU 70530, Nonesuch H 71246.
——*Stratégie* for two orchestras (1962, Salabert).

8 Moments of Parting

'At the first opportunity there was a break-out from the stifling prison of *number,* and then EVERYTHING was allowed including the most idiotic and vulgar exhibitionism. Did anyone expect thus to escape the only reality? And what did this permissiveness and these long holidays from thought signify, if not a continued flight from responsibility?'[1]

Boulez's dismay at the directions music was taking in the early 1960s contrasts markedly with the optimism which he and his colleagues had shared a decade earlier. The search for 'a grammatical expression which would fix the language in precise ways, and which would fix it for a long time to come'[2] had certainly had its successes, but by 1962, when Boulez was writing, it was plain that the possibility of a common language based on the principles of serialism was becoming ever more remote. The unity of concerted effort, which had given strength to Stockhausen, Boulez, Nono and Pousseur in the early 1950s, was no more to be found; perhaps it had always been an illusion. No more were there clear lines of development in the art, and this chapter serves therefore to take note of the situation before the diverse compositional activities of the later 1960s and 1970s are considered.

CHALLENGES TO SERIALISM

Among the young composers who arrived at Darmstadt in the late 1950s were many who eagerly embraced the prevailing orthodoxies and set themselves to producing close copies of works by the leaders of the avant garde. Boulez, whose music had more definable characteristics of style than did the ever-fresh departures of Stockhausen, attracted a number of imitators, particularly from among those French musicians who had learned their musical modernism at the concerts of the Domaine Musical. The early works of Gilbert Amy, for instance, give clear evidence of the beguiling lures of the Boulez manner: his *Cantate brève* for soprano, flute, xylorimba and vibraphone (1957) could hardly fail to show the imprint of *Le marteau sans maître*, and his Piano Sonata (1957–60) is a direct descendant of Boulez's Third.

Boulez himself, while appearing to condone imitation by conducting many works moulded on his patterns, was still more critical of epigonism than of the deficiencies of Cage, Bussotti and others whose work he polemically derided in his survey of contemporary music.[3] It had been his aim to forge a language; he had found himself initiating a style. And in drawing on that style his juniors had ignored his lesson that each work demanded a system of coherent thought uniquely its own. One could not simply take over materials and procedures from a contemporary, any more than one could from the past, for to do so was to overlook the need for determined relationships binding together every level of invention, from general aspects of form and instrumentation down to the details of small-scale structures and the serial data. Paradoxically, therefore, serial thought was being undermined by those who were adopting it most willingly.

Serialism was equally and more openly under attack from those who, like Xenakis,[4] detected a discrepancy between intention and result in certain examples of the most recent serial music. Ligeti, though a subtler critic than Xenakis, makes some of the same points in his 'Metamorphoses of Musical Form',[5] in which he cites examples from Boulez, Stockhausen and others to show how serial principles have proved self-defeating or else have been abandoned in favour of 'higher order' principles, such as those governing the temporal structure of *Gruppen*. From his analysis he derives the notion of 'permeability' in music: a musical structure is said to be 'permeable' if it admits a free choice of intervals and 'impermeable' if it does not (he gives the example of Palestrina's music as being strictly defined by rigid harmonic laws and hence 'impermeable' to an unusual degree). He decides that contemporary works depend for their formal shape more on matters of texture than of harmony, counterpoint or thematic working, and suggests that composition with textures requires attention to be paid to degrees of permeability.

Using the example of *Gruppen,* he notes that 'a dense, gelatinous, soft and sensitive material can be penetrated *ad libitum* by sharp, hacked splinters. . . . "Soft" materials are less permeable when combined with each other, and there are places . . . of an opaque complexity beyond compare'[6] – beyond compare, that is, in late 1958, when Ligeti wrote the article. By the next year he had completed his orchestral piece *Apparitions,* whose première at the 1960 ISCM Festival caused quite a stir in avant-garde musical circles.

Until then Ligeti had been known as a musician who, fleeing from Hungary in 1956, had eventually found refuge with Stockhausen in Cologne, and as the painstaking analyst of Boulez's *Structures Ia.*[7] His concentration in *Apparitions* on effects of texture was bound to seem like a defection, even though the technique was not yet applied as thoroughly or as masterfully as in *Atmosphères* for orchestra (1961) or *Volumina* for organ (1961–2). In these works there is no attempt to work with units of pitch, duration, loudness and timbre in a serial manner, or indeed in any other. Ligeti appears to have concluded that his contemporaries were deluding themselves in supposing that musical minutiae could be composed into meaningful structures, and so he took the drastic step of limiting himself to transformations and oppositions on the largest scale, whether by adopting an imprecise style of graphic notation (in *Volumina*) or by ensuring that smaller musical differentiations are suppressed (in *Atmosphères*). Rhythmic movement is readily eliminated by staggering instrumental entries and avoiding all sense of pulse; harmonic progress can similarly be suspended by the use of sustained clusters in the orchestra, a technique in which Ligeti found the means to create a searing expressive tension, held immobile. From a different standpoint he had arrived at the position of Boulez in *Structures Ia* or Cage in the *Music of Changes:* he had reacted to the immediate past by effacing it, and his later works were to show a progressive rediscovery of modes of particularization which could be distinctive and comprehensible.

Ligeti's critical approach to composition is revealed also in other, very different works of the same period. The *Trois bagatelles* for pianist and the *Poème symphonique* for 100 metronomes are satirical reactions to the kind of 'action music' favoured by Bussotti and to the Cageian 'happening'. But, like Schoenberg in his *Drei Satiren,* Ligeti indicated that he knew also how to take these things seriously, and in his *Aventures* for three singers and seven players (1962) he composed a comic entertainment from scraps of non-verbal communication[8] and instrumental horseplay, a work that acts out the humorous, almost vocal streams of electronic sound in his variously textured tape piece *Artikulation* (1958). He even felt confident enough to direct his wit and cynicism against his own 'cloud' technique in *Fragment* (1961), scored for an unlikely ensemble of heavyweight instruments (double bassoon, bass trombone, double bass tuba, three double basses) and percussion.

Atmospheric 'texture music' appears to have been in the air around 1960, the year in which Stockhausen's *Carré* and Penderecki's *Threnody* for large string orchestra appeared. The latter was one of the first works in which Penderecki displayed his skilled handling of sound masses – principally clusters and glissandos, with frequent use of new performing techniques (see Example 42) – to generate fiercely expressive effects. Though his means sometimes

Ex. 42

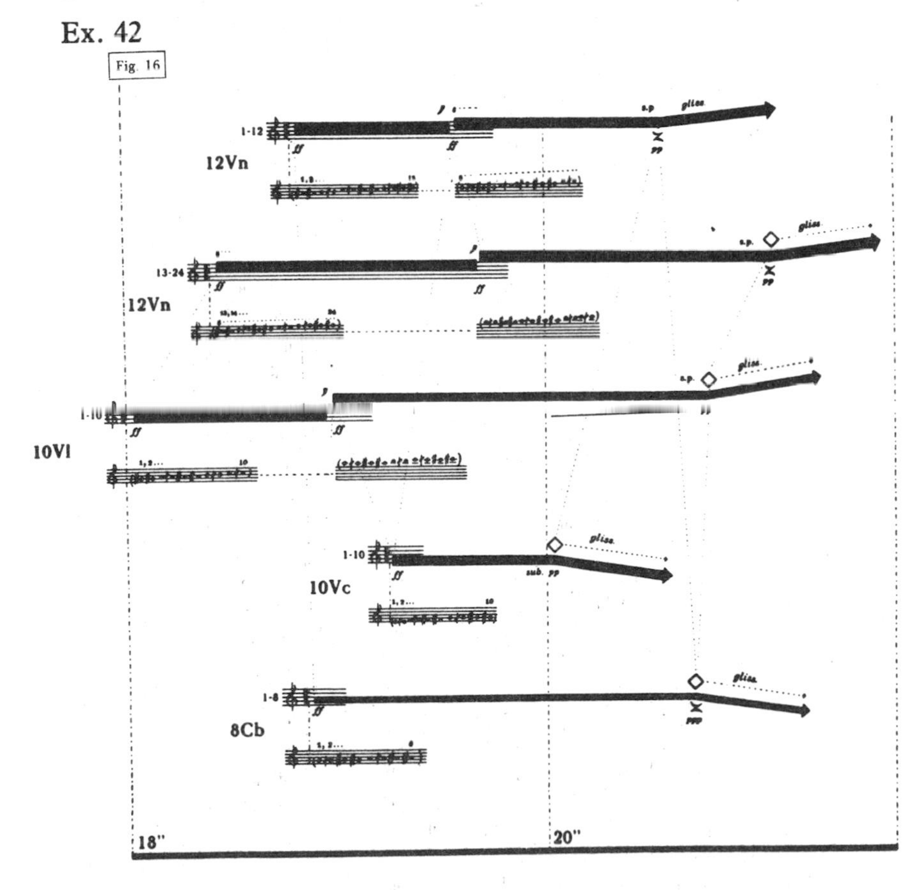

resemble those of Ligeti, his notation is cruder (*Volumina* remains the only serious piece in which Ligeti has suspended his notational exactitude) and his gestures correspondingly simpler. Often his name is associated also with that of his compatriot Lutosławski, though the two share little apart from the fact of having been musically liberated by the Polish cultural thaw of 1958. This allowed Lutosławski to bring forward his *Funeral Music* for string orchestra (1954–8), a work whose slight connections with serialism are less significant than its appealingly straightforward approach to problems of harmonic cohesion: cells consisting only of minor 2nds and tritones are developed in a harmony bereft of 3rds and 6ths. Such a harmonic method made it possible for Lutosławski to react to the experience of Cage's *Concert* by developing aleatory textures in which small elements in each instrumental part may be repeated out of synchrony, for since the form is satisfactorily engineered on the large scale by a unified harmonic consistency, local variability is perfectly acceptable. In *Venetian Games* for small orchestra (1960–61), and in most of the works that have followed, Lutosławski has been able to bring about a combination, based on close harmonic control, of fully notated, metrical music with aleatory, ametrical counterpoint.[9]

This civilization of Cage's innovations, giving function to ideas and procedures which had been invented in the hope of making music purposeless, is almost exclusively a European phenomenon, manifest not only in the music of Lutosławski but also, as noted in the preceding chapter, in that of such otherwise very different composers as Stockhausen, Boulez, Bussotti and Berio. By contrast, serial composers in the U.S.A. have found little to interest them in aleatory liberation: Babbitt, for instance, has never permitted the intervention of chance or choice into his music. Cage's ideas have appealed rather to composers who share his leaning towards performance rather than prescription, towards the unique event rather than the permanent work of art, towards action rather than structure. In the early 1960s his influence was instrumental in the foundation of the Fluxus movement,[10] which brought about a resurrection of dada in performances combining comedy, cheek and perhaps a certain amount of groping after new creative possibilities. Typical, though unusual in its charm, is Composition 1960 no. 5 by LaMonte Young:

Turn a butterfly (or any number of butterflies) loose in the performance area.

When the composition is over, be sure to allow the butterfly to fly away outside.

The composition may be any length but if an unlimited amount of time is available, the doors and windows may be opened before the butterfly is turned loose and the composition may be considered finished when the butterfly flies away.

Rather closer to what is conventionally regarded as music is Young's Composition 1960 no. 7, which consists simply of a notated perfect 5th with the instruction 'to be held for a long time', and which therefore fits into the mainstream of the composer's concerns with pure frequency ratios and with sounds of long duration.[11]

Many of those associated with the Fluxus movement had been pupils of Cage in New York; Young was unusual in having discovered Cage's music and ideas at, of all places, the Darmstadt courses of 1959. Another young composer present on that occasion was Cornelius Cardew, whose music of this period shows an openness to indeterminacy and an unfettered approach more characteristic of an American than of a European musician. Cardew, like Young, had started out as a serial composer: his two string trios (1955–6) and three piano sonatas (1955–8) display an early commitment, unparalleled among English composers at the time, to what was then being accomplished by Boulez and by Stockhausen, whose assistant he became in 1958. However, he responded to the experience of Cage and Tudor at Darmstadt that year by composing a number of works, including the *Two Books of Study for Pianists* (1959), where the influence of recent American music is apparent in the notational innovations and in the complexity of the instructions, which demand from the performer a full engagement of his intellect, technique and taste. If nothing else, Cardew's works suggested that the Cageian revolution was not for much longer to be contained within European notions of art, while the contemporary compositions of other non-serial composers – Ligeti, Xenakis, Kagel, Bussotti and others – were opening up terrain which could neither be accommodated within serialism nor ignored.

THE OLD GUARD OF THE AVANT GARDE

One of Cardew's principal tasks as Stockhausen's assistant was to work on the score of *Carré* for four choral-orchestral formations (1959–60),[12] a work which recalls *Gruppen* in its layout for spaced groups but has quite a different character. Where the earlier work had originated in the theoretical idea of magnifying sound spectra, *Carré* was stimulated by a particular experience of sound, marking a change, characteristic of this period in Stockhausen's career, from abstract speculation to concentrated listening, and a new emphasis on the quality of each sound as an individual event rather than on relationships among sounds. Stockhausen has recalled how the idea of *Carré* came to him when he was spending a lot of time flying across America: 'I was always leaning my ear . . . against the window, like listening with earphones directly to the inner vibrations. And though a physicist would have said that the engine sound doesn't change, it changed all the time because I was listening to all the partials within the spectrum'.[13]

The translation of this experience into orchestral terms resulted in Stockhausen's purest and most comprehensive essay in timbre composition, and so in music which, like the second movement of his *Spiel*, calls for active contemplation of a wide repertory of sounds which succeed one another without any strong sense of logical connection. Attention is directed to what is happening within a sound, to gradual changes created, for example, by slow glissandos or to more precisely figured movements playing on the sonic surfaces, though the tranquil unfolding of *Carré* is several times interrupted by the insertion of contrasting episodes, these vigorously exploiting, as at the climax of *Gruppen*, the possibility of spinning sounds in the centrifuge of the ensembles.

Meanwhile in the electronic studio Stockhausen was at work on *Kontakte* (1958–60), similarly designed for four sound sources and also resembling *Carré* in its slowly changing sonorities and its swirling of sounds through space. But he was more concerned in *Kontakte* with opportunities unique to the medium, and these he outlined in a radio talk of 1961 which used his latest electronic work as example.[14] He mentions two abiding interests – the composition and 'de-composition' of timbres, and the establishment of scales between pitched tone and noise – both of which can be more easily and thoroughly pursued in a medium offering the possibility of smooth transition between dissimilar states. Another of his 'criteria' distinguishing electronic from instrumental music is the new possibility of creating scales of loudness, a parameter which has an important function in *Kontakte* when, by means of carefully regulated levels of volume and reverberation, he creates the illusion of separate screens of sound receding from the listener: in some passages the nearer screens are drawn back to reveal layers extending beyond. This creation of artificial space, as important in the work as the real space which separates the loudspeakers, also makes possible the projection of sounds which appear to come from the distance and then, dropping in pitch to imitate a Döppler effect, fly past the listener, irresistibly suggesting the aeroplane engines which stimulated *Carré*.

But the most significant special feature of electronic music, and the one Stockhausen places first, is the opportunity it provides for demonstrating and exploiting thc cohcrcnt unity of 'coloristic composition, harmonic-meloduc composition and metrical-rhythmic composition'. The continuity of the parameters, their common basis in the phenomenon of vibration, had of course been a matter of interest in the preceding group of works associated with the essay '. . . how time passes . . .', but *Kontakte* is a still more concrete expression of Stockhausen's theory. Example 43 shows an exemplary

Ex. 43

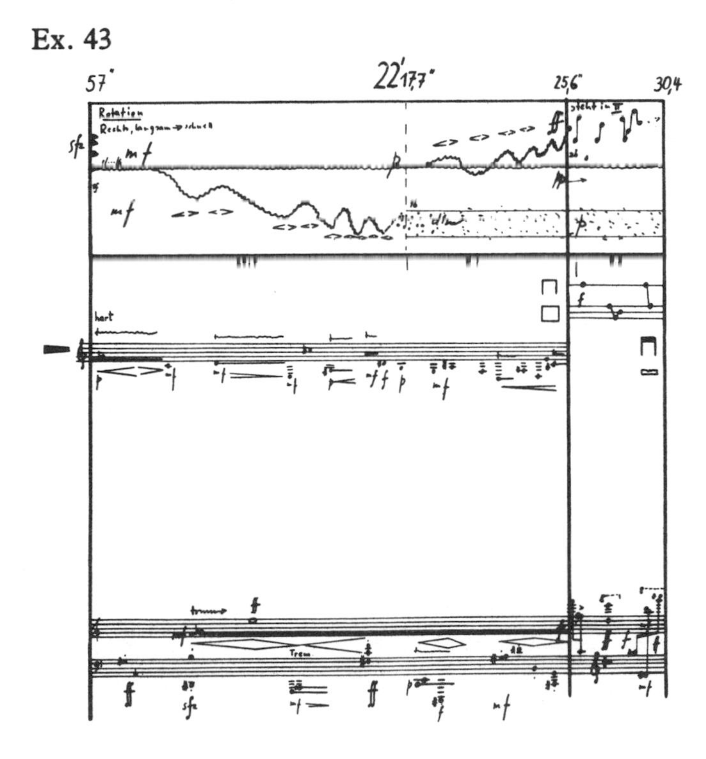

instance where a complex sound is progressively stripped of its components, each of which appears to float away and degenerate into the basic material of single impulses. Progressive deceleration of the constituents therefore takes them from the realm of timbre to that of pitched sound and thence to that of rhythm.

The 'contacts' of the title may thus be seen as referring to the links which are established between the parameters and also between the domains of pitched sound and noise. But at the same time *Kontakte* extends in a smooth continuum from sounds which appear familiar, usually because they resemble those of percussion instruments (though everything in the work is artificially synthesized), to sounds which are entirely unfamiliar, and in the alternative version with piano and percussion joining the tape (see Example 43) the contacts with the instrumental world are dramatized: the performers may seem to capture sounds emerging from the loudspeakers, or the tape may appear to take over material from the instruments and develop it in unforeseen ways. To quote Stockhausen's graphic description: 'The known sounds give orientation, perspective to the listening experience; they function as traffic signs in the unbounded space of the newly discovered electronic sound world.'[15] Examples of such aural direction can be found, for instance, in the short passage which begins at 22′ 25.6″ and is shown in Example 43, both players joining the tape in blobs of sound in the upper register.

Kontakte well displays, in such passages as that of Example 43 and in its general character, Stockhausen's avowed interest in the process of forming rather than in the making of a form.[16] He has, indeed, said that the work's ending is arbitrary,[17] though this spinning swish of sound, gradually disappearing into the far distance, makes a perfectly effective withdrawal; and *Carré* also suggests a relative disinterest in larger design, for whole sections of it may be omitted. Both works, like Boulez's mobile-form compositions of the same period, question the need for temporal progression, but they do so in quite a different manner. Instead of introducing multiple routes and flexibilities of coordination, they obscure the passing of time by their long durations (*Kontakte* lasts for over half an hour and *Carré* can take almost an hour, both playing continuously) and their lack of causal relationships linking one event to the next. As Stockhausen has said of *Kontakte:* 'The musical events do not take a fixed course between a determined beginning and an inevitable ending, and the moments are not merely consequents of what precedes them and antecedents of what follows; rather the concentration on the Now – on every Now – as if it were a vertical slice dominating over any horizontal conception of time and reaching into timelessness, which I call eternity: an eternity which does not begin at the end of time, but is attainable at every *moment*'.[18]

This is the first and basic statement of Stockhausen's concept of 'moment form',[19] a kind of musical structure in which the 'moments', each with its own distinctive character, are to be savoured for their individual qualities rather than understood as links in a chain of musical argument. Where Schoenberg in his serial works (and Babbitt in his) had attempted to find forces to compensate for that directed thrust which had been lost with diatonic harmony, Stockhausen and his colleagues in the European avant garde had concluded by the end of the 1950s that music could exist without such a temporal arrow. Barraqué had determined that the inevitable answer was music which constantly strives for completion but must remain unfinished, Boulez that a musical work might be, as he wrote of the second book of *Structures*, 'a fantastic succession, in which the "stories" have no rigid relationship, no fixed order'.[20] Stockhausen at the same time came up with the idea of 'moments', and if these were truly 'not merely consequents . . . and antecedents' then there was no reason why they should not be, like the elements in a Boulez mobile or in Stockhausen's own Piano Piece XI, subject to variable ordering: this he reintroduced in his grandest celebration of 'the Now', his *Momente* for soprano, four choral groups, brass octet, two electric organs and three percussionists (1961–4).

Momente is an assembly of notionally separate units, the 'moments' of the title, which can be put together in various arrangements; it may be presumed, like the earlier *Punkte* and *Gruppen*, to have been designed as the triumph of a declared technique. However, the variability of the work is greatly circumscribed, particularly in the final version of 1972, by Stockhausen's concern for mediation and by his sense of occasion, which leads him to give the definitive score a long and exhilaratingly dramatic section that could never be anything but an opening.[21] The moments are not freely interchangeable but must be organized, like planets, around the three suns which are moments each emphasizing one of the fundamental attributes of duration, melody and timbre; the planetary moments mix these categories to varying degrees, or else ignore them, and the permissible forms are governed by associations of similarity and contrast. Moreover, Stockhausen sprinkles the work with foretastes of moments to come or reminiscences of moments past, thus encouraging exactly the kind of sense of linear progression that moment form was ostensibly devised to minimize.

In this way *Momente* becomes not a haphazard succession of isolated elements but a spectacular achievement of synthesis.[22] It follows on from *Gesang der Jünglinge* in ignoring any boundary between speech and music, the solo soprano and the choirs enjoying a vast repertory of modes of vocal and non-vocal behaviour. Similarly, it shares with *Kontakte* a refusal to acknowledge any dividing line between the pitched and the unpitched, and it also ranks with *Kontakte* as a crowning work of timbre composition, using its superficially limited but in fact very versatile ensemble to create a wealth of complex sonorities, often dark and enclosed in the music of 1961–4, more outward and brighter in the sections added afterwards.

Momente became a momentous public statement only in the later stage of its development, but while Stockhausen was working on the earlier version several of his colleagues were already concerning themselves increasingly with music directed beyond the circuit of modern-music festivals. Nono's *Intolleranza* (1960–61) was the first opera by a member of the 1950s avant garde, and a work which projects on to the stage that spirit of revolt against bourgeois thinking which its composer had seen as inherent in the new serialism.[23] The opera is a protest against capitalist society's heartless treatment of an immigrant, cast in short scenes which encapsulate incidents of inhumanity and, through the almost constant presence of the chorus, universalize them. At the same time the work brings to a culmination the most broad and vigorous features of Nono's previous output: the strident handling of orchestral sonorities in *Diario polacco* and *Incontri,* the range of choral writing from finely divided textures to powerful mass effects, and the solo vocal lines of large expressive amplitude. But for the first time these are combined with electronic sounds of penetrating force (Nono had made a belated acquisition of studio techniques in his tape piece *Omaggio a Emilio Vedova* of 1960), and after completing his next major work, the *Canti di vita e d'amore* (1962), he was to turn his back for the moment on the resources of conventional concert life.

Meanwhile Berio was producing his own exposé of the destructive social pressures which operate on an individual, his *Passaggio* (1962) enacting the transition of an unnamed female character from human being to chattel. She, alone on the stage, is musically and psychologically stormed by the chorus, who are placed among the orchestra and the audience and so, in a simple but effective manner, involve everyone in the degradation. The vocal writing, both for the soloist and for the chorus, draws on all the new techniques Berio had evolved in *Circles*, in *Epifanie* and in the more recent *Visage* (1961), a tape drama based on the voice of Cathy Berberian. Following the example of *Gesang der Jünglinge* (but not of his own *Thema*, which had used only vocal sounds), Berio here presents a mélange of the vocal and the purely electronic, with the difference that the voice by no means resists interpretation as a character. She is heard in a natural recording almost throughout, but only at two points does she stumble towards verbal expression, towards the enunciation of 'parole' ('words'). For the rest she laughs, moans, sighs, cries and gabbles in nonsense language, all the while evoking an emotional turmoil admitting violent swings from anguish to erotic excitement.

Pousseur's tape ballet *Electre* (1960) occupies the middle ground between Berio's theatrical wielding of the electronic voice and Stockhausen's analytical study of it, while his electronic *Trois visages de Liège* (1961) skilfully graft *Gesang*-like interjections from children's voices on to sonic expanses in the manner of *Kontakte*. These are not negligible achievements, but Pousseur is more individual in those instrumental works of the same period which continue to explore the possibilities of harmonic liaison he had uncovered in his *Exercices*, these works including the *Madrigal* series (1958–62) and *Caractères* for piano (1961), of which the latter also takes further the aleatory variability of his *Mobile*. *Madrigal I* for clarinet (1958) was the first work in which he attempted what Jean-Claude Eloy has described as a 'reactivation of the harmonic values that post-Webernian music had almost neutralized':[24] in other words, he reintroduces a sense of harmonic progression through a subtle emphasis on focal pitches or intervals which manages to avoid any open acknowledgement of tonality. The technique was in essence a development, like so much in the music of the 1950s, from hints in *Kontra-Punkte*, but in that it presaged a more wholesale attempt at integration with the past, it looked forward to the vastly more heterogeneous 1960s and 1970s.

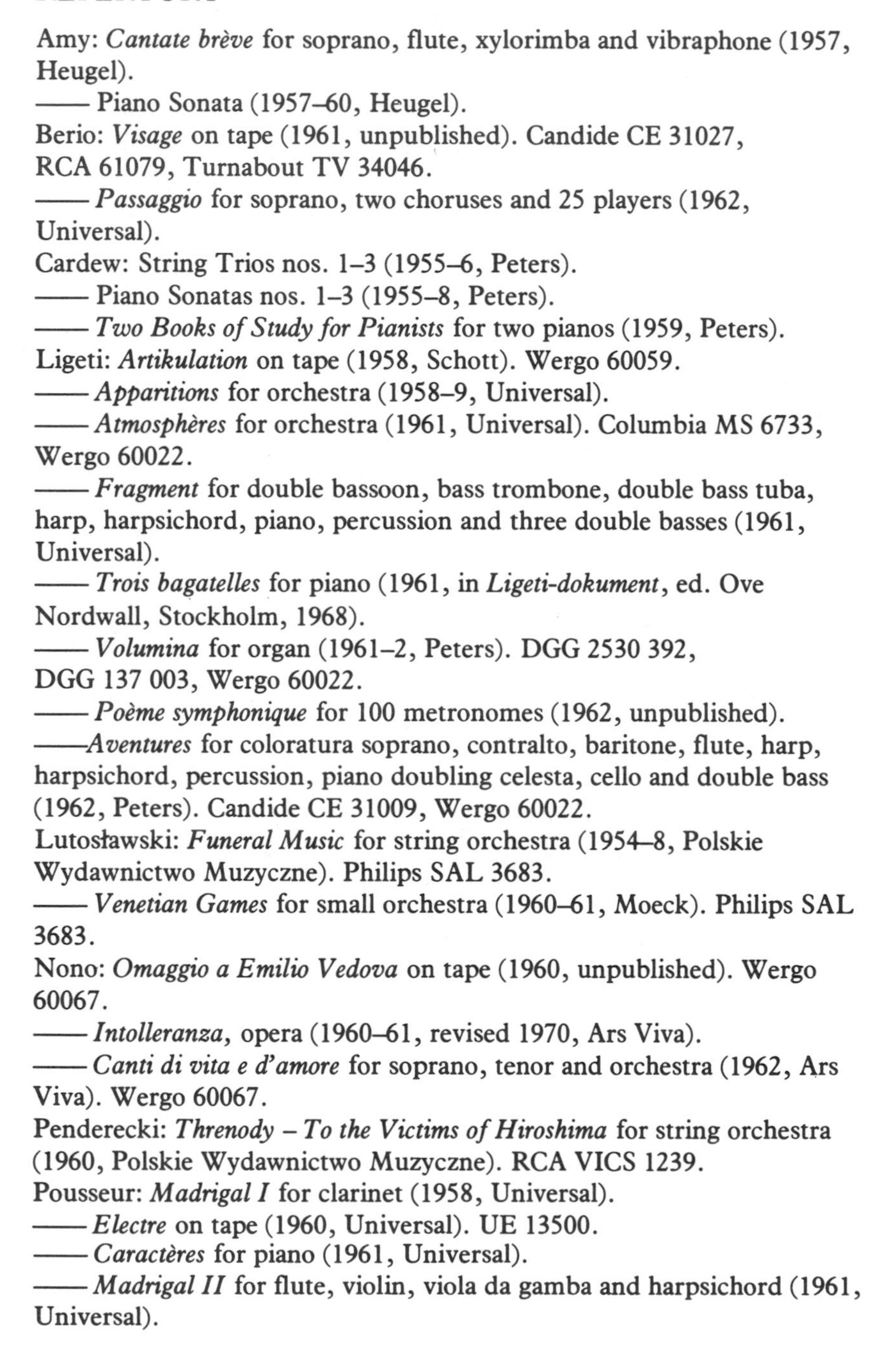

REPERTORY

Amy: *Cantate brève* for soprano, flute, xylorimba and vibraphone (1957, Heugel).

—— Piano Sonata (1957–60, Heugel).

Berio: *Visage* on tape (1961, unpublished). Candide CE 31027, RCA 61079, Turnabout TV 34046.

—— *Passaggio* for soprano, two choruses and 25 players (1962, Universal).

Cardew: String Trios nos. 1–3 (1955–6, Peters).

—— Piano Sonatas nos. 1–3 (1955–8, Peters).

—— *Two Books of Study for Pianists* for two pianos (1959, Peters).

Ligeti: *Artikulation* on tape (1958, Schott). Wergo 60059.

—— *Apparitions* for orchestra (1958–9, Universal).

—— *Atmosphères* for orchestra (1961, Universal). Columbia MS 6733, Wergo 60022.

—— *Fragment* for double bassoon, bass trombone, double bass tuba, harp, harpsichord, piano, percussion and three double basses (1961, Universal).

—— *Trois bagatelles* for piano (1961, in *Ligeti-dokument*, ed. Ove Nordwall, Stockholm, 1968).

—— *Volumina* for organ (1961–2, Peters). DGG 2530 392, DGG 137 003, Wergo 60022.

—— *Poème symphonique* for 100 metronomes (1962, unpublished).

——*Aventures* for coloratura soprano, contralto, baritone, flute, harp, harpsichord, percussion, piano doubling celesta, cello and double bass (1962, Peters). Candide CE 31009, Wergo 60022.

Lutosławski: *Funeral Music* for string orchestra (1954–8, Polskie Wydawnictwo Muzyczne). Philips SAL 3683.

—— *Venetian Games* for small orchestra (1960–61, Moeck). Philips SAL 3683.

Nono: *Omaggio a Emilio Vedova* on tape (1960, unpublished). Wergo 60067.

—— *Intolleranza*, opera (1960–61, revised 1970, Ars Viva).

—— *Canti di vita e d'amore* for soprano, tenor and orchestra (1962, Ars Viva). Wergo 60067.

Penderecki: *Threnody – To the Victims of Hiroshima* for string orchestra (1960, Polskie Wydawnictwo Muzyczne). RCA VICS 1239.

Pousseur: *Madrigal I* for clarinet (1958, Universal).

—— *Electre* on tape (1960, Universal). UE 13500.

—— *Caractères* for piano (1961, Universal).

—— *Madrigal II* for flute, violin, viola da gamba and harpsichord (1961, Universal).

—— *Trois visages de Liège* on tape (1961, unpublished). Columbia MS 7051.
—— *Madrigal III* for clarinet, two percussion and piano trio (1962, Universal). Adès 16001.
Stockhausen: *Carré* for four choral-orchestral groups (1959–60, Universal). DGG 137 002.
—— *Kontakte* on tape, with or without piano and percussion (both versions 1958–60, Universal). DGG 138 811 (tape), Vox STGBY 638 (with instruments), Wergo 60009 (with instruments).
—— *Momente* for soprano, four choral groups and 13 players (1961–4, extended 1969–72, Universal). DGG 2709 055 (final version), Nonesuch H 71157, Wergo 60024 (both earlier version).
Young: Compositions 1960 nos. 1–15, prose scores for various activities (1960, in LaMonte Young and Jackson MacLow: *An Anthology*, Munich, 2nd edition 1970).

Part II
Music in the 1960s and 1970s

9 American Serialism → Computer Music

It seems appropriate to begin the second and necessarily more diffuse part of this survey by considering a branch of contemporary music – that drawing on the ideas of Milton Babbitt – which has grown without momentous interruption from origins covered in Part I. Babbitt has described his goal as that of 'attempting to make music as much as it might be, rather than as little as one obviously can get away with music's being under the present egalitarian dispensation',[1] and he has pursued that aim in forever increasing the complexity, subtlety and integrated wholeness of his compositions. At the same time his high ideals, together with the highly developed techniques of serial composition which make them attainable, have influenced and guided many younger American composers.

Very often, and particularly in Babbitt's music, the fine structuring of musical parameters demands unusual precision in performance, creating problems that do not arise in the medium of tape music. Composers sharing the Princeton regard for rigour have therefore tended to be at the forefront of developments in the electronic medium, and several of them have been active in exploiting computer-programmed sound synthesis.

BABBITT

Some indication of the complexity of Babbitt's more recent music is given by Example 44, the first bar of his *Post-Partitions* for piano (1966). The 12-note aggregate here is partitioned into dyads, each struck twice, so that there are 12 attacks. These attacks occur at 12 different time points (though not with a one-to-one correspondence) in six simultaneous meters, a feature that the dynamic levels are

Ex. 44

designed to clarify, at least to the eye. Throughout the piece a direct relationship is maintained between dynamic level and time point on the scale *ppppp* = 1, *pppp* = 2, . . . *fffff* = 12 (i.e. 0). Thus, for example, the first C in Example 44 is at time point 1 (meter counted in units of a triplet quaver) while the A flat occurring with it is at time point 2 (meter counted in triplet semiquavers); the second occurrence of the dyad is at time point 4 (meter counted in quintuplet semiquavers). In this bar there are two time points used in each of the six metrical streams: 8 and 0 in the semiquaver stream, for instance, and 3 and 7 in that of septuplet semiquavers. These 'time-point dyads' are the rhythmic equivalents of the pitch-class dyads introduced, since by convention C is ascribed the pitch-class number 0, C sharp 1, D 2, and so on; hence, for example, the dyad A flat–C has the numbering 8–0, and the dyad E flat–G is 3–7. There is thus a close connection between the pitch organization and the rhythmic organization, while the latter, as has been mentioned, is intimately linked with the organization of dynamics. Nor does this exhaust Babbitt's repertory of means for increasing his music's density of thought, for there is significance also in the registral placings and in the durations employed.

Babbitt's concentration of musical meaning, his use of every parameter to assist in conveying structure, is evident too in an orchestral work from the same period, *Relata I* (1965), on which he has written one of his rare exegetical articles.[2] *Relata I*, like *Post-Partitions*, has a time-point structure based on divisions of the crotchet into units of a third, a quarter, a fifth, a sixth, a seventh and an eighth, and again like *Post-Partitions* it has an unvarying tempo, the perceived speed being altered by changes in the number of simultaneous metrical streams and hence in the density of events. But the availability of a large ensemble makes possible an organization, unlike that of the piano work, in which timbre can play a rich part, there being a different instrument or homogenous group for each of the 48 fundamental serial forms. Though Babbitt in his analysis emphasizes such ' "atomic" musical features', he also suggests how large sections of the work are connected together in ways which parallel the smaller relationships of the music, right down to those of its pre-compositional data. In this respect *Relata I* may be regarded as leading towards what John M. Peel has distinguished as Babbitt's 'third period'[3] (he specifically mentions *Post-Partitions* as a transitional work). According to Peel, the music of this period is preoccupied 'with polyphony, that is, fundamental "lines" or "voices" (in whatever musical dimensions these be interpreted) contributing ordered subsets or segments to form a larger, more complex, ordered set which itself may then be regarded as a new or derived line subject to the same transformations and the same interpretation in a musical dimension as a fundamental line'. Babbitt himself raises similar expectations when he writes of his Third Quartet (1969–70) that 'further recalling should lead the listener from those local coherences and immediate modes of progression and association which are instantly apparent through those analogously constructed and related larger units which subsume them, on to the total foreground as a totality'.[4]

The Third Quartet is another work to show typical 'third-period' features of metronomic stability, of changes of velocity engineered by changes in metrical density, of sectional formation, and of the use of every musical parameter, here including the distinction between arco and pizzicato, to project the structure of integrated polyphony. A ramified construction of this kind inevitably imposes severe burdens on performers: the example from *Post-Partitions* is enough to suggest how much exactitude in the playing of rhythms and dynamics is expected – indeed, must be expected if the time-point structure is to be made unequivocally plain. And given the marked tempo here, which makes the smallest metrical unit equivalent to a 12th of a second, the problem is no mean one. For a soloist or a small ensemble the demands of Babbitt's music are probably still within the bounds of the practical (though it is, of course, another matter whether such fine subtleties as the time-point structuring of Example 44 can be perceived and interpreted, even in a perfect performance). An orchestra, under present conditions of work, is most unlikely to be able to give a fair account of a work so rhythmically complex as *Relata I*, and Babbitt drew a bitter lesson from his experience of the work's first performances, noting that 'only about 80 per cent of the notes of the composition were played at all, and only about 60 per cent of these were played accurately rhythmically, and only about 40 per cent of these were played with any regard for dynamic values'.[5] Until things can be improved, he suggests, 'composers of such works who have access to electronic media will, with fewer and fainter pangs of renunciation, enter their electronic studios with their compositions in their heads, and leave those studios with their performances on the tapes in their hands'.[6]

Apart from conferring the benefit of accuracy, the electronic medium also makes possible those rehearings which are essential if Babbitt's structures are to be appreciated, and it is perhaps significant that since he began working in the electronic studio, in 1960, Babbitt's concern has moved to ever deeper levels of structure, to the extent that the obvious patterning of his earlier music has tended to disappear: the symmetries and the clear processes of his Second Quartet (1954), for instance, had long been outgrown by the time he came to write his Third, which he almost congratulates himself 'does not instance any cherished surface "formal" pattern'.[7] There is a similar contrast, though less extreme, between his first two works for tape alone, the Composition for Synthesizer (1960–61) and *Ensembles for Synthesizer* (1962–4). The Composition develops with more obvious continuity to a climax which shakes at a single chord, while *Ensembles* is a composite of many tiny and ingeniously worked fragments, beginning as an alternation between short counterpoints and chords from which notes are successively removed, then continuing as a closely integrated mosaic of more diverse 'ensembles'.

All of Babbitt's electronic works have been created with the aid of the RCA Synthesizer[8] at the Columbia–Princeton Electronic Music Center in New York. This machine, which has little in common with the voltage-controlled synthesizers later produced by Robert Moog and others, is able to generate a wide variety of sounds or else to alter sounds in quite precise ways. Oscillators and noise generators provide the raw materials which the composer, giving the synthesizer its instructions on a punched paper roll, can obtain at will with a high degree of control over pitch, timbre and volume. The apparatus is thus a kind of super-instrument, one with an enormous range of quasi-instrumental voices, and one which appears most happily employed when, as in Babbitt's compositions, working within the equal-tempered 12-note scale. Babbitt readily acknowledges the instrumental character of his electronic music and doubts the value of works which, like Stockhausen's *Gesang der Jünglinge* or *Kontakte*, are based on entirely new premises unimaginable without electronic means of creating and transforming sound. 'Perhaps', he has written, 'a system founded on the unique resources of the electronic medium, and on premises hitherto unknown and not as yet even foreseeable, will be discovered and vindicated. Meanwhile, if it is only meanwhile, there is still an unforeseeably extensive domain in which the electronic medium uniquely can enrich and extend the musical systems whose premises have been tested, and whose resources barely have been tapped.'[9]

Yet Babbitt's caution does not keep him from taking advantage of the dramatic possibilities of the medium in his *Philomel* for soprano and tape (1963). This work, effectively a scena for the soloist accompanied by recorded soprano and synthesized sounds, is set at the instant when the tongueless Philomel of Ovid's story undergoes metamorphosis into a nightingale, and that transformation can be accomplished, as it were, through the mirror of the loudspeakers, the vocal contribution coming now from the human soloist, now from a disembodied entity: an echo song brings out the transitions particularly clearly. At the same time the dense interweaving of electronically synthesized polyphony gives the work a sure musical continuity and also makes a poetic contribution in evoking the nocturnal forest through which Philomel flees and flies. There is, in addition, some proximity in terms of technique between John Hollander's punning text – 'Feel a million filaments; fear the tearing, the feeling trees, that are full of felony' – and the perpetual reinterpretation of basic elements central to Babbitt's music.

Parallels between verbal and musical structures are further exploited in his other major work for soprano and tape, *Vision and Prayer* (1961), as well as in his Composition for Tenor and Six Instruments (1960). In both, vowels are associated with particular timbres, and in *Vision and Prayer* the music is very clearly shaped to offer correspondences at various levels with the forms of Dylan

Thomas's stanzas, patterned on the page in diamond and X shapes; in this respect the piece is a continuation from the Two Sonnets of 1955. A different approach is shown in *Sounds and Words* for soprano and piano (1960) and *Phonemena* for soprano and piano or tape (1969–74), both of which set nonsense phonemes associated with pitches according to rules of 12-note organization, so that here music gives rise to a 'text' instead of, as more normally, being derived from one.

THE BABBITT CIRCLE

Among those who have been pupils of Babbitt at Princeton, Peter Westergaard stands out for his contributions to serial theory[10] and also for his compositions, in which a Webernian delight in symmetry and mirror relationship is allied with a Babbitt-like regard for the systematic and integrated use of all the musical parameters. Example 45*a*, from his Quartet of 1960, may indicate his cast of mind. The series of the piece, Example 45*b*, is symmetrically partitioned in this

Ex. 45a

Ex. 45b

excerpt into three-note units which preserves the shapes of its constituent trichords, and these units are assigned respectively to the four instruments; thus the series controls both the total pitch succession, which is a serial statement, and the pitch succession in each of the instrumental lines. In this way Westergaard achieves one aim which he shares with Babbitt, that of creating a genuine 12-note polyphony in which the basic set determines not only linear successions but also other aspects (harmony, instrumental disposition, formal structure and so on), and in which the polyphony is not necessarily one of discrete instrumental lines but one of underlying serial functions.[11] From this viewpoint the opening of Babbitt's *Post-Partitions* (Example 44) is a six-part polyphony which is condensed in its expression, while the extract from Westergaard's Quartet (Example 45*a*) is a monody, a single serial statement, expanded to reveal its polyphonic potential. There is also an interesting contrast of rhythmic technique. Westergaard does not draw on the intricate possibilities of association provided by time-point serialism but instead uses simpler patterns which are correspondingly more easily perceived. For example, if one counts duration as the distance between attack points within the structure under consideration, then the first trichord of the series has the durations 3–2–1 quavers and the later statement of the same motif, transposed up a perfect 5th in the vibraphone, also has the durations 3–2–1 quavers. Its transposed retrograde in the total serial statement, A–C sharp–C, again has the durations 3–2–1 quavers, but this time the uniform instrumental projection, in the cello, has the duration sequence 7–6–5 quavers, which may be regarded as an 'octave transposition' of the rhythmic motif, adding four to each value.

Westergaard's other works are composed with no less concern for clear, beautiful and audible patterning on a variety of levels. His use of instruments to convey serial relationships sometimes draws him, as in his Variations for Six Players (1963), to ask musicians to match their sonorities one with another. For instance, a violin harmonic played with a marked attack can make a connection with a glockenspiel note, or a slap-tongue clarinet tone can be made to resemble a snap pizzicato in the cello. Such techniques make it possible for the composer to create two intermeshed polyphonies, as foreshadowed in the extract above from the Quartet: one is projected in the instrumental lines and one in those lines which, though given to different instruments, proceed in matched timbres. In his vocal works, which include a cycle of cantatas and the brief chamber opera *Mr and Mrs Discobbolos* after Edward Lear (1965), Westergaard is similarly economical and inventive, using verbal syntax to make explicit, at least in some measure, the musical syntax of his coherent and multi-dimensional polyphony.

The transparency of Westergaard's music removes it far from the world of Babbitt's later works, nor are his profusely motivic and imitative surfaces at all typical of music composed under the influence of Babbitt's ideas. It is, indeed, more usual to find American serial composers attempting to combine constructive rigour proceeding from Babbitt with ample instrumental gestures which suggest the influence of the characterful chamber music of Elliott Carter or Stefan Wolpe, or else partake of Schoenbergian expressive force. Such is the case with the brilliant and prolific Charles Wuorinen. His output includes a large number of works which feature a solo instrument, whether alone, spotlit within a chamber group or heard against an orchestra: working in any of these genres he is able to engage himself with performance as a matter of projection, to create solo parts that encourage a rhetorical mode of presentation. His setting of abundant and often extravagant imagery within clear forms and calculated contrapuntal textures suggests a peculiarly modern form of neo-classicism, rather as in the writing of John Barth. There is a framework of 18th-century security, sometimes upheld by the Augustan references of such titles as *Time's Encomium* or *The Politics of Harmony,* but it is filled with an imaginative torrent of unmistakably 20th-century power, abounding as it does in the irregular and the asymmetrical.

Example 46 shows the opening of the bass aria which is among the

Ex. 46

most musically elaborate of the encapsulated numbers from Wuorinen's 'masque' *The Politics of Harmony* (1966–7), a theatre piece scored for alto, tenor and bass soloists with a chamber orchestra consisting of flutes, tubas, violins, double basses and harps in pairs with piano and percussion (a total, significantly enough, of 12 players).[12] Drawing on ancient Chinese sources, the masque is a moral fable warning against the corrupting power of bizarre music: the thirst of two dukes for novel sounds brings calamity and disorder to the realm. Wuorinen's message is clear, and needs no more emphasis than is provided by the sophisticated orderliness of his music, as exemplified in Example 46. The vocal line begins with one of the work's two basic hexachords, C–E flat–D flat–D–F–E, and then links this to a transposed inversion of the same hexachord, E–. . .C, and finally to a transposed retrograde, C– . . . G sharp. The word-setting is determined in part by correspondences between phoneme and pitch class which are maintained throughout the aria; short *i*, for instance, is always associated with the pair C–D flat (or C sharp), so that the verse rhymes, whether internal or overt, are musically pointed. Wuorinen thus shows himself profiting from his teacher's experience in such works as the Two Sonnets, *Sounds and Words* and *Vision and Prayer*, and he similarly uses Babbittian principles in the instrumental music. This begins with the first hexachord of the vocal part and then continues with a complementary hexachord, F sharp–G–A–B flat–G sharp–B, this 12-note aggregate being associated with a set of 12 time points, 0–1–3–6–7–8–9–10–11–2–4–5. The remainder of the example presents a content-invariant inversion of the first hexachord in the tubas over a sustained middle C, followed by a complementary transposed retrograde of that hexachord in the flutes.

It is impossible in a short extract to give more than a faint impression of the manner in which Wuorinen weaves together his contrapuntal lines, often passing from instrument to instrument, and winds those lines through chords spaced with almost Stravinskyan finesse. Even so, it should be clear that his constructive procedures, which have been no more than sketched here, do not inhibit the creation of music that is poetically apt and fluently expressive. Indeed, it is entirely characteristic of Wuorinen that his music should appear, unlike that of Babbitt or Westergaard, quite spontaneous despite its evident density of working.

His approach to composing tape music is guided by rather different musical concerns, arising from his view that 'the rhetoric of performed music cannot create meaningful structures and articulations in the electronic medium'.[13] 'That medium', he goes on, 'must present musical structures which *are*, rather than those which *become* (by performance)', the distinction implying different methods of handling rhythm. Whereas in performed music 'rhythm is largely a qualitative, or accentual matter' because the musician 'stresses events he judges important', in electronic music the composer must direct his attention to 'the proportions among absolute lengths of events'.[14] In working with tape, therefore, Wuorinen feels bound largely to forgo those strong, purposefully directed rhythms which are such a feature of his music for instruments; his most ambitious electronic work, *Time's Encomium* (1968–9), depends on less dynamic, more calculated methods of structuring time. The use in this composition of the RCA Synthesizer immediately suggests a link with Babbitt's tape pieces, and Wuorinen similarly confines himself to the equal-tempered 12-note scale and uses time-point serialism. But, unlike Babbitt's works, *Time's Encomium* has a spaciousness and a grandeur gained from the combination of pure synthesized material with synthesized sounds which have been electronically processed, almost always with the addition of reverberation. The music thus spreads out from a foreground of clearly defined ideas to an outer space of more or less modified sounds, and in general the former pursue a steady development while the latter take off into decorative digressions.

TAPE MUSIC

Although Wuorinen has stressed the essential difference between music for performance and music for reproduction, and although his *Time's Encomium* bears witness to his awareness of that difference, the work has an instrumental feeling if only because it uses the familiar gamut of chromatic pitches and employs the RCA Synthesizer as a source of differentiated voices; the same features have already been noted in the electronic works of Babbitt. Such an approach to the medium is characteristic of much American tape music, and has been so ever since the early experiments of Luening and Ussachevsky with transformed instrumental sounds. The invention of new sounds and new ways of handling sound, so important in the electronic music of Stockhausen, is not a priority for Babbitt, as has been mentioned, nor is it a matter of first importance in the tape music even of composers distant from Babbitt in style and interests.

It became much easier to produce electronic music of an instrumental character when voltage-controlled synthesizers became available in the mid-1960s. The Moog synthesizer, perhaps still the most famous of the breed thanks to the music created with it by Walter Carlos, usually has a keyboard attachment which may encourage musicians to use it as a super-electronic organ. The Buchla synthesizer, though most commonly activated by finger pressure on a touch-sensitive plate rather than by performance on a keyboard, similarly suggests an instrumental style, and is so used in the colourful electronic poems of Morton Subotnick. It is typical of Subotnick's music that electronic devices, such as the sequencer, which can store a cycle of instructions and so give rise to an ostinato, should be used in his *Silver Apples of the Moon* (1967) and *The Wild Bull* (1968) to bring about a flamboyant energy suggestive of nothing so much as a jazz improvisation. The composer thus becomes a virtuoso performer on his instrument, and it is not surprising that synthesizers should have found use in live performance, in rock as well as in art music, even though their limitations (many, for instance, are monophonic instruments) would seem to suit them more to studio work.

Another indication of the instrumental approach to the electronic medium shown by many American composers is the fact that they have been eager to exploit combinations of live music with tape. And by contrast with Stockhausen's *Kontakte*, where the instrumentalists can only point to events happening in realms beyond, such works as Luening's *Gargoyles* for violin and tape (1960) or Davidovsky's cycle of *Synchronisms* (1963–76) place the two media on an equal footing. Luening's piece gives the impression of two energetic partners taking part in a game of imitation: the tape is more at home in rolling gambols than in the lyrical flights that are the violin's province, but it it most frequently through copying that the compact variations of the piece are fused. Davidovsky's methods are different, in that he makes witty and effective use of mimicry of timbre rather than of musical idea, but the result is again a close coupling of live and recorded music. Indeed, in *Synchronisms no. 5* for percussion quintet and tape (1970) it is often very difficult to be sure which sounds are synthetic and which are being obtained from the large array of instruments at the players' disposal. And *Synchronisms no. 6* for piano and tape (1970) presents itself as a solo piece, not a dialogue like the earlier works for flute (no. 1, 1963) and cello (no. 3, 1964–5), almost tempting one to believe that the instrument's capacity has been extended to encompass the more or less piano-like sonorities which emerge from the loudspeakers. Yet another way of making electronic music instrumental in nature is illustrated in the Concerted Piece for tape and orchestra (1960) jointly composed by Luening and Ussachevsky, where the model is evidently that of the grand romantic concerto: there is a heraldic orchestral introduction before the electronic component saunters on to the stage, and the 'soloist' in this cheerful little piece even has a cadenza of whirling cartwheels.

COMPUTER MUSIC

Given the quasi-instrumental variety of electronic music favoured by many American composers, and given too the concern of many of them, stimulated by the example of Babbitt, with the precise definition of musical qualities, it is natural that computer sound synthesis should have been welcomed as offering the most flexible and accurate means of determining every aspect of sound. Important work in this area has been carried out in London by Peter Zinovieff (in whose studio Harrison Birtwistle and others have worked) and in Utrecht by Gottfried Michael Koenig, but the principal developments have taken place in the U.S.A., and have been in the hands of a group of composers working at the Bell Telephone Laboratories and at the universities of Columbia and Princeton.

It is important to distinguish between computer sound synthesis and those forms of computer composition essayed by Hiller, Xenakis and others from the mid-1950s onwards. Those earlier efforts involved the computer in making decisions about the choice and arrangement of musical events; its output then had to be converted by a quite separate process into a musical score or electronic tape. Computer sound synthesis, by contrast, uses the computer as an instrument of storage and performance in the creation of the sounds themselves. Charles Dodge, one of the composers most active in this field, has explained that a composer using a computer program for sound synthesis 'must typically provide: (1) *Stored functions* which will reside in the computer's memory representing waveforms to be used by the *unit generators* of the program. (2) "Instruments" of his own design which logically interconnect these *unit generators*. (*Unit generators* are subprograms that simulate all the sound generation, modification, and storage devices of the ideal electronic music studio.) The computer "instruments" play the *notes* of the composition. (3) *Notes* may correspond to the familiar "pitch in time" or, alternatively, may represent some convenient way of dividing the time continuum'.[15] Thus for Dodge the computer is in essence a very versatile synthesizer (though its output, being in digital form, requires conversion before it may be experienced as sound), an apparatus similarly to be used in the generation of 'instrumental' (or indeed 'vocal') parts, but released from the synthesizer's limitations and, since no manual control is involved, very much more accurate.

A not untypical example of computer-synthesized music, and one that shows the importance of Babbitt's thinking to many composers working in this area, is Benjamin Boretz's *Group Variations* (1964–73), a work composed for chamber orchestra and only later 'rescored' for computer, thus neatly demonstrating the common view of the instrumental and electronic media as near alternatives, not as fundamentally dissimilar. Boretz's statement that the piece is to be heard as 'polyphonic ensemble music, whose sonic surfaces are the fused images of networks of musical qualities', and that each 'image' is a part of 'a still larger, single, complex, image', indicates how much he shares Babbitt's interpretation of polyphony, while his long essay 'Meta-Variations',[16] springing from this work, gives further proof that his attitudes are no less rigorous, his approach no less systematic. The electronic medium here is most certainly not the message, but only the means of achieving with precision a complex, interlocking web of musical relationships, rather as in Babbitt's *Ensembles for Synthesizer*.

The computer works of Charles Dodge and James K. Randall show a greater willingness to make use of the unique capacities of computer sound synthesis. Notwithstanding the fact that the score of Randall's *Quartets in Pairs* (1964) had been written in the abstract (i.e. without instrumentation) before the composer began to work with computer sound synthesis, it is a piece which calls for features, particularly the ability of an instrumental voice to function over a wide pitch range, which are not readily available in other media.[17] His *Quartersines* (1969), another short sketch, is also a conceit which could not easily have been realized except with the aid of a computer, being a monophonic glissando shaped after the pattern of quarter parts of sine curves. Dodge's much more ambitious *Changes* (1970) similarly draws on ideas which can be worked out relatively simply with the aid of a computer but which would require long and laborious hours of work with more conventional electronic apparatus. The work is a 12-note composition which has three basic constituents: flowing counterpoints of lines, irregularly placed chords and percussive interplays, of which the first are the most conspicuously affected by 'changes'. Put simply, every time a chord appears the timbres of the lines are altered, rather as if with each new chord a different coloured filter were placed in front of the polyphony.

Dodge's ingenuity in working with computer sound synthesis is further demonstrated by his *Earth's Magnetic Field* (1970), where pitch successions are obtained through a musical translation of indices of change in the magnetic field of the earth: the interpretation of the indices is appealingly diatonic in the first half, polyphonic and 12-note in the second. Another work by Dodge, his *Extensions* for trumpet and tape (1973), cleverly joins the live and recorded forces by using the same principle, that of equally dividing the pitch space, in both. Thus the free-flowing trumpet line emphasizes tritones, 3rds and 2nds, these being equal divisions of the octave, while the computer-generated tape scans across in wide glissandos, gradually accumulating further equal divisions of its own pitch space so that the original 16 regularly spaced tones have become 1024 by the end.

Computers can be used not only in the de novo synthesis of sound, as in these works by Boretz, Randall and Dodge, but also in the reproduction and transformation of sound material which has been submitted to them. All the techniques of *musique concrète* are therefore available, though with a degree of control and a versatility not easily matched in the standard electronic studio. Birtwistle's *Chronometer* (1971), created with Zinovieff's assistance from clock sounds analysed by and stored in a computer, provides a rare example of this method being used other than in vocal music, which has been a special interest of Dodge's. His *In Celebration* (1975) shows how computer re-synthesis can provide real speech melodies, so that music and language can be unified as they are in Stockhausen's *Gesang der Jünglinge*, with which the Dodge piece has something in common in the variety of textures it derives from a single voice (not least some close harmony redolent of the Beach Boys).

Dodge also uses computer speech synthesis in *The Story of our Lives* (1974), a miniature 'opera' for a couple who read the story of their lives in a book which itself speaks through strange glistening streams of glissandos. The re-creation of sound by computer has not yet been perfected – Dodge's characters sound irredeemably catarrhal – but the few examples of computer music so far composed hold the promise that this will be an extremely fruitful field. It may even be that, as in Ussachevsky's Two Sketches for a Computer Piece (1971), the computer will become a performing instrument, its manifold potentialities available to the composer–performer in real time, though that would be to sacrifice the fine precision which makes computer sound synthesis an irresistible field for composers who still hold the view that music is a matter of significant relationships.

REPERTORY

Babbitt: Composition for Tenor and Six Instruments (1960).
—— *Sounds and Words* for soprano and piano (1960, Marks).
—— Composition for Synthesizer on tape (1960–61, unpublished). Columbia MS 6566.
—— *Vision and Prayer* for soprano and tape (1961, Associated). CRI SD 268.
—— *Philomel* for soprano and tape (1963, Associated). Acoustic Research AR 0654 083.
—— *Ensembles for Synthesizer* on tape (1962–4, unpublished). Columbia MS 7051, Finnadar 9010 Q.
Relata I for orchestra (1965, unpublished)
—— *Post-Partitions* for piano (1966, Peters). New World NW 209.
—— String Quartet no. 3 (1969–70, Peters). Turnabout TV 34515.
—— *Phonemena* for soprano and piano (1969–70, Peters), also for soprano and tape (1974). New World NW 209 (both versions).
Birtwistle: *Chronometer* on tape (1971, unpublished). Argo ZRG 790.
Boretz: *Group Variations* for chamber orchestra (1964–7), also on tape (1969–73). CRI SD 300 (tape).
Davidovsky: *Synchronisms no. 1* for flute and tape (1963, McGinnis & Marx). CRI SD 204.
—— *Synchronisms no. 3* for cello and tape (1964–5, McGinnis & Marx). CRI SD 204.
—— *Synchronisms no. 5* for percussion quintet and tape (1970). CRI SD 268, Turnabout TV 34487.
—— *Synchronisms no. 6* for piano and tape (1970). Turnabout TV 34487.

Dodge: *Changes* on tape (1970, unpublished). Nonesuch H 71245.
—— *Earth's Magnetic Field* on tape (1970, unpublished). Nonesuch H 71250.
—— *Extensions* for trumpet and tape (1973, unpublished). CRI SD 300.
—— *The Story of our Lives* on tape (1974, unpublished). CRI SD 348.
—— *In Celebration* on tape (1975, unpublished). CRI SD 348.
Luening: *Gargoyles* for violin and tape (1960, Peters). Columbia MS 6566.
Luening and Ussachevsky: Concerted Piece for tape and orchestra (1960, Peters). CRI SD 227.
Randall: *Quartets in Pairs* on tape (1964, unpublished). Nonesuch H 71245.
—— *Quartersines* on tape (1969, unpublished). Nonesuch H 71245.
Subotnick: *Silver Apples of the Moon* on tape (1967, unpublished). Nonesuch H 71174.
—— *The Wild Bull* on tape (1968, unpublished). Nonesuch H 71208.
Ussachevsky: Two Sketches for a Computer Piece (1971, unpublished). CRI SD 268.
Westergaard: Quartet for clarinet, vibraphone, violin and cello (1960, Schott).
—— Variations for Six Players on flute, clarinet, piano, percussion, violin and cello (1963, Alexander Broude). Acoustic Research AR 0654 088.
—— *Mr and Mrs Discobbolos,* chamber opera (1965, Alexander Broude). CRI SD 271.
Wuorinen: *The Politics of Harmony*, masque (1967, Peters).
—— *Time's Enconium* on tape (1968–9, unpublished). Nonesuch H 71225.

10 Indeterminacy → Changing the System

This chapter, like the last, is concerned largely with American music, but with a quite different branch which can usefully be distinguished as 'experimental'. In the words of Michael Nyman, who has set out what separates the 'experimental' from the 'avant-garde' musician: 'Experimental composers are by and large not concerned with prescribing a defined *time-object* whose materials, structuring and relationships are calculated and arranged in advance, but are more excited by the prospect of outlining a *situation* in which sounds may occur, a *process* of generating action (sounding or otherwise), a *field* delineated by certain compositional "rules" '.[1]

The experimental tradition (not so much a contradiction in terms as perhaps it should be) goes back to the music produced by Cage and his associates in the early 1950s, and perhaps still further to the work of other American composers who were unencumbered by European notions of what a musical composition should be: Cowell, Partch and Ives. In the 1950s, as has been shown, the main thrust of experimental music had been in the direction of indeterminacy, of moving away from the fixed composition to the unique performance, and of enlarging the scope of music so much that sound is no longer a prerequisite, whether in Cage's *4′ 33″* or in the events composed by Young and others associated with the Fluxus movement. All this was to remain characteristic of much experimental music in the 1960s and 1970s, but there were also new developments which call for most comment here: the use of electronic apparatus in performance and the emergence of ensembles specializing in live electronic music; the rise of compositional 'systems' or 'minimal' music based on simple, gradual processes of change within a context of repetition; and the growing feeling, shared by many composers on the avant-garde flank, that music must serve or at least express a political commitment.

LIVE ELECTRONIC MUSIC

Cage's *Cartridge Music* (1960) has already been noted as the ancestor of live electronic music, and it was not long before its innovations were taken up by other composers. Stockhausen, for instance, after setting aside *Momente,* applied techniques of electronic amplification and modification to a large tam-tam in his *Mikrophonie I* (1964), to an orchestra in his *Mixtur* (1964) and to a small chorus in his *Mikrophonie II* (1965). Within the terms set out above, however, Stockhausen is an avant-garde rather than an experimental composer: he defines the sounds he wants, the ways in which they are to be produced and the forms into which they are to be built. The gulf between his approach and that of an experimental musician may be illustrated by a comparison of *Mixtur* with Cage's *Atlas eclipticalis* (1961–2), also scored for orchestra and allowing scope for live electronic participation. Where Stockhausen writes for a determined ensemble, Cage provides 86 parts which may, like those of the earlier *Concert for Piano and Orchestra,* be used in whole or in part. Again, Stockhausen stipulates the role of electronic transformation with some exactness, devoting his attention to the effects obtained by the ring modulation of orchestral sonorities, while Cage leaves his performers to decide what, if any, electronic modifications are used (in the recorded version *Cartridge Music* is taken as a source of instructions). And Stockhausen's work is fully notated, though the separate 'moments' can be arranged in different orders, whereas the parts of *Atlas eclipticalis* do not greatly limit the performer's imagination, offering little squiggles of enigmatic notation which follow patterns obtained from star maps: Example 47 is typical.

Even this degree of prescription is rare in Cage's music of the period after *Fontana Mix.* The score of his *Variations II* (1961), like that of *Variations I,* is simply an assortment of straight lines and points printed on 11 transparent sheets which may be overlaid in any manner; the performer then has to draw perpendiculars from each point to each line and measure the lengths to determine, for each musical event, the values to be assigned to the parameters of pitch, volume, duration, timbre, point of occurrence and structure. Tudor's version of the piece uses the piano as a reservoir of sounds

Ex. 47

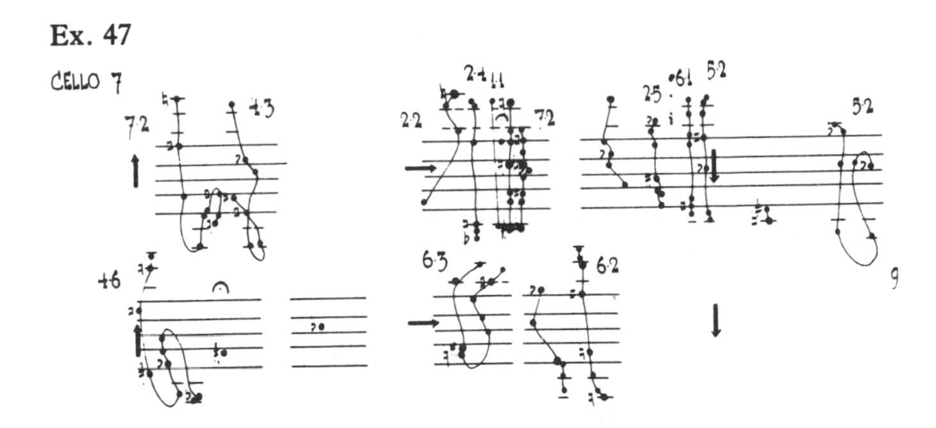

ranging from the most fragile resonances to the ugliest scrapes, all drawn from the instrument by the application, as in *Cartridge Music*, of gramophone cartridges and contact microphones. In Cage's catalogue of works *Variations II* is described simply as being for 'any number of players, any sound-producing means', and so there is no reason why it should be performed as live electronic music. However, such works of Cage invite interpretation in this manner, partly because of the composer's evident preference at the time for electronic systems, and partly because scores so minimally directive can be adapted to the widely varying styles and practices which have arisen in live electronic music. The medium almost demands an empirical approach to the choice of means (perhaps including the construction of instruments as well as the use and adaptation of conventional instruments and electronic devices), to the discovery of sounds and, if more than one player is involved, to the development of ensemble relationships. Furthermore, it is obviously difficult for a composer to give exact notations for instruments, playing techniques and electronic linkages which have not been standardized. For these reasons live electronic music has tended to be the province of specialist ensembles, usually including one or more composers, and often confining themselves to their own repertories. Such ensembles may well be closer in their mode of working to a jazz band or a rock group, where similarly the performers' ideas override or at least greatly constrain the composer's, than to a conventional chamber ensemble.

The variety of resources available to a live electronic ensemble is apparent from a publicity statement put out by Musica Elettronica

Viva, a group of American composer–performers formed in Rome in the mid-1960s: 'Tapes, complex electronics – Moog synthesizer, brainwave amplifiers, photocell mixers for movement of sound in space – are combined with traditional instruments, everyday objects and the environment itself, amplified by means of contact mikes, or not. Sounds may originate both inside and outside the performing-listening space and may move freely within and around it. Jazz, rock, primitive and Oriental musics, Western classical tradition, verbal and organic sound both individual and collective may all be present'.[2]

Musica Elettronica Viva began by playing determined compositions by their members but soon turned rather more to improvisatory pieces, among which *Spacecraft*, performed on numerous occasions in 1967–8, had the programme of leading each player from his 'occupied space' of personal inclination to 'a new space which was neither his nor another's, but everybody's'.[3] Such a view of music as social therapy, even as an instrument for political consciousness-raising, underpinned the subsequent development of the ensemble. Frederic Rzewski, a founder-member of Musica Elettronica Viva and a major influence on the group, asked in *Free Soup* (1968) that the audience should play with the ensemble, who were 'to relate to each other and to people and act as naturally and free as possible, without the odious role-playing ceremony of traditional concerts'.[4] His *Sound Pool* (1969) is even more a model of utopian social behaviour: 'In an environment', the score remarks, 'where painful noise is being produced by other human beings, the object of the performance must be to cast a living net of softness across space, to guide these beings from peaks of pain to valleys of pleasure in which all are able to hear each other and harmony becomes possible'.[5]

Other live electronic ensembles have been inspired less by reforming principle than by the dominant personality of a composer (this is particularly the case with Stockhausen's group, which was originally formed for performances of *Mikrophonie I* and which has rarely played music other than his) or else by a curiosity in the investigation of new ways of creating and handling sound. This latter is especially a feature of the work of the Sonic Arts Union, a quartet formed in the mid-1960s by Robert Ashley, David Behrman, Alvin Lucier and Gordon Mumma, all American musicians. Unlike their colleagues in Musica Elettronica Viva, they have consistently concerned themselves with their own individual compositions, and each of them has followed his own interests, though they share a preference for pieces which are almost natural outcomes of particular configurations of resources. In Behrman's *Wave Train* (1967), for instance, magnetic guitar pickups are attached to the strings of two pianos, and loudspeakers are placed so that they cause the strings to vibrate. There is thus a feedback loop: vibrations in the strings are transmitted to the pickups and so to the loudspeakers, which thus perpetuate the vibrations.

More sophisticated electronic systems have been developed by Gordon Mumma, who regards the construction of special 'cybersonic' equipment for each piece as an essential part of composition. His *Mesa* for bandoneon and electronics (1965) uses circuitry not only to transform the quality of the sound but also to change its apparent position and the space it seems to occupy, while his *Hornpipe* (1967) requires the player, on horn, to wear a 'cybersonic console' which reacts to the resonances produced by the instrument and makes its own response. In *Conspiracy 8* (1969–70) Mumma includes a computer as a member of his octet and so creates 'a theatre of communication under hazardous conditions' where 'the forces of social regulation', represented by the computer, 'are neither predictable nor necessarily just'.[6] But to contrast with this sinister vision of machine domination there is *Cybersonic Cantilevers* (1973), a model of communicated fun in which the audience is invited to bring sounds to the electronic circuitry for instant and unforeseen transformation. Mumma's music thus offers various images of man–machine interaction, of technological relationships which live electronic music is particularly qualified to interpret, clarify and influence.

Inventive applications of electronics are also to be found in the music of Ashley, whose *Wolfman* (1964) employs feedback to add grotesque smears to vocal sound, and in that of Lucier, who has interested himself particularly in exploiting the acoustic qualities of the performance space. His *I am Sitting in a Room* (1970) demonstrates how a spoken sentence is progressively obscured as resonances accumulate on tape in a perpetual cycle of playback and re-recording; and in his *Vespers* (1968) he asks his performers to explore a darkened room, using click generators and listening to the echoes generated so that, bat-like, they collide neither with each other nor with stationary objects but go about their business of taking 'slow sound photographs' of their surroundings.[7]

MINIMAL MUSIC

The origins of minimal music, a very different current in the experimental stream, may be traced to the early works of La Monte Young, concerned as they were with sounds of long duration. In 1962 Young formed his own performing ensemble, the Theatre of Eternal Music, and he has worked with them ever since on his static and highly repetitive drone-based music, using carefully chosen frequencies in simple ratios. His changeless 'dream music' is intended for continuous performance in 'dream houses' as 'a total environmental set of frequency structures in the media of sound and light.[8] The frequency structures in sound may be simply of two or more sine tones, drifting very slightly in phase relationship and hence in perceived volume (*Drift Studies,* 1964–), or the performers may contribute 'additional frequencies at prescribed time intervals',[9] while a visual complement is provided by the 'ornamental lightyears tracery' of patterned slides and coloured lights designed by the composer's wife, Marian Zazeela.

Since 1964 the Theatre of Eternal Music has been dedicated to performing excerpts from a continuously evolving work, *The Tortoise, his Dreams and Journeys,* so called in honour of an animal that has the Youngian virtues of longevity and slowness. The titles of these excerpts, such as *The Obsidian Ocelot, the Sawmill, and the Blue Sawtooth High Tension Line Transformer Refracting the Legend of the Dream of the Tortoise Traversing the 189/98 Lost Ancestral Lake Regions Illuminated Quotients from the Black Tiger Tapestries of the Drone of the Holy Numbers,* have a baroque splendour which contrasts oddly with the pure control of the music. The performers have to be expert in attuning their contributions to the frequency structure in use and, in the case of vocalists, employing different parts of the vocal cavity to bring forward different harmonics. Young himself has studied the Kirana style of Indian singing with Pandit Pran Nath, and this has undoubtedly had a profound effect on his way of using the voice and more generally on the nature of his music: his scrupulous selection of frequency structures with reference to their supposed moods, for example, bears comparison with an Indian musician's attitude to the raga. However, his insistence on just intonation suggests a link with Partch, and his readiness to confine himself to a narrow range of possibilities makes him a central figure among contemporary American and English minimalists, many of whom have been influenced by him.

Terry Riley, indeed, was an early member of the Theatre of Eternal Music, though since the mid-1960s he has appeared most frequently as a solo improviser. His music, like Young's, uses a small repertory of pitches and a high degree of repetition, but he replaces the inwardly directed concentration of 'dream music' by flights of fantasy and an exuberant pleasure in bright modal harmonies: where Young is a priest of music, Riley is a virtuoso and a child. Electronic means are often used to provide background textures of ostinatos against which he weaves further patterns of reiteration on soprano saxophone (*Dorian Reeds,* 1966, and *Poppy Nogood and the Phantom Band,* 1968) or electronic organ (*A Rainbow in Curved Air,* 1969, and *Persian Surgery Dervishes,* 1971). But perhaps Riley's best-known piece is not a solo improvisation but one for ensemble, *In C* (1964), in which the pulsed background is generated for each player by his fellows, all of them deciding individually how and when to choose from the 53 motifs supplied by the rudimentary score, though the expectation is that there will be a more or less unanimous progression through the material. Depending on how many musicians are involved, therefore, the effect is of gradually changing figures proceeding through an Ionian landscape: Example 48 shows the first six motifs.

Ex. 48

Philip Glass and Steve Reich have both sought to bring strict system to a Riley-like music of repetition, and have both formed their own ensembles to play music which demands a streamlined rhythmic precision. Both have also, like Young, been influenced by extra-European musical traditions: Glass worked with Ravi Shankar while pursuing more orthodox studies in Paris with Nadia Boulanger, and also studied the tabla under Alla Rakha before composing any of his acknowledged works, while Reich studied African drumming in Accra and Balinese gamelan playing in Seattle, though only after he had embarked on his career as a composer and performer. In neither case, however, are the exotic connections overt, and indeed Reich has criticized those who imitate the sound of some non-Western music, implicitly including Young in his criticism. For him, as also for Glass, the concern is rather with models of structure: 'One can study the rhythmic structure of non-Western music', he has written, 'and let that study lead one where it will while continuing to use the instruments, scales, and any other sound one has grown up with'.[10]

In Glass's music the basic principle of rhythmic structure is that of adding, repeating or removing units in a context of repetition and harmonic stasis. Example 49 shows four bars from his *Music in*

Ex. 49

Similar Motion (1969): each bar is repeated over and over again until the composer gives a signal to move on to the next; instrumentation is not specified, as is usual in Glass's music, for he is not interested in having his works performed other than by his own ensemble, which may vary in constitution, though generally it comprises about half a dozen players on electronic keyboards and woodwind instruments. Since the music is usually played fast and at a high volume level, the effect is of a forward motion at high pressure, jolted by the changes of figure and more seriously by sudden alterations in density.

The simple parallel harmony of Example 49 is characteristic of Glass's earlier pieces: *Two Pages* (1969) is in unison, *Music in Fifths* (also 1969) is a pair of lines spliced at the named interval. His later works, including *Music with Changing Parts* (1970) and *Music in Twelve Parts* (1971–4), are richer and more varied in harmony, and the rather severe rhythmic processes are joined by sustained chordal movements, giving layered textures of musical planes in different but meshing tempos. The result is sometimes strikingly close to Balinese gamelan music, though Glass has also begun a process of re-investigating his Western heritage. In *Another Look at Harmony* (1975) he 'took a VI–II–IV–V–I cadence with some altered things in it' and applied additive processes as in his earlier music so that 'you start hearing this cadence that you've heard all your life in a very different way'.[11] His opera *Einstein on the Beach* (1975), to a scenario by Robert Wilson, uses similar techniques, and he has spoken of his particular interest in thus using the simplest donnés of musical history in a manner seemingly 'unconscious of their historical weight'.[12]

Reich's music has the same feeling of a totally naïve approach to musical fundamentals, and the same foundation in repetition, but he differs from Glass in fixing the scoring of his pieces and in concerning himself with continuous, single processes of change rather than with abrupt shifts. 'I want', he has said, 'to be able to hear the process happening through the sounding music',[13] and he has noted that: 'It is quite natural to think about musical processes if one is frequently working with electro-mechanical sound equipment'.[14] Indeed, his interest in repetitive processes came from working with tape loops, which he put to creative use for the first time in *It's Gonna Rain* (1965), a tape piece created by working with loops of speech, as he has explained: 'Two loops are lined up in unison and then gradually move out of phase with each other, and then back into unison. The experience of that musical process is, above all else, impersonal: *it* just goes *its* way. Another aspect is its precision; there is nothing left to chance whatsoever. Once the process has been set up it inexorably works itself out'.[15]

It is interesting to note that Reich here approaches Cage's aesthetics of the early 1950s in placing a value on musical impersonality, and that his route to that goal is diametrically opposed to Cage's, requiring absolute control. He continued his exploiting of 'phasing' processes in another tape work, *Come out* (1966), and then in pieces for live performance, beginning with *Piano Phase* for two pianos and *Violin Phase* for four violins (both 1967), of which the latter brought him to a realization of 'the many melodic patterns resulting from the combination of two or more identical instruments playing the same repeating pattern one or more beats out of phase with each other'.[16] 'Since', he goes on, 'it is the attention of the listener which will largely determine which particular resulting pattern he or she will hear at any one moment, these patterns can be understood as psycho-acoustic by-products of the repetition and phase shifting. When I say there is more in my music than what I put there, I primarily mean these resulting patterns.' Example 50 shows one bar from *Violin Phase*, where the phase shifting has reached a point where the second violin is a minim ahead of the first and the third a minim ahead of the second; the fourth violin picks out resulting patterns, such as the one shown (three others are also projected

Ex. 50

during the repetitions of this bar). Similar processes of phasing and of bringing out resultant patterns are involved in *Phase Patterns* for four electronic organs (1970) and *Drumming* for voices, piccolo and percussionists (1971).

The latter work, playing for about an hour and a half, also introduces new techniques, among which Reich enumerates 'the process of gradually substituting beats for rests (or rests for beats) within a constantly repeating rhythmic cycle, the gradual changing of timbre while rhythm and pitch remain constant, the simultaneous combination of instruments of different timbre [earlier works had been for homogeneous groupings], and the use of the human voice to become part of the musical ensemble by imitating the exact sound of the instruments'.[17] In subsequent compositions he has tended to abandon simple phasing processes and to develop rather the new methods of *Drumming* and the process of progressive rhythmic augmentation first employed in *Four Organs* (1970), where a nine-note chord, played by four electronic organs, grows one note at a time so that melodic patterns emerge from it and are then obscured again as the chord comes to fill the available time. At the same time, these later works, such as *Music for Mallet Instruments, Voices and Organ* (1973) and *Music for Eighteen Musicians* (1974–6), have a breadth and a glamour which perhaps reflect the public success the composer had come to enjoy.

Although the music of Young, Riley, Glass and Reich has had some effect on other composers, particularly in England and Germany (Young's influence on Stockhausen, for instance, is unmistakable in *Stimmung* and is perhaps to be detected also in the raw repetitions of Piano Piece XI), minimal music appears a peculiarly circumscribed and American phenomenon: American in its ability to ignore most of European tradition (or come to it afresh) and to draw with equal readiness on exotic cultures, circumscribed in its happy neglect of any device for the communication of complex thought. Its materials are the most basic elements of the art, typified by the sine tones of Young or the simple repeating rhythms of Glass and Reich; it is music in a state of nature. Therein, perhaps, lies both its appeal and its limitation.

MUSIC AND POLITICS

'The ideology of a ruling class is present in its art implicitly; the ideology of a revolutionary class must be expressed in its art explicitly. Progressive ideas must shine like a bright light into the dusty cobwebs of bourgeois ideology in the avantgarde, so that any genuinely progressive spirits working in the avantgarde find their way out, take a stand on the side of the people and set about making a positive contribution to the revolutionary movement.'[18]

The words are those of Cornelius Cardew, whose earlier career had progressed under the influences of Stockhausen and then of American indeterminacy. This latter phase had reached a culmination with *Treatise* (1963–7), a magnum opus of graphic design (Example 51 shows a representative extract) quite independent of any sounding

Ex. 51

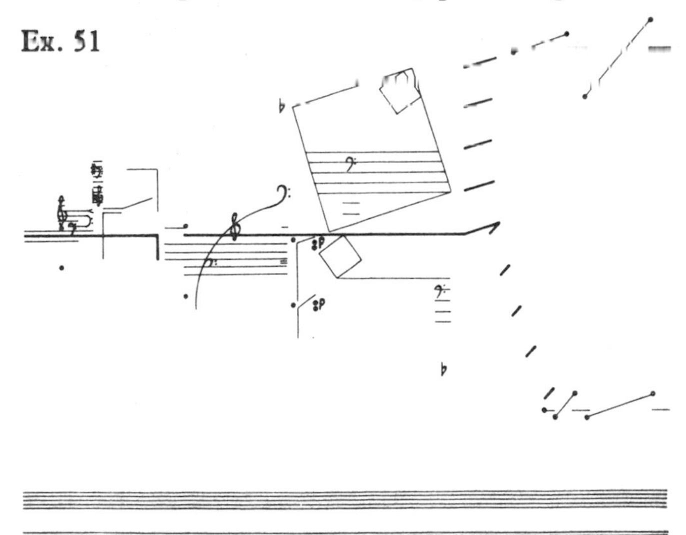

interpretation it might be given, as Cardew was despairingly aware: 'Psychologically', he wrote, 'the existence of *Treatise* is fully explained by the situation of the composer who is not in a position to make music'.[19] Yet he was 'in a position to make music' at this time as a member of the London performing group AMM, who worked with conventional instruments and electronics and who engaged in 'free improvisation' without reference to existing traditions of jazz or art music but with a strong sense of communal concentration and discipline, as is clear from their one commercial recording.

For Cardew, however, the private music of AMM was not enough. He wanted to work with larger groups, and he wanted to involve not only professional musicians but also interested amateurs; and so in his settings of the first seven paragraphs of *The Great Learning,* one of the classic texts of Confucianism, he provided materials which might bring professionals and novices together in an educative exercise. Paragraph 2, for instance, simply offers 26 drum rhythms and 25 elementary melodies of five or six notes. The performers are divided into several groups, each consisting of a drummer and singers; the drummer chooses one of the rhythms and repeats it continuously while the singers, following a leader, proceed slowly through one of the melodies, and then all move on.

Work on this piece led to the formation in 1969 of the Scratch Orchestra, a group of composers, musicians and non-musicians who joined together in a spirit of high idealism to break down 'the barrier between private and group activity, between professional and amateur'.[20] A musical training conferred no special privilege and might even be a handicap; the atmosphere, as in the exactly contemporary work of Musica Elettronica Viva, was one of benign anarchy. Scratch Orchestra programmes included compositions by American experimental musicians (Young, Riley, Rzewski) and by members of the orchestra, scratch performances of popular classics, and 'improvisation rites' which were designed so that they did not 'attempt to influence the music that will be played' but which went no further than to 'establish a community of feeling, or a communal starting-point, through ritual' (here again there is a connection with Rzewski's work with Musica Elettronica Viva).

Like a revolutionary cadre the Scratch Orchestra was from the first to be alert to its own evolution, and almost inevitably that evolution led it from the modelling of egalitarian relationships to active political engagement. The Scratch Orchestra Ideology Group was established in 1971 to make a study of socialist thought, and before long the orchestra's allegiance had switched from Confucius to Mao. For a performance of the first two paragraphs of *The Great Learning* in 1972 Cardew made a new translation of the characters, so that Pound's call for keen introspection – '*The Great Learning* takes root in clarifying the way wherein the intelligence increases through the process of looking straight into one's own heart and acting on the result; it is rooted in watching with affection the way people grow' – took on an unambiguous political cast: '*The Great Learning* means raising your level of consciousness by getting right to the heart of a matter and acting on your conclusions. *The Great Learning* is rooted in love for the broad masses of the people'. Cardew also began now to criticize Cage and Stockhausen, and his own earlier works, for what he saw as an implicit support of the status quo.[21] As the quotation at the head of this section makes clear, he came to regard avant-garde (and experimental) music as pernicious or irrelevant in terms of its political content, but it is of course another question how the composer is to give explicit expression to 'the ideology of a revolutionary class'. Cardew's answer has been to offer simple didactic songs, such as *Soon* (1971, see Example 52), to make

Ex. 52

arrangements of the East–West confections put out as revolutionary art by the Chinese régime in the last years of Mao, or, as in his Piano Albums of 1973 and 1974, to make decorated transcriptions of Chinese and Irish revolutionary songs.

Cardew was not alone in his conversion to China-style socialism, for both Rzewski and Wolff, each at some time associated with the

Scratch Orchestra, took the same road at much the same time. Wolff's *Accompaniments I* for singing pianist (1972) has a text which solemnly praises advances made in sanitation, contraception and infant care under Chairman Mao, but for Wolff the adoption of a clear political stance did not necessitate a sudden change of style like Cardew's: there are evident links with his earlier music, the score being an outline which requires the performer to decide on the vocal melody and on the choice of accompaniment chords from those provided.

Rzewski's first outspokenly political works, *Coming Together* and *Attica* (both 1972), also bear the residue of his background in experimental music. Both call for an instrumental ensemble of unspecified constitution to give cumulatively aggressive expression to a melodic line, rather as in his earlier improvisation piece *Les moutons de Panurge* (1969), and there is also some connection with the systematic methods of Glass, though the spoken texts, taken from statements of noble humanity made by prisoners involved in the Attica revolt of September 1971, place these works firmly in the world of political activism. Rzewski's later works, which include sets of piano variations on 'No place to go but around' and on the Chilean song 'El pueblo unido jamas sera vencido' (both 1973), contain a political message only in the references of their subject material; apart from that they oddly recall nothing so much as the large-scale virtuoso pieces of a Liszt or a Busoni.

It may be that Cardew and Rzewski are both drawing the same lesson from their critical appraisal of the avant garde, the lesson that composers must concern themselves with a presumed common currency, and that that currency turns out to be what is, in their own terms, the musical language of the 19th-century capitalist apogee. One may reasonably doubt that music can ever have a predictable effect on the political thinking of its audience, except perhaps to encourage the faithful, but if it is truly to have a part in changing opinion, then it is probably by presenting new models of integration that it may lead its listeners to recognize the possibility and the desirability of a fuller human community. That is the utopian prospect which has guided the work of such composers as Pousseur, though his later works, representing the avant garde rather than the experimental wing of music, must await consideration in the next chapter.

REPERTORY

AMM: Improvisation (1968, unpublished). Mainstream MS 5002.
Ashley: *The Wolfman* for amplified voice and tape (1964, *Source* magazine no. 4). ESP 1009, Source 1.
Behrman: *Wave Train* for two to four players using guitar pickups and two pianos (1967, *Source* magazine no. 4). Source 1.
Cage: *Variations II* for undetermined forces (1961, Peters). Columbia MS 7051 (amplified piano version by Tudor).
—— *Atlas eclipticalis* for orchestra (1961–2, Peters). DGG 137 009 (with *Winter Music* and *Cartridge Music*).
Cardew: *Treatise* for undetermined forces (1963–7, Gallery Upstairs).
—— *The Great Learning* in seven paragraphs for various forces (1968–70, Experimental Music Catalogue in part).
—— *Soon* for voice or voices with or without accompaniment (1971, Experimental Music Catalogue).
—— Piano Album 1973 (1973, Experimental Music Catalogue). Cramps CRSLP 6106 (excerpts).
—— Piano Album 1974 (1974, Experimental Music Catalogue). Cramps CRSLP 6106 (excerpts).
Glass: *Two Pages* for ensemble (1969, unpublished). Folkways FTS 33902, Shandar 83 515.
—— *Music in Fifths* for ensemble (1969, unpublished). Chatham Sq LP 1003.
—— *Music in Similar Motion* for ensemble (1969, unpublished). Chatham Sq LP 1003.
—— *Music with Changing Parts* for ensemble (1970, unpublished). Chatham Sq LP 1001–2.
—— *Music in Twelve Parts* (1971–4, unpublished).
—— *Another Look at Harmony* for ensemble (1975, unpublished).
—— *Einstein on the Beach,* opera (1975, unpublished).
Lucier: *Vespers* for players with echo-location devices (1968, *Source* magazine no. 7). Mainstream MS 5010.
—— *I am Sitting in a Room* for tape and slides (1970, *Source* magazine no. 7). Source 3.
Mumma: *Mesa* for bandoneon and electronics (1965, unpublished). Odyssey 32 16 0158.
—— *Hornpipe* for horn and electronics (1967, unpublished). Mainstream MS 5010.
—— *Conspiracy 8* for seven performers and computer (1969–70, unpublished).
—— *Cybersonic Cantilevers* for audience and electronics (1973, unpublished). Folkways FTS 33904.

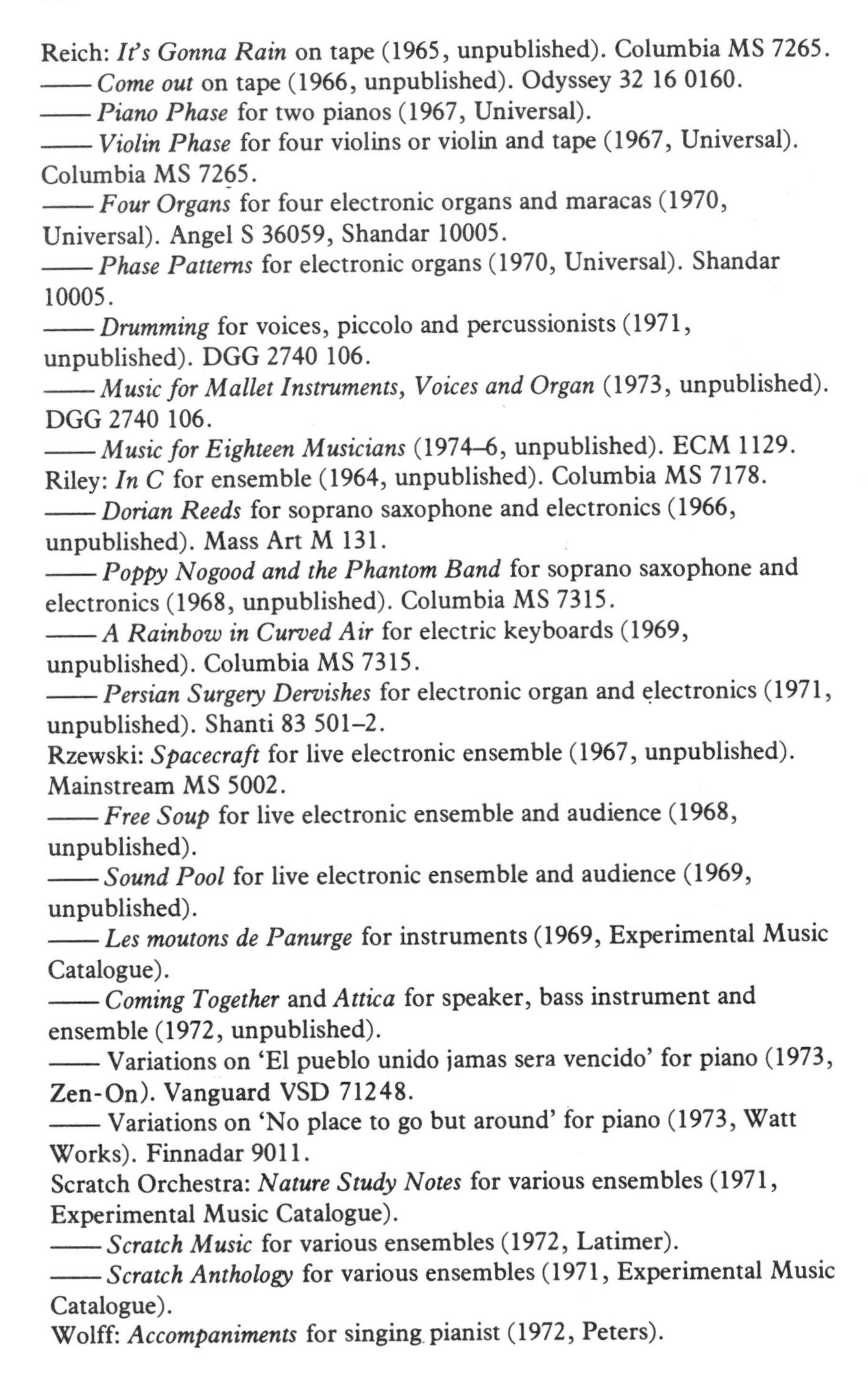

Reich: *It's Gonna Rain* on tape (1965, unpublished). Columbia MS 7265.
—— *Come out* on tape (1966, unpublished). Odyssey 32 16 0160.
—— *Piano Phase* for two pianos (1967, Universal).
—— *Violin Phase* for four violins or violin and tape (1967, Universal). Columbia MS 7265.
—— *Four Organs* for four electronic organs and maracas (1970, Universal). Angel S 36059, Shandar 10005.
—— *Phase Patterns* for electronic organs (1970, Universal). Shandar 10005.
—— *Drumming* for voices, piccolo and percussionists (1971, unpublished). DGG 2740 106.
—— *Music for Mallet Instruments, Voices and Organ* (1973, unpublished). DGG 2740 106.
—— *Music for Eighteen Musicians* (1974–6, unpublished). ECM 1129.
Riley: *In C* for ensemble (1964, unpublished). Columbia MS 7178.
—— *Dorian Reeds* for soprano saxophone and electronics (1966, unpublished). Mass Art M 131.
—— *Poppy Nogood and the Phantom Band* for soprano saxophone and electronics (1968, unpublished). Columbia MS 7315.
—— *A Rainbow in Curved Air* for electric keyboards (1969, unpublished). Columbia MS 7315.
—— *Persian Surgery Dervishes* for electronic organ and electronics (1971, unpublished). Shanti 83 501–2.
Rzewski: *Spacecraft* for live electronic ensemble (1967, unpublished). Mainstream MS 5002.
—— *Free Soup* for live electronic ensemble and audience (1968, unpublished).
—— *Sound Pool* for live electronic ensemble and audience (1969, unpublished).
—— *Les moutons de Panurge* for instruments (1969, Experimental Music Catalogue).
—— *Coming Together* and *Attica* for speaker, bass instrument and ensemble (1972, unpublished).
—— Variations on 'El pueblo unido jamas sera vencido' for piano (1973, Zen-On). Vanguard VSD 71248.
—— Variations on 'No place to go but around' for piano (1973, Watt Works). Finnadar 9011.
Scratch Orchestra: *Nature Study Notes* for various ensembles (1971, Experimental Music Catalogue).
—— *Scratch Music* for various ensembles (1972, Latimer).
—— *Scratch Anthology* for various ensembles (1971, Experimental Music Catalogue).
Wolff: *Accompaniments* for singing pianist (1972, Peters).

Young: *The Tortoise, his Dreams and Journeys* for performers and electronics (1964–, unpublished). Shandar 83 510 (section *13 1 73 5: 35–6:14:03 PM NYC*, 1969–73).
—— *Drift Study 14 VII 73 9:27:27–10:06:41 PM NYC* for sine tones (1973, unpublished). Shandar 83 510.

11 Quotation → Integration

Though the passage of time irrevocably obscures novelty of any kind, one of the most striking features of the music of the early 1950s remains its isolation, in so many respects of aim and technique, from any immediate precedent. It is arguable, indeed, that the revolution initiated by such works as Stockhausen's *Kreuzspiel* and Boulez's first book of *Structures* represented a more complete shift in musical history even than the great tide of change of the years just before World War I, for never before had composers concerned themselves so assiduously with matters of organization and construction, never before had they required their listeners to attend to separate processes unfolding in terms of pitch, rhythm and other qualities at the same time. Of course, the total serial dogma was soon compromised in all manner of ways, but it had a lasting influence in making composers impatient with anything that suggested the music of the past: all must be made new, as it was in the bright dawn of 1951–2.

Boulez has been the most vociferous spokesman for this position, despite his work as a conductor in the museum of musical tradition. Writing in the mid-1970s, at the time of the establishment of his research institute in Paris, he insisted that: 'Our age is one of persistent, relentless, almost unbearable inquiry. In its exaltation it cuts off all retreats and bans all sanctuaries; its passion is contagious, its thirst for the unknown projects us forcefully, violently into the future. . . . Despite the skilful ruses we have cultivated in our desperate effort to make the world of the past serve our present-day needs, we can no longer elude the essential trial: that of becoming an absolute part of the present, of forsaking all memory to forge a perception without precedent, of renouncing the legacies of the past, to discover yet undreamed-of territories'.[1]

For other composers, however, the legacies of the past have been too alluring to be renounced, too richly suggestive to be ignored, too much a part of the present, in that works from before 1900 still form the bulk of the concert and recorded repertory, to be overlooked.

OUT OF THE PAST

Too close to be approached without taint of conservatism, the music of the 18th and 19th centuries has been of use to composers of the 20th only if, like Stravinsky, they could preserve a large measure of ironic detachment, or if, like Henze among musicians of the postwar generation, they have been able and willing to return wholeheartedly to earlier modes of thought. The more distant musical past offers less problematic territory, partly because the music of the medieval and Renaissance periods is sufficiently separate from the present to be no danger to the composer for whom compromise with the past would be obnoxious, but also because the methods of pre-Baroque composers may often be in surprisingly close accord with those of their contemporary successors. The growth of a new public interest in 'early music', which began in the mid-1960s, may be seen as evidence of a more widespread community of feeling and thought; it has also made it possible for composers to write for previously extinct instruments, as Kagel did in his quite un-Renaissance-sounding *Musik für Renaissance-Instrumente* (1965). As for matters of compositional technique, the medieval view of rhythm as an incarnation of number suggests comparison with the attitudes of Messiaen and of those composers who, influenced by him, developed methods of rhythmic serialization: Barraqué drew attention to this in his article on rhythm, where, with no sense of incongruity, he moves straight from Machaut's *Messe de Notre Dame* to *The Rite of Spring.*[2] Moreover, as Wuorinen has pointed out, the rhythmic complexities cultivated by composers of the post-Machaut generation are such as to make *Le marteau sans maître* seem quite normal.[3]

But these are instances of correspondence rather than influence. True examples of interaction between the medieval and the modern are provided by the music of three English composers, Peter Maxwell Davies, Harrison Birtwistle and Roger Smalley, of whom the first two were fellow students in the mid-1950s, while Smalley arrived at similar conclusions independently a little later; Birtwistle and Smalley both developed away from using early music during the

1960s, but Davies's concern with the past has remained intense. The role of pre-Baroque music in his work is various and profound, though so too are the transformation processes which usually leave little kinship of sound or expression between his works and their models or sources: even in straight transcriptions – and he has made many, of works by Machaut, Dunstable, Purcell and others – the original is often twisted into very alien harmonic or instrumental territory. Thus it is that, though a great deal of his music is founded in plainsong, this is rarely apparent, for by combining 15th-century techniques of parody with 20th-century techniques of variation he contrives to create melodies which have little of the Gregorian about them. At the simplest level, a plainsong theme may be subjected to octave displacement of its pitches, melodic variation and a very un-chant-like rhythmic presentation: Example 53 shows an instance of this in a comparison of the opening of the sequence *Victimae paschali laudes,* transposed up a semitone (Example 53*a*), with the related cello solo from the final scene of Davies's opera *Taverner* of 1962–70 (Example 53*b*), the plainsong here serving, as Stephen

Arnold has noted,[4] not only as a musical source but also as a symbol of the Resurrection by virtue of its text. This use of Gregorian themes both for their musical qualities and for their associative meanings is common in Davies's music, as it is also in that of his medieval and Renaissance predecessors, and often the plainsong functions too in the manner of a series, a basic source of melodic variants and harmonic potentialities.

In parenthesis it is worth noting the very different use of plainsong in some contemporary works of Messiaen. Like Davies, Messiaen is alive to the textual weights borne by the melodies he chooses: one important theme in his *Couleurs de la cité céleste* for piano, wind and percussion (1963), for instance, comes from the Alleluia for the Eighth Sunday after Pentecost, *Magnus Dominus,* which tells of the New Jerusalem, and there are similarly apt quotations in most of his later works. Unlike Davies, however, Messiaen accepts the plainsong as given material. He neither alters nor develops the melodies but accepts them into his music, along with much else, effecting an integration by his choice of rhythmic, harmonic and instrumental presentation. Example 54, from *Couleurs,* shows the above-

Ex. 54

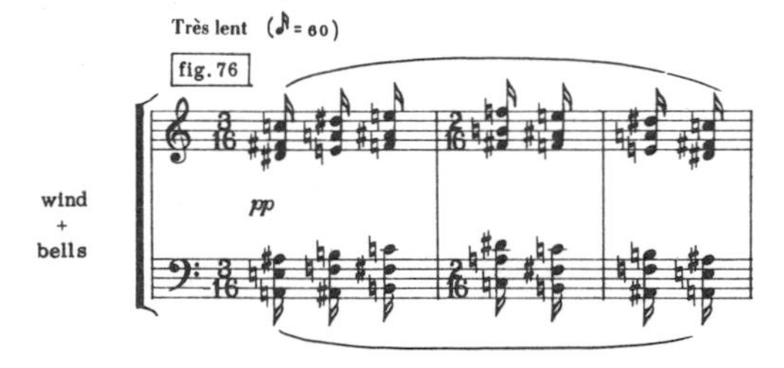

mentioned Alleluia harmonized in Messiaen's fourth mode of limited transposition and illustrates his manner of integration, which is made musically possible by the modal character of his music and spiritually essential because the whole effort of his work, he has said, is 'to highlight the theological truths of the Catholic faith'.[5] For a composer of this persuasion it is as necessary to draw on the great musical tradition of the church – i.e. plainsong, the only proper liturgical music in Messiaen's view[6] – as it is to draw on her great dogmatic tradition, represented by the texts from the New Testament, the Missal and St Thomas Aquinas in *La Transfiguration de Notre Seigneur Jésus-Christ* (1963–9).

Davies's standpoint is very different. His is a music not of exposition but of interpretation and, still more, questioning, even to the extent of negation. It is surely not by chance that one of his favoured musical techniques is a process of gradual melodic transformation by which a melody is converted into its inversion,[7] nor is it possible to ignore his abiding concern with betrayal, which stands especially explicit in his dramatic works. Outside the theatrical context betrayal may still be expressed – and is expressed very often in Davies's music – in parody. As a musical technique this came of course from his study of pre-Baroque music, for in the parody masses of the 15th and 16th centuries he found models for his own handling of plainsong melodies and also sources, in some measure, for the parody methods he applied to other material: to a Dunstable motet in *Alma redemptoris mater* for six wind (1957), to Monteverdi's Vespers in his String Quartet (1961), or to Taverner's *Gloria Tibi Trinitas* mass not only in the opera *Taverner* but also in two orchestral fantasias (1962 and 1964) and in the Seven in Nomine for chamber ensemble (1963–5). In these works the parody is to a large degree secret and expressively neutral (not a term, though, which could be applied to other aspects of the music), for the music's relationship to its source is generally far from plain and so the processes of distortion remain largely hidden. In later pieces, however, parody becomes overt and takes on its modern sense, dramatized in the theatre works but no less disturbingly present in the concert compositions which followed Davies's foray into music-theatre in the late 1960s. Indeed, it infects the very substance of these works.

Davies has described his 'foxtrot for orchestra' *St Thomas Wake* (1969) as based on 'three levels of musical experience – that of the original sixteenth century "St Thomas Wake" pavan, played on the harp, the level of the foxtrots derived from this, played by a foxtrot band, and the level of my "real" music, also derived from the pavan, played by the symphony orchestra',[8] but there remains the question of how the composer is to be sure of what his 'real' music is, how he is to find his true face among so many masks (a problem to be played out in theatrical terms in *Blind Man's Buff,* 1972). That question is bound to arise for any composer who, in the wake of Stravinsky, turns consciously to models of form and style from the past; but it was particularly acute for Davies, who by this stage in his career had proved himself an accomplished imitator and pasticheur of everything from 15th-century polyphony to 1930s dance music, from Monteverdi's melodic floridity to Schoenberg's harmonic strain. There was no obvious reason why his post-Schoenbergian style, so powerfully enshrined in the Second Taverner Fantasia, should be presumed to have a 'reality' not held equally by the other guises his music was capable of taking. This he recognized himself in concluding the fantasia with the brief dispatch of a grotesque parody of itself, throwing off the weight of pathos accumulated through a long and troubled development, but redoubling the tension of the piece by questioning the very foundations of that tension: by questioning the honesty of the style. In the orchestral work which followed, *Worldes Blis* (1966–9), he again built an immense musical edifice from a seed of given material, a medieval monody, but now, without the blatant self-destruction of the fantasia, the music is deeply concerned at every stage with testing its own validity. As Stephen Pruslin has observed: 'The main allegro pays only lip-service to closure and after the transition the music careens through a whole series of sections, all of them unclosed. The effect is that of amassing a series of left-hand parentheses without bothering about the corresponding right-hand ones, so that one builds up a huge "structural overdraft" '.[9] Where the Second Taverner Fantasia had presented a steady process of growth whose premises were alarmingly shaken at the close, *Worldes Blis* advances in momentous instability and only at its end comes overwhelmingly to affirmation. The work is thus not only a gigantic musical exploration of its 13th-century source but also a 20th-century gloss on the medieval poet's bitter awareness of the vanity of the material world, an exercise in self-revelation such as few composers since Schoenberg have felt able to undertake, and a quest not so much for religious enlightenment as for self-definition, which is the spiritual goal of so much of Davies's music.

In this light his use of past material cannot be seen as prompted by nostalgia, by a longing for past certainties, for in his music all assumed certainties must be ruthlessly tested for their truth to himself, tested by his formidable weaponry of techniques of distortion. The great conflict in many of his works up to and including *Worldes Blis* is that between the true and the travesty, the good and the evil, and it is perhaps only in his fierce belief in the existence of these as principles that he may be said to hold a medieval outlook. In his earliest works, such as the *St Michael Sonata* for 17 wind (1957) or the orchestral *Prolation* (1959), he tests his musical ideas against the most rebarbative techniques of his medieval predecessors (mensuration canon, isorhythm, etc.) and of his contemporaries (the serial apparatus of Boulez); the *St Michael Sonata* is explicitly a work of judgment not only in its title but also in its use of the 'Dies irae' plainsong. Only by the stringent application of technique to dissect his ideas, Davies would appear to be suggesting, can the composer have security in the genuineness of his creation; and again and again his music offers images of purgation in which the false is caricatured, the true celebrated with intensity. Even in those works which, following *Worldes Blis,* have evinced a greater certainty and a surer wholeness – such as the chamber piece *Ave maris stella* (1975), First Symphony (1973–6) and the orchestral *A Mirror of Whitening Light* (1977) – there remain the elaborate technical artifices by means of which Davies separates himself from the dishonest and the easy. Indeed, these compositions are all based on a tightly restricting constructive method by which, as David Roberts has shown,[10] a plainsong theme is converted into a 'magic square' of nine by nine elements determining successions of pitch classes and durational values. And the spiritual function of such practices is indicated when Davies remarks of *A Mirror of Whitening Light* that its title 'is alchemical, referring to the purification or "whitening" process by which a base metal may be transformed into gold and, by extension, to the purification of the human soul'.[11]

Two short examples from this work, one from towards the end of the second allegro development (Example 55*a*) and the other from the start of the final 'Lento assai' (Example 55*b*), may serve to illustrate, though in a simple way, Davies's techniques of transformation. The same plainsong-derived theme appears in both,

Ex. 55a

harmonized in the marimba and woodwind in Example 55*a* and melodically presented by the oboe in Example 55*b*. Both are also riddled with other quasi-medieval features, from the parallel 12ths in the strings in Example 55*a* to the characteristic polymetrical counterpoint of Example 55*b*, while in character the two extracts suggest more recent exemplars, perhaps Schoenberg and Mahler, both of whom are invoked as witnesses in many another Davies score. Yet the resultant music, not only in these brief excerpts but throughout the work's concentrated, continuous development, belongs unmistakably to Davies. Past materials and procedures are held in a perfect if tension-filled balance, without the earlier amplification of irony into parody, and the synthesis is that of Davies himself.

Ex. 55b

OUT OF THE EAST

Though few composers have joined Davies in his deep engagement with the music and thought of the Middle Ages and the Renaissance, the lure of the East, exerted both by its philosophies and by its musical traditions, has left few untouched in the period since World War II. Asian influences on European music are, of course, to be detected in every era from the Crusades to the time of Debussy and Mahler, but only in comparatively recent times have those influences altered the essential nature of music being composed in the West. Messiaen was one of the first to show an enthusiastic acceptance of alien materials, whether the 'Hindu rhythms' which appear in many of his works, or the Balinese-style metallophone scoring of the *Turangalîla-symphonie, La Transfiguration* and other orchestral compositions, or the complete tradition copied in the 'Gagaku' movement from the *Sept haïkaï* for piano and small orchestra (1962). Yet Messiaen's approach still exemplifies a tendency to absorb and integrate which may be regarded as characteristically European; those American composers who have been drawn to Eastern sources have felt freer to abandon the European heritage, as Cage's history well shows, and as is also demonstrated in the music of such younger composers as Young and Reich. There are few European parallels for Cage's attachment to Zen Buddhism in the late 1940s and 1950s, or for Young's later wholesale adoption of an Indian view of the function and performance of music. Even Stockhausen's mystical excursions, taking place in such works as *Stimmung* (1968), *Mantra* (1970) and the contemporary collections of pieces for 'intuitive' music-making, can be understood, as Jonathan Harvey has pointed out,[12] within a German tradition which includes such writers as Meister Eckhart and Novalis; and Stockhausen's insistence on a finely tuned meditative approach to his music dates back to 1952,[13] long before his encounter with the thought of Sri Aurobindo.

For European composers, therefore, exotic musical traditions have been valuable as sources of materials rather than metaphysics, and in particular for the stimulus they have given to the search for new instrumental combinations, new modes of performance and new possibilities of form. The instruments themselves have not generally been seen as exportable, except by Kagel in his *Exotica* for six players on at least 60 extra-European instruments (1971), but the percussion-based ensembles of Stockhausen's *Kreuzspiel* and *Refrain* or Boulez's *Le marteau sans maître* and *Improvisations sur Mallarmé I–II* have obvious and acknowledged exotic resonances, as has been mentioned. Both these composers have also learned from meetings with musicians from alien cultures: Boulez has recounted how the experience of hearing Peruvian Indians play the harp affected his writing for the instrument in the second *Improvisation sur Mallarmé*;[14] and Stockhausen's use of vocal interjections in *Mantra* is in explicit homage to the music of the nō drama, though this is a case where the composer's inventiveness had already led him to similar effects, for in works composed before he first visited Japan in 1966, notably *Refrain* and *Carré*, vowel sounds are joined to percussive attacks in a manner which, since the composition of *Mantra*, has gained a perhaps unwarranted but certainly enriching oriental echo.

The few compositions of Boulez's pupil Jean-Claude Eloy bear comparison with these works of Stockhausen and Boulez as instances of analytic integration, of the choice of particular Eastern features which can be accommodated within a Western avant-garde style. His *Equivalences* for 18 players (1963), for instance, is a typical Boulez-school essay in the play of opposites – groupings of wind and percussion, extremes of density, registral fixity against mobility of pitches, and so on – but he has also remarked that: 'In the long silences, the immobility, the sustained high woodwind notes or the deep sequences in the brass there seems to break through a memory of music from the Far East, Japan or Tibet'.[15] In the late 1960s Eloy made a study of Indian music *in situ*, but still his compositional use of his findings remained careful and considered. His *Faisceaux-diffractions* for 28 players (1970) may suggest the East in some of its gestures and in its ornamental decoration of static chords on wind, electric guitars or Hammond organ, but again the music has stronger links with Boulez and Varèse in its dialectical organization and in its projection of sound masses as material for 'diffraction' into new dispositions. Eloy goes further in invoking Indian philosophical ideas in his *Kamakala* for three choral-orchestral groups (1971) and *Shanti* for voices, instruments and electronics (1972–3), but even in these works he is sufficiently analytical to avoid imitation. The pace, as in *Faisceaux-diffractions*, is slow and the ambience contemplative, but contemplation is firmly directed to what is happening within the gradually changing textures, and in particular to the genesis of language from the elements of vocal articulation.

It is curious that most of the comparable exercises in East–West synthesis that have come from the Asian side, from such composers as Toru Takemitsu and Isang Yun, have tended to be biased strongly in favour of the West. If Takemitsu's delight in evanescent, apparently unwilled sonorities seems on the surface to be a Japanese trait, on further reflection it may be found to link him at least as much with Feldman, while his orchestral writing draws much more from Debussy and Boulez than from indigenous traditions. Even in those of his works which employ Japanese instruments, such as *November Steps* for shakuhachi, biwa and orchestra (1967), the manner is distinctly Western. So it is too in the music of Yun, who, born in Korea but long resident in Berlin, has progressively distanced himself from the oriental sound world of his *Loyang* for chamber ensemble (1962).

Certainly the works of Takemitsu and Yun do not show oriental traditions providing new formal models for composition in a Western style, whether models of rhythmic structuring as in the music of Reich or instances of open form such as Boulez was to find. Boulez has recorded that, when he first heard examples of African and Far Eastern music on records, he was struck not only by their beauty but also 'by the conception governing their elaboration'.[16] 'Nothing in them', he goes on, 'is based on the "masterpiece", on the closed cycle, on passive contemplation, on purely aesthetic enjoyment. Music is a way of being in the world, becomes an integral part of existence, is inseparably connected with it; it is an ethical category, no longer merely an aesthetic one.' Though one may doubt whether Boulez has ever relinquished the view of music as an 'aesthetic category', still less the need for the 'masterpiece', the mobile form of the Third Piano Sonata was devised to respect 'the "finished" aspect of the Occidental work, its closed cycle' while introducing 'the "chance" of the Oriental work, its open development'.[17] And the third *Improvisation sur Mallarmé* clearly shows both aspects of his borrowing from the East: the material in its long sustained sounds, its heterophonies for homogeneous percussive groupings (two xylophones, three harps, etc.) and its immense opening soprano melisma delicately inflected with quarter-tones; the formal in its provision of alternatives and its loosening of temporal coordination among overlapping blocks. That Boulez has not proceeded further in this direction is perhaps to be attributed to his wariness of anything retaining some reference to worlds beyond the work in which it is contained. He has praised his teacher Messiaen for providing the lesson 'that *all* can become music',[18] but in his own work he could never accept such anecdotal materials as Hindu rhythms, plainsong and gagaku imitations: all must be analysed and then transmuted into materials and means concordant with the musical system and with it alone.

By contrast, Stockhausen in his tape piece *Telemusik* (1966) accepts the music provided by extraneous cultures exactly as it comes, in the form of recordings, and then applies techniques of modification and integration to achieve a coherent whole. As he has explained, the work contains ' "electronic" passages, which are of today, together with tape recordings of music, for example from the south Sahara, from the Shipibo of the Amazon, from a Spanish village festival, Hungarian, Balinese music, recordings from temple ceremonies in Japan, . . . music of the highland dwellers of Vietnam, etc.'.[19] But he has also insisted that *Telemusik* is not a collage nor yet a synthesis but rather 'an untrammelled spiritual encounter'[20] of the components, 'a music of the whole world'.[21] The stage for this encounter is provided by the purely electronic sounds, often piercing high frequencies which give a suggestion of shortwave reception to the piece, while meetings are engineered by studio techniques which the composer has also explained: 'I modulate the rhythm of one event with the dynamic curve of another. Or I modulate electronic chords, regulated by myself, with the dynamic curve of a priestly chant, then this with the monotonous song (therefore the pitch line) of a Shipibo song, and so on'.[22] This technique of 'intermodulation', to use Stockhausen's own term, 'generates complex textures and dense events in which the original recordings, when they can be distinguished at all, sound as if they are being jammed by interference, colliding with and obscured by alien music.

Telemusik, the first of Stockhausen's works to include any open reference to music other than his own, prompted and was prompted by a new view of his music as continuous with that of other times and cultures. The work was composed during a period in Tokyo, and its use of Japanese percussion instruments to signal each new section is an obvious gesture of deference to the composer's hosts. But in dedicating his piece to the Japanese people Stockhausen was concerned with deeper issues: 'I have learnt', he wrote, '– especially in Japan – that tradition does not simply exist, but that it must be created anew every day. . . . Let us not forget that everything we do and say must be considered as a moment in a continuing tradition'.[23]

From now on, as Robin Maconie has observed, Stockhausen 'is eager to discover parallels between his own and other music (especially traditional music of oral cultures) as proof that his personal intuitions are in tune with universal forms of musical expression'.[24] And not for the first time Stockhausen was acting for his generation in searching for roots and linkages.

COLLAGE

The most obvious technique by which a composer may claim (or deny) roots in the past is that of quotation, and from the time of *Telemusik* the use of quotations, usually from well-known classics of the Western repertory, becomes a cliché of contemporary music. It is possible that the rediscovery of Ives played some part in this, though it is perhaps more likely that, as in other respects, Ives provided confirmation rather than influence. In any event, the more significant reasons for such borrowings have been those of an aesthetic or even a moral order: the need to test the present against the past and vice versa, the desire to improve contact with audiences by offering known subjects for discussion, the wish to find musical analogues for the multiple and simultaneous sensory bombardment in the world. This last is uppermost in those Cage pieces, such as the tape works *Williams Mix* and *Fontana Mix*, which present an image of undirected complexity by bringing together a whole variety of sounds. These and other similar collages proceed from the composer's view that electronic technology can and should be used for creative rather than reproductive ends, a view earlier enshrined in his *Credo in Us* (1942), where a gramophone record is irreverently treated as just another voice in a rhythmic counterpoint for piano and percussion. Cage merely suggests the use of something by Dvořák, Beethoven, Sibelius or Shostakovich, but the choice of the 'New World' Symphony in the only commercial recording contrives to give the work a belligerent edge as the charter of a musical Monroe doctrine, and encourages one to read the last word of the title in capital letters.

Among the more diverse, less prescriptive and often theatrical congregations of musical activity with which Cage was associated in the 1960s, *Variations V* (1965) extends the notion of collage in several directions at the same time. The score is confined to 37 'remarks re an audio-visual performance'; the real creative work for the first performance was carried out by Tudor and Mumma, who devised complex circuitry to derive sounds directly from the movements of dancers. As the dancers moved towards and away from sensitive antennae, or interrupted light beams directed at photocells, so they triggered the release of sounds from tape recorders, record players and radios, and there were also films and slides contributing to what Mumma described as 'a superbly poly: -chromatic, -genic, -phonic, -meric, -morphic, -pagic, -technic, -valent, multi-ringed circus'.[25] Similarly demanding of omni-attention are *Variations IV* (1963), which in the sanctioned recordings becomes a vast sweep of musical excerpts and other sound detritus, *HPSCHD* for up to seven harpsichordists, up to 51 tapes and visual entertainments ad libitum (1967–9) and the 'musicircus' (1967) for which Cage assembled numerous composers and performers in uncoordinated activities, as well as light shows, refreshment stalls, large balloons and an audience.

Cage's influence on 'multi-media' events, through such works as *Variations V*, *HPSCHD* and the earlier *Theatre Piece*, has been strongly felt in the U.S.A.: Eric Salzman's *The Nude Paper Sermon* (1968–9) is only one of the more clever essays in pastiche, stylistic heterogeneity and deliberate abandonment of linear consequence, where the 'sermon', read by an actor, leads a circuitous path through assortments of speech, song and instrumental playing, including a madrigal set in fake 16th-century style as a 'ruin'. The man-centred sensibility of the Renaissance, it is suggested, has given way to new modes of thought in which there are no fixed poles, no definite directions; Salzman remarks on his use of electronic technology to 'interrelate a variety of electronic age experiences'.[26]

Other composers, particularly in Europe, have been less tempted to invoke the dawn of a new age in order to justify collage techniques, but rather have used quotations and copies for their expressive associations. There are abundant examples in the music of Davies and also in that of George Crumb, whose works, though showing a certain superficial closeness to Davies in their extravagant instrumental writing and their delight in pastiche, make no attempt at the integrated development of Davies's best music. Crumb's use of quotations is correspondingly more a matter of acceptance than of interrogation. He has expressed himself as having 'an urge to fuse unrelated stylistic elements and juxtapose the seemingly incongruous',[27] but the fusion is less easy to discern than the juxtaposition, and the borrowed material tends to appear either as aural décor, as when flamenco arrives in the Lorca piece *Ancient Voices of Children* (1970), or as expressive of a melancholy and sentimental nostalgia. Richard Steinitz has aptly remarked of *Night of the Four Moons* for contralto and four players (1969) that: 'The direct quotations from Bach, Schubert or Chopin, heard through Crumb's strange and unworldly soundscape, acquire an amazing aura of distance both cultural and temporal. Surrealist museum exhibits, their mummified beauty seems utterly remote, like a childhood memory of warm, homely security'.[28] Such an effort to return to the musical womb has its not so distant counterpart in the composer's predilection exhibited elsewhere, notably in *Black Angels* for amplified string quartet (1970) and *Lux aeterna* for soprano and four players (1971), for images of death and the macabre, the paraphernalia of the latter work – 'the performers, masked and wearing black robes, sit in lotus position and in near-darkness around a lighted candle; sung phrases of the Requiem text alternate with a refrain for sitar, recorder and tabla'[29] – suggesting nothing so much as the excoriating excesses of the contemporary cinema.

The problem of integrating quotations into a foreign musical substance, which barely arises in the otherwise very different outputs of Cage and Crumb, is tackled in most of the works Zimmermann wrote in his last decade. Some earlier compositions, such as the C major trumpet concerto *Nobody knows the trouble I see* (1954), show an openness to sources which few of his Darmstadt colleagues would then have found worthy of attention, but his first statement of musical pluralism was the opera *Die Soldaten* (1958–64); this not only presents different scenes simultaneously on different stage levels, not only uses a wide gamut of vocal, instrumental and electronic sounds, but also introduces quotations from Bach and other composers at emotionally appropriate moments. Zimmermann's method here evidently derives from the Violin Concerto of Berg, whose *Wozzeck* is a determining, almost overbearing influence on the opera as a whole. Smaller works by Zimmermann, however, make use of past materials in a more subtle and individual manner: the oppositions of *Antiphonen* (1962), for instance, exist between recalled and original materials as well as between the viola soloist and the orchestra, and also between instrumental sound and speech by the players. Different musical worlds are brought together in similar fashion in two of the composer's imaginary ballets, the 'concerto scénique' *Présence* for piano trio (1961) and the 'ballet noir' *Musique pour les soupers du Roi Ubu* (1967), of which the former casts the three players as characters – the violinist Don Quixote, the cellist Molly Bloom and the pianist Ubu – which the music leads through diverse musical situations sharpened by quotations from Bach, Prokofiev and others. Example 56 shows a passage from another similar work, *Monologe* for two pianos (1960–64), and may suggest how quotations arise in Zimmermann's music from a containing stream of discourse. In the later *Photoptosis* for orchestra (1968), however, he relinquishes such command over the cited extracts, and here Beethoven, Wagner and the rest gather to observe, as it seems, the passing of a tradition, while he frames and supports them with brilliant but empty rhetoric.

Other ghosts from the musical past appear in near-contemporary works by two composers of an earlier generation, Shostakovich and Tippett, both of them more selective in their borrowings than Zimmermann, Cage or Crumb. The excerpts from Wagner and from Rossini's *Guillaume Tell* overture in Shostakovich's 15th Symphony (1971) can hardly fail to appear as alien presences, but since they occupy only a small part of the work, and since that work, being tonal, can to some degree fuse with them, they can largely retain their original expressive functions: they are not immediately set in relief, as are the quotations in Zimmermann's *Monologe*, for example. The case is similar in Tippett's Third Symphony (1972), which takes the *Schreckensfanfare* from the finale of Beethoven's Ninth Symphony to introduce not an ode to joy but a modern gloss on the earlier composer's optimistic humanism, cast in the form of a cultured blues solo for soprano. Divorced from its original context, however, the gesture cannot have the same disruptive and arresting force, while its exposure in the Tippett symphony carries some risk of devaluing that force in the Beethoven, so readily can quotation turn to travesty.

But for a composer like Kagel, whose critical inspection of musical mores leads him by aim and inclination to travesty of a humorous kind, the great are fair game for deflation. Accordingly his chamber orchestral version of his *Ludwig van* (1969) is a skit on Beethoven themes, reducing them to banality by empty repetition and distortion. Kagel's film of the same title, however, has more serious points to make, for here, in a surreal fantasy which has Beethoven revisiting his birthplace after two centuries, he takes his predecessor's part in examining how the myth has obscured and distanced the music. And in his *Variationen ohne Fuge* for orchestra (1971–2) he pays curious

Ex. 56
fig. 4
♩ = 76 Bach "Wachet auf, rufet uns, die Stimme"
quasi Organo
m.d.
p come prima, ben portato
(genaue Dynamik)
pp
lo stesso tempo
quasi spicc.
♩ = 60 Messiaen "Alléluias sereins d'une âme qui désire le ciel"
quasi Oboe
sempre espr. dolce
cresc.
pp murmurando
----- (Pedale giusto)

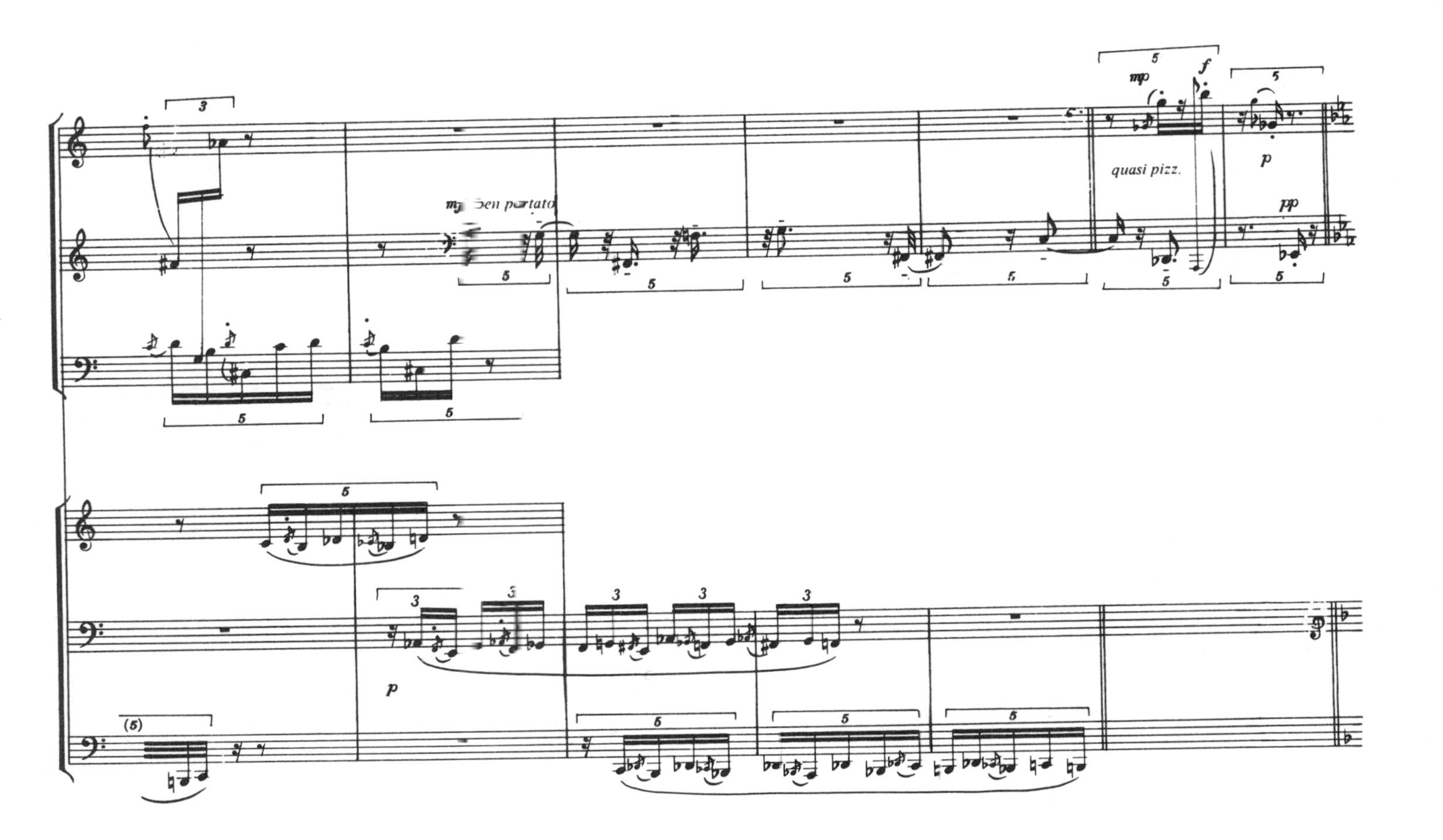
quasi pizz.

tribute to Brahms, 'the Varèse of the nineteenth century',[30] by liberally orchestrating and altering the Handel Variations, so providing a 20th-century gloss on a 19th-century commentary on 18th-century music. The result cannot but seem disrespectful, and Kagel is surely expressing his dissatisfaction with a musical culture which prizes the past above all contemporary work; yet the piece suggests also that an inventive dialogue with the past can be more illuminating than another rehearing of a masterwork. His method here is almost the reverse of Tippett's and quite distinct from those of other composers who have been mentioned in this section: instead of taking fragments from history, each loaded with its own weight of association, he acts within a single work, and it may appear that it is Brahms who is quoting Kagel.

The Beethoven bicentenary of 1970 prompted other composers than Kagel to subject 'Ludwig van' to their scrutiny. André Boucourechliev, in his *Ombres* for string orchestra, directed his attention principally to the quartets and concerned himself, like Kagel but in a quite different manner, with our experience of the music as much as with the material itself. As he has written: 'I tried hard to *integrate* the Beethovenian elements into my own style, in the perspective of a musical unity on several levels: a whole scale of thematic states is engendered, from the fragment which is barely recognizable, fugitive, ambiguous, to deliberate quotation considered as a goal. Even the distortion of a theme in our memory, its "mythic state", so to speak, here finds a place'.[31] The absorption of Beethoven into a new musical world is more radically attempted in Stockhausen's *Opus 1970,* a realization of his *Kurzwellen* in which taped fragments from Beethoven's works and from the Heiligenstadt Testament replace shortwave radios as sources of material for intuitive elaboration by live electronic ensemble. The performers may thus be enabled 'to hear familiar, old, pre-formed musical material with new ears, to penetrate and transform it with a musical consciousness of today',[32] so that the composer proves, as in *Telemusik,* that he can encompass and reinterpret given music, proceeding from the known to the new.

Many different ways of treating 'old, pre-formed musical material' from the Western repertory have been mentioned here, but certain basic attitudes stand out as options for the composer. He may feel able to take over a fragment, and retain its original meaning even while giving it a new context; this will be most readily achieved if that context shares some common features with the original, as in the examples from Tippett and Shostakovich. Alternatively, the composer may wish to use quotations within music of dissimilar style, and to take advantage of the inevitable disparities; the works of Crumb, Zimmermann and Boucourechliev show different ways of achieving this. Then again, quotations may be used as generative seeds of a totally alien musical development (Stockhausen) or strands in a complex collage (Cage), both techniques tending to neutralize the associations of the original material. Or those associations may become the main subject matter, as in Kagel's encounters with tradition.

There are of course other possibilities. Henze, a composer stylistically closer to the central tradition than any of those named above, has used quotations either to exorcize brooding giants (Wagner in his *Tristan* for piano, orchestra and tape, 1973) or simply to express, without any deeper qualms of musical conscience, an affectionate respect for earlier music (Byrd in his Fourth String Quartet, Bach in his wind quintet *L'autunno*, both works dating from the mid-1970s). His response to other musical cultures, notably that of Cuba in his Sixth Symphony (1969) and other works, is similarly one of uninhibited enthusiasm, involving no more than an enlarged eclecticism and not, as in Boulez or Stockhausen, the development of fundamentally new methods of composition. Only in his dramatic works does quotation become what it is in many collage works from Berg's Violin Concerto onwards: an outward sign that the continuity of tradition has been irrevocably lost.

INTEGRATION

Although the distinction between 'collage' and 'integration' may appear to imply a judgment of value, and certainly does so in Stockhausen's vocabulary, it is convenient to distinguish those works in which quotations are frankly acknowledged and presented as incidents (the collage model) from those in which cited excerpts have their original functions more or less suppressed in order to serve the needs of a new musical form; Stockhausen's *Telemusik* and *Opus 1970* have already provided instances of the latter.

The central movement of Berio's *Sinfonia* (1968–9) provides an extraordinary example of the new musical form being itself a quotation (this is not the case in Kagel's *Variationen ohne Fuge*, where not only is the fugue omitted but the number, order and formal dimensions of the variations are all changed). Berio takes over the whole scherzo from Mahler's Second Symphony as a stream in which to float a host of quotations from Debussy, Strauss, Wagner and many others, as well as prominent allusions to composers ranging from Bach to himself, all this being interwoven with a further current of verbal material impinging on a recitation from Beckett's *The Unnameable*. Example 57 shows the opening of the movement, where the first discernible quotations come from the start of the 'Jeux de vagues' from Debussy's *La mer* (bars 4–5: clarinets 1 and 3, oboe 1, bassoons, glockenspiel, harp, violins B, cellos, basses) and from the beginning of Mahler's Fourth Symphony (bars 2–7: flutes 1 and 2, snare drum); these are duly recognized by the sopranos, but the second alto has noticed also the beginning of the wholesale borrowing of the Mahler scherzo (bars 7–10: cor anglais, bassoons, timpani). There is no attempt to establish any kind of mediation among the diverse excerpts, and yet the flux of material is so rich, and so astutely handled, that one may reasonably speak of this assembly as a totally original creation. It can also be seen as an image of the weight of musical history which a composer may feel to bear down upon him at a time when virtually any music from the past is available to anyone within reach of a gramophone; but unlike the similarly intended collages of Cage, the Berio movement is a thoroughly organized picture of disorder, its quotations judiciously stitched into the Mahler scherzo.

Moreover, the welter of quotation and reference occupies only one movement, though that the largest and inevitably the most striking, in a five-part work which successfully contains it by reflecting elsewhere its heterophonies, its harmonic characters (perhaps unavoidably, these being so various) and its scoring. In particular, the first and fifth movements present fuzzy memories of the primitive roots of music, using words from Lévi-Strauss's *Le cru et le cuit* in a musical fabric suggestive of a long past dawning, voices and instruments being called upon in varied combinations to contribute to a dappled and harmonically static texture. Heard in this context, the middle movement is a parallel excursion into more recent musical history, plumbing the last 250 years or so rather than as many millennia, and in turn it gave rise to a more open encounter with folk music in *Questo vuol dire che* for voices, instruments and tape (1969).

Berio had earlier, in his *Folk Songs* for mezzo-soprano and en-

Ex. 57

acc...
Tempo dello Scherzo (III mov.) della II Sinfonia di G. Mahler

semble (1964), fashioned a cycle of sophisticated arrangements in a manner not so far from that of Stravinsky or Ravel, but *Questo vuol dire che* is a much more elaborate piece, offering the possibility for diverse folk materials and modes of performance to co-exist within the all-embracing medium of a Youngian perfect 5th. His later essays in the purposeful integration of sound materials have taken place in dramatic works: the opera *Opera* (1960–70, revised 1977) and the music-theatre piece *Recital I (for Cathy)* (1972), designed for Berberian with accompaniment for small orchestra. In this latter work the quotations, which include an early tonal song by the composer to prove his musical voluptuousness of long standing, are brought in by the singer as she recalls snatches of her repertory in what is a portrayal of mental disintegration.

Stockhausen's dedication to Berio of one of the four 'regions', or sections, of his tape work *Hymnen* (1966–7), his grandest essay in the integration of pre-existing music, is perhaps to be understood as recognition of a common interest, though in fact the German composer's aims and methods are very different from the Italian's. To compare their works based on folk music, where Berio in *Questo vuol dire che* is interested in folk styles of performance as exemplifying music-making in a natural, innocent state, Stockhausen in *Telemusik* is concerned with folk-musical objects, with recordings. In *Hymnen* he uses the techniques of the earlier work, though on a larger scale and in a more continuous manner, to create a fluid stream of electronic sound evolving from the national anthems of many nations. Again he intermodulates recordings one with another, but now the sources are much nearer the surface and the form is much looser and more ample, with none of the severely sectional structuring of *Telemusik*. *Hymnen* is much more in the world of radio experience, drifting as it does from what sounds like poor reception to the clear exposure of an anthem, or from passages which take up the methods of *Kontakte* in operating processes of transformation and 'decomposition' upon the recordings to naturalistic dream sequences, like the multi-lingual litany on the word 'red' or the ominous calls of a croupier. And the variety of the material is matched by the versatility of the work, which is, Stockhausen has said, 'composed in such a way that various screenplays or librettos for films, operas and ballets can be written to the music'.[33] And he goes on: 'The order of the characteristic sections and the total duration are variable. Depending on the dramatic requirements, regions may be extended, added or omitted'. He himself has not sanctioned such drastic alterations, though he has prepared versions of the work with live electronic ensemble participating throughout, imitating what they hear and forging connections between anthems, and also with an orchestra playing in the third region.

If all this suggests that *Hymnen* is more the basic matrix for a composition than a fully composed work, attention must also be drawn to the processes which make it a two-hour piece of continuous interest: the processes by which anthems are made to emerge from backgrounds of fragmented allusions, by which they are dismembered, or by which their component sounds are electronically changed. Example 58 shows a simple instance from the second region (the quotation is from the 'listening score' devised merely to guide the ear, not to show how the piece was made). Here the German anthem is torn between a unison chorus ('CH') and an orchestral accompaniment ('B') with jolting internal repetitions; then the choral and orchestral sound is magically sustained, gradually pulled towards opposite extremes of pitch as if by magnets, and finally allowed to continue when the octave interval has been reached. In this extract, as so often in the work, the electronic transformations bring about a dislocation of time, freezing its passage to simulate an eternal present or cutting back to the past in the middle of a continual unfolding. The work even contains its own past, for in one remarkable passage later in the second region the development of German and African anthems is cut off for the insertion of a conversation between Stockhausen and his assistant recorded during the composition of the piece.

Yet it is hard to accept *Hymnen* only as an exercise in musical and temporal displacement and transition, to ignore its implications as an image of universal brotherhood. Stockhausen has suggested that he used national anthems because they are 'the most familiar music imaginable'.[34] 'If one integrates familiar music', he goes on, 'into the composition of unfamiliar, new music, the listener can hear particularly clearly how it has been integrated: untransformed, more or less transformed, transposed, modulated, etc.' But his choice for the close of the work, a majestic passage floated on the sounds of his own breathing, is not of any familiar music but of a manufactured anthem 'which belongs to the utopian realm of *Hymunion* in *Harmondy* under *Pluramon*';[35] a realm which the puns barely conceal is one of union and world harmony guided by a being who, like Stockhausen himself

Ex. 58

I. ZENTRUM
CH=CHOR einstimmig
mit B=Begleitung
akkordisch
M ca 67 (B etwas schneller als CH)
IIIII = zerhackt
Deutschland
CH
Kl. Tr.
B
ff
harmonisiert in D
11' 46"
52, 5"
dim. poco a poco
gliss.
12' 27"
42, 5"
13' 23"
32, 5"
43, 2"

in this work, is both pluralist and monist, treasuring the many but seeking to provide a single ground for their encounter.

Pousseur takes up this point when, in a context where he mentions both *Hymnen* and Berio's *Questo vuol dire che,* he speaks of recent music as 'the organizer of a space for cohabitation, where all previous musical acquisitions (or parallel ones, for it is clear that original lexicological discoveries are always possible) may find their most suitable places, existing together and contributing to a new *corporate harmony*'.[36] He also makes the interesting suggestion that there is a link between the polyphonic conception of *Hymnen,* where distinct musical strata are often presented simultaneously, and Stockhausen's notion of moment form, which nominally allows the juxtaposition of unrelated events: in both cases connections come about as a result of the listener's mental activity, whether in shifting his attention from one layer to another or in using memory to establish links through time, so that the dictatorial function of the composer, inimical to a musician of Pousseur's political persuasion, is diminished. Pousseur sees too a more overt social message in the works of his colleagues, not only in Stockhausen's use of national anthems but also in the 'corporate harmony' of divergent materials as a model of a utopian order among men. To pursue this interpretation a stage further, one might even suggest that such works as *Questo vuol dire che* and *Telemusik* can be construed as attempts to demonstrate, whether consciously or not, that modern man (electronic techniques, advanced compositional methods) need feel no alienation from the natural world (the voice, spontaneous music-making, folksong).

Pousseur's own creative inclinations, towards the reintroduction of harmonic function, and the importance to his political thinking of Charles Fourier[37] have together led him to the elaboration of harmonic systems in which networks of relationships exist among chords of all possible types. His largest work based on such systems is the opera *Votre Faust* (1960–67), which has, through a technique of proliferating variation characteristic of his music, spawned a number of related compositions, including two sets of *Echos de Votre Faust* (for cello, 1967, and for mezzo-soprano and trio, 1969), the piano work *Miroir de Votre Faust* (1964–5) and the latter's electronic commentary *Jeu de miroirs de Votre Faust* (1967). Among these, *Miroir* shows with exemplary clarity the direction Pousseur's harmony was taking, from the use of chosen interval groupings as norms in the works of the late 1950s and early 1960s to the employment of a more comprehensive chordal repertory: its first section, 'Le tarot d'Henri', is a mobile made up of materials with specific harmonic characters on a scale from the diatonic to the chromatic, and its second part, 'Le chevauchée fantastique', is a virtuoso potted history of harmony, travelling by means of allusion from Bach to the present.

In his orchestral work *Couleurs croisées* (1967) Pousseur uses similar techniques to serve an unambiguous political message, for here the civil rights song 'We shall overcome' is made the 'matrix from which the whole composition is strictly derived'.[38] The composer continues: 'In particular, it is projected through a whole system of melodic-harmonic fields, beginning with a disjunct, chromatic, expressionist musical reality and ending . . . in a diatonic state which is relatively, hypothetically at peace', and so the music contrives 'to "recount a story – musically", a story more hoped-for than yet effective, at least in full (Martin Luther King: "I have a dream")'. Pousseur's golden vision of a future society of perfect equity and peace is further expressed in his *Invitation à l'utopie* (1971), where the recitation and singing of a poetic almanac by Michel Butor is grafted on to his *Les éphémerides d'Icare 2* for soloist, concertino trio and ripieno ensemble (1970), and where a benign collaboration is established between individual and small group, small group and totality, in a harmonic ambience of seductive concord.

The harmonic systems which Pousseur has used in his works since *Votre Faust* have been evolved through a searching musical and more generally cultural analysis of the past, and particularly of the 20th-century past. Instead of castigating Schoenberg for his attachment to earlier models, as had been the habit in the 1950s, Pousseur praises that 'stylistic polyphony' which can bring together, in the sixth of the Orchestral Variations op. 31, the Viennese waltz, memories of Bach's three-part inventions and of Mozart's minuets, and 'the most convoluted post-Wagnerian harmony'.[39] His second big dramatic work, *Die Erprobung des Petrus Hebraïcus* (1974), carries Schoenberg criticism to the creative forum, where, drawing partly on those means of encouraging the collaboration of performers which he had introduced (going beyond *Répons*) in the 'systems of improvisation' offered by *Mnemosyne II* (1969) and *Icare apprenti* (1970), he actively questions the role of the leader in relation to the group, whether that leader be composer or prophet (the scenario is based on biblical events) or both.[40] At the same time *Die Erprobung* is concerned with testing not only the function of the gifted or inspired individual but also the properties of closed musical systems, whether tonal or serial. Any such system, Pousseur argues, is the expression of a restrictive society, and it is the composer's duty to demonstrate that constraints may be lifted without music thus falling into the anarchy of Cage's world, that harmonic order is possible without a fixed hierarchy.

In addressing himself to his other great 20th-century predecessor, Stravinsky, Pousseur has remarked that before that composer's harmony can be adequately described 'we will have to wait for the search for (if not the discovery of) a much more general harmonic system which will allow us to integrate the chromatic harmony of the Viennese as well as the more consonant harmonies of our history, including all the attempts of preserial music, and to open the way to envisioning the integration of extra-European harmonies, as well as the opening up (now partially reclosing) of possibilities which are new by virtue of their very material (non-tempered scales, relationships of "harmonic" containing primary factors greater than 5; micro-intervals: all things whose exploration *does* to my knowledge absolutely require the aid of *simple consonances*)',[41] this grand design of harmonic integration being sparked off by a consideration of *Agon*. Pousseur's *Racine 19* for cello (1977) marks a step in the exploration of the new possibilities of which he writes, using as it does an equal-tempered scale of 19 intervals to the octave; but his richest and most consistent attempts at general harmonic integration have come in *Die Erprobung* and in two homages to Stravinsky: *L'effacement du Prince Igor* for orchestra and *Stravinsky au futur* for voice, solo instrument, ensemble and electronics (both 1971).

The latter consists of 'collective musical inventions prepared on the basis of pre-existing elements',[42] on which Pousseur worked with a group of fellow composers and performers in redirecting and recombining not only Stravinsky's musical ideas but also his mythical characters: Apollo, Pulcinella, Persephone, Oedipus, Noah and Orpheus. Thus the piece is able to propose schemes of communication among musicians, among the principles and products of Stravinsky's mind, and further between performers and listeners, since the audience is 'invited, by means of a somewhat enigmatic "programmatic" description of the music they are about to hear, to *follow* it, to try to establish a correspondence between what they hear and the description they have been given'.[43] Even though this may be the situation of any audience faced with a programme note, nothing could better illustrate Pousseur's view of professional musicians as teachers and guides, offering suggestions to each other and to the audience, suggestions which may be acted upon or rejected. Equally the piece shows his use of integrating procedures not in order to lay claim to foreign material but rather to question the premises of the past, to expose what history may contain by way of warning or promise.

L'effacement du Prince Igor, a fixed composition, provides a much clearer example of Pousseur's harmonic integration at work. He takes his cue from, again, Stravinsky's *Agon,* in which he finds 'a variation of *stylistic colors,* according to which we can certainly see that it is very far from being a simple *collage,* since it rests on an extraordinarily active metabolism, on the omnipresent circulation of molecular elements, common to all the specialized organizations'.[44] His analysis of the unified harmonic variety of *Agon* leads him to a technique of generating the most diverse harmonic characters from the series of Webern's Variations op. 30, a work itself tied to *Agon* as source of Stravinsky's 'Pas de deux'. *L'effacement,* cast largely in block chords for homogeneous groups of instruments, is a dance of these harmonic characters, which impinge on each other to varying degrees and project a gradual withdrawal in terms of dynamic level and of complexity.[45] Example 59 shows a passage which is relatively rich in characters from the tonal past.

Another attempt at encompassing all harmonic possibilities is to be found in the more recent scores of Peter Schat, whose earlier works, such as the Improvisations and Symphonies for wind quintet (1960), had proved him a gifted pupil of Boulez. As in the case of Pousseur, his concern with a less exclusive harmony has developed in parallel with a socialist commitment expressed in such works as *To You* for mezzo-soprano and ensemble (Adrian Mitchell text, 1970–72) and *Canto general* for mezzo-soprano, violin and piano (Neruda text, 1974). The first of these has the words declaimed to powerful music for electric guitars, but this encounter with rock was short-lived, and in subsequent works Schat has concentrated on developing techniques of melodic and harmonic permutation which ensure that a wide range of intervallic material can be gradually revealed in a continuous musical process. Example 60, taken from the instrumental introduction to *Canto general,* shows his technique

Ex. 59

of 'permuteration', by which 'no new tone is introduced in a series . . . until all the relations between the tones already present have been exploited as fully as possible',[46] and shows too his liking for repetitive textures influenced by Reich and Riley.

The harmonic systems of Schat and Pousseur, though they propose means by which composers may use the previously banned sounds of major triads and so on, carry no sense of restoration or

Ex. 60

nostalgia; the laws of relationship are new, and the music is directed not to the past but to a utopian future. Other composers, however, have seen return to former certainties as holding the only possibility of genuine achievement – a view adopted by a considerable number of composers, particularly in America and Germany, during the early 1970s. Perhaps the most distinguished convert to tonality was George Rochberg, who has recalled how he 'came to realize that the music of the "old masters" was a living presence, that its spiritual values had not been displaced or destroyed by the new'.[47]

Rochberg's creative career from the late 1940s to the early 1960s had shown a not unusual evolution from the shadow of Hindemith, Stravinsky and Bartók in such works as his First String Quartet (1952), through areas close to Schoenberg (and, in his Second Symphony of 1955–6, Mahler) to a finely wrought and expressively poignant Webernian style in his *Blake Songs* (1957, revised 1962) and other compositions. This led him to formulate a theory of the 'spatialization' of music, of modern music as breaking with the temporal continuity assured by thematic development, by metrical regularity and, most important, by the directed progressions of diatonic harmony, substituting a 'spatial image' of music as eternal present, as aspiring 'to Being, not Becoming'.[48]

But the death of his son in 1964 brought him to the conclusion that he 'could not continue writing so-called "serial" music . . . it was finished . . . hollow . . . meaningless'.[49] His next works, including the instrumental quartet *Contra mortem et tempus* (1965), the orchestral *Music for the Magic Theater* (1965) and the Third Symphony (1968), were based largely on quotations and suggest, like the roughly contemporary works of Zimmermann, an examination of the present in terms of the past and a testing of the past's relevance to the present: the second 'act', or movement, of *Music for the Magic Theater* is certainly composed from this viewpoint, grafting as it does a miscellany of ideas on to the continuing thread of a movement from Mozart. The procedure is close to that which Berio was to adopt in the central movement of his *Sinfonia*, but the expressive character is utterly different. In the Rochberg there is none of Berio's exultation but instead a hopelessness in the comparison of past and present, as if Mozart's music had come from a civilization whose skills have been lost beyond recall. There is, therefore, some logic in his subsequent move, in such works as his Third String Quartet (1972–3) and Violin Concerto (1975), to adopt past styles for his own; and where the imitations even of late Beethoven (in the third movement of the quartet) are so expert and evidently not ironic, one cannot speak of quotation, nor of integration, but of complete recapture.

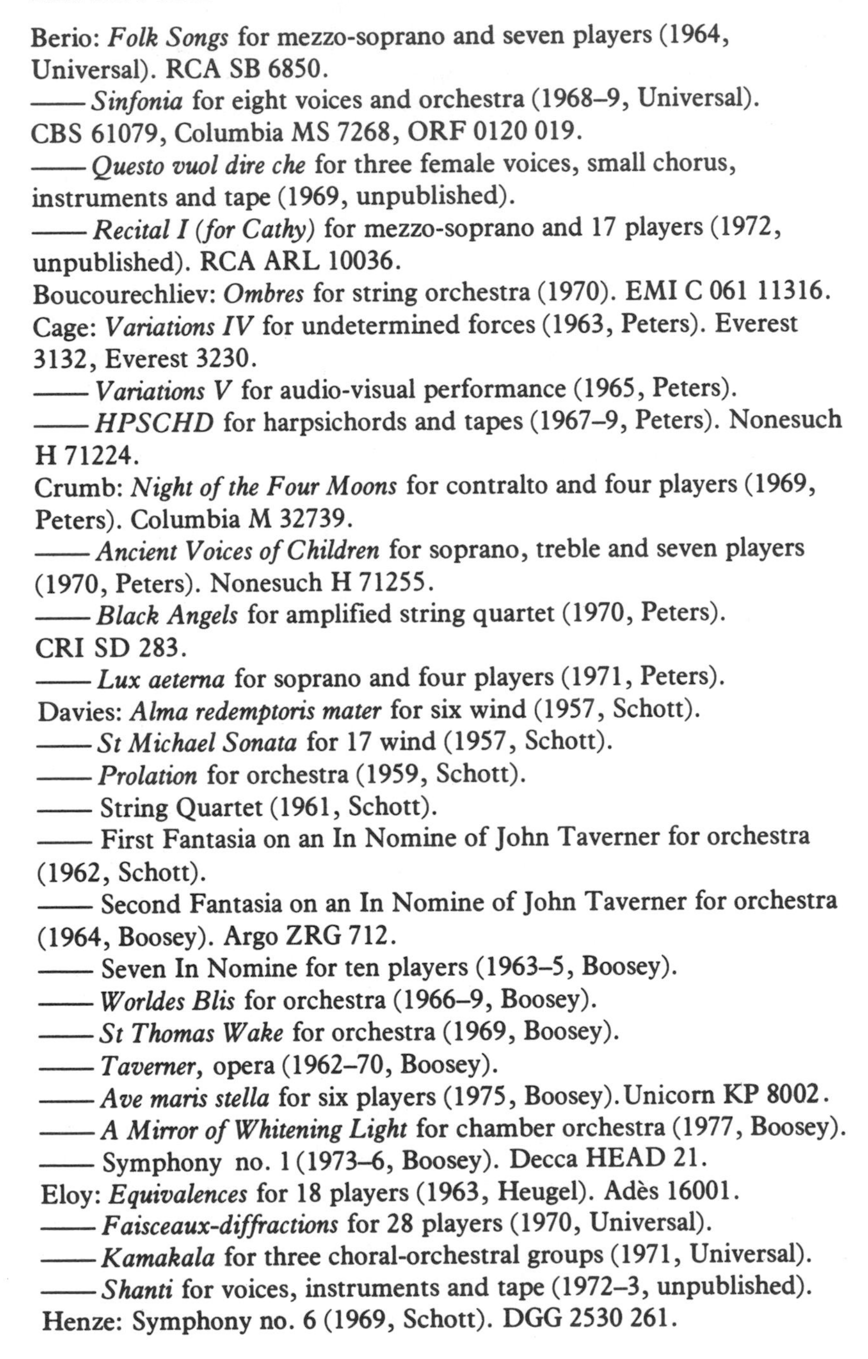

REPERTORY

Berio: *Folk Songs* for mezzo-soprano and seven players (1964, Universal). RCA SB 6850.
—— *Sinfonia* for eight voices and orchestra (1968–9, Universal). CBS 61079, Columbia MS 7268, ORF 0120 019.
—— *Questo vuol dire che* for three female voices, small chorus, instruments and tape (1969, unpublished).
—— *Recital I (for Cathy)* for mezzo-soprano and 17 players (1972, unpublished). RCA ARL 10036.
Boucourechliev: *Ombres* for string orchestra (1970). EMI C 061 11316.
Cage: *Variations IV* for undetermined forces (1963, Peters). Everest 3132, Everest 3230.
—— *Variations V* for audio-visual performance (1965, Peters).
—— *HPSCHD* for harpsichords and tapes (1967–9, Peters). Nonesuch H 71224.
Crumb: *Night of the Four Moons* for contralto and four players (1969, Peters). Columbia M 32739.
—— *Ancient Voices of Children* for soprano, treble and seven players (1970, Peters). Nonesuch H 71255.
—— *Black Angels* for amplified string quartet (1970, Peters). CRI SD 283.
—— *Lux aeterna* for soprano and four players (1971, Peters).
Davies: *Alma redemptoris mater* for six wind (1957, Schott).
—— *St Michael Sonata* for 17 wind (1957, Schott).
—— *Prolation* for orchestra (1959, Schott).
—— String Quartet (1961, Schott).
—— First Fantasia on an In Nomine of John Taverner for orchestra (1962, Schott).
—— Second Fantasia on an In Nomine of John Taverner for orchestra (1964, Boosey). Argo ZRG 712.
—— Seven In Nomine for ten players (1963–5, Boosey).
—— *Worldes Blis* for orchestra (1966–9, Boosey).
—— *St Thomas Wake* for orchestra (1969, Boosey).
—— *Taverner,* opera (1962–70, Boosey).
—— *Ave maris stella* for six players (1975, Boosey). Unicorn KP 8002.
—— *A Mirror of Whitening Light* for chamber orchestra (1977, Boosey).
—— Symphony no. 1 (1973–6, Boosey). Decca HEAD 21.
Eloy: *Equivalences* for 18 players (1963, Heugel). Adès 16001.
—— *Faisceaux-diffractions* for 28 players (1970, Universal).
—— *Kamakala* for three choral-orchestral groups (1971, Universal).
—— *Shanti* for voices, instruments and tape (1972–3, unpublished).
Henze: Symphony no. 6 (1969, Schott). DGG 2530 261.

—— *Tristan* for piano, orchestra and tape (1973, Schott). DGG 2530 834.
—— String Quartet no. 4 (1975–6, Schott).
—— *L'autunno* for wind quintet (1977, Schott).
Kagel: *Musik für Renaissance-Instrumente* for 23 players (1965, Universal). DGG 104 933.
—— *Ludwig van* for undetermined forces (1969, Universal), versions for chamber orchestra and on film. DGG 2530 014.
—— *Exotica* for six players (1971, Universal). DGG 2530 251.
—— *Variationen ohne Fuge* for two actors and orchestra (1971–2, Universal).
Messiaen: *Sept haïkaï* for piano and small orchestra (1962, Leduc). Adès 16001.
—— *Couleurs de la cité céleste* for piano, wind and percussion (1963, Leduc). CBS 72471.
—— *La Transfiguration de Notre Seigneur Jésus-Christ* for seven instrumental soloists, chorus and orchestra (1963–9, Leduc). Decca HEAD 1–2.
Pousseur: *Miroir de Votre Faust* for piano with soprano ad libitum (1964–5, Universal).
—— *Couleurs croisées* for orchestra (1967, Suvini Zerboni).
—— *Jeu de miroirs de Votre Faust* on tape (1967, unpublished). Heliodor Wergo 2549 021, Wergo 60039.
—— *Echos de Votre Faust I* for cello (1967, Universal), *II* for mezzo-soprano, flute, cello and piano (1969, Universal).
—— *Mnemosyne I—II* for undetermined forces (1968–9, Suvini Zerboni).
—— *Les éphémerides d'Icare 2* for soloist, trio and ensemble (1970, Suvini Zerboni), also with speaker, two female voices and chorus as *Invitation à l'utopia* (1971, Suvini Zerboni).
—— *L'effacement du Prince Igor* for orchestra (1971, Suvini Zerboni).
—— *Stravinsky au futur* for voice, solo instrument, ensemble and electronics (1971, unpublished).
—— *Die Erprobung des Petrus Herbraïcus,* music theatre (1974, unpublished).
—— *Racine 19* for cello (1977, unpublished).
Rochberg: String Quartet no. 1 (1952, Presser). CRI SD 337.
—— Symphony no. 2 (1955–6, Presser). Columbia AMS 6379.
—— *Blake Songs* for soprano and eight players (1957, revised 1962, Leeds). Nonesuch H 71302.
—— *Contra mortem et tempus* for flute, clarinet, violin and piano (1965, Presser). CRI 231 USD.
—— *Music for the Magic Theater* for orchestra (1965, Presser). Desto 6444.

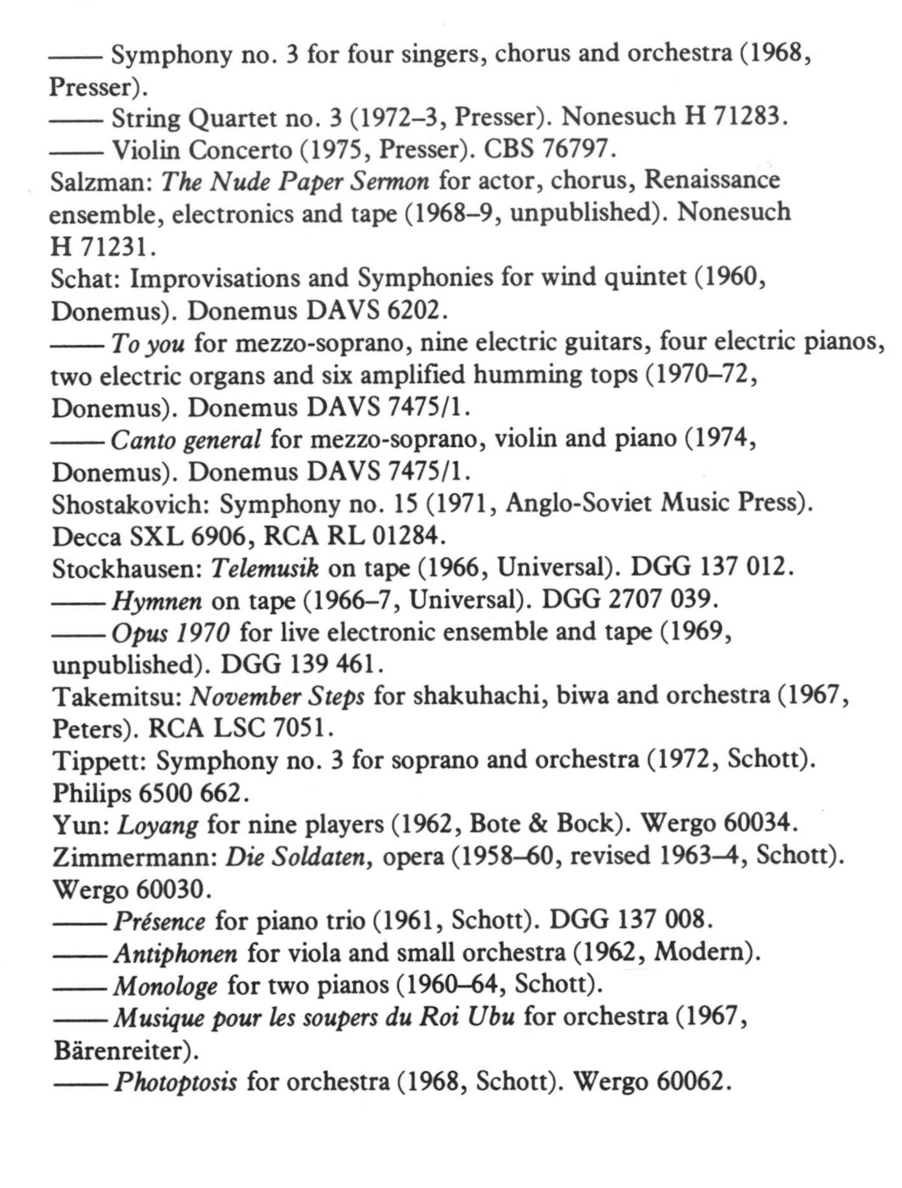

—— Symphony no. 3 for four singers, chorus and orchestra (1968, Presser).
—— String Quartet no. 3 (1972–3, Presser). Nonesuch H 71283.
—— Violin Concerto (1975, Presser). CBS 76797.
Salzman: *The Nude Paper Sermon* for actor, chorus, Renaissance ensemble, electronics and tape (1968–9, unpublished). Nonesuch H 71231.
Schat: Improvisations and Symphonies for wind quintet (1960, Donemus). Donemus DAVS 6202.
—— *To you* for mezzo-soprano, nine electric guitars, four electric pianos, two electric organs and six amplified humming tops (1970–72, Donemus). Donemus DAVS 7475/1.
—— *Canto general* for mezzo-soprano, violin and piano (1974, Donemus). Donemus DAVS 7475/1.
Shostakovich: Symphony no. 15 (1971, Anglo-Soviet Music Press). Decca SXL 6906, RCA RL 01284.
Stockhausen: *Telemusik* on tape (1966, Universal). DGG 137 012.
—— *Hymnen* on tape (1966–7, Universal). DGG 2707 039.
—— *Opus 1970* for live electronic ensemble and tape (1969, unpublished). DGG 139 461.
Takemitsu: *November Steps* for shakuhachi, biwa and orchestra (1967, Peters). RCA LSC 7051.
Tippett: Symphony no. 3 for soprano and orchestra (1972, Schott). Philips 6500 662.
Yun: *Loyang* for nine players (1962, Bote & Bock). Wergo 60034.
Zimmermann: *Die Soldaten,* opera (1958–60, revised 1963–4, Schott). Wergo 60030.
—— *Présence* for piano trio (1961, Schott). DGG 137 008.
—— *Antiphonen* for viola and small orchestra (1962, Modern).
—— *Monologe* for two pianos (1960–64, Schott).
—— *Musique pour les soupers du Roi Ubu* for orchestra (1967, Bärenreiter).
—— *Photoptosis* for orchestra (1968, Schott). Wergo 60062.

12 Virtuosity → Improvisation

The history of music has repeatedly shown difficulty of performance to be a transitory quality of a work, evaporating as innovations become absorbed within the common practice of executants. Even so, certain works of the 1950s, such as Boulez's *Le marteau sans maître* or Stockhausen's *Zeitmasze,* would appear to reach to the borderlands of the feasible, certainly in terms of temporal precision, and one may doubt that such works will ever lie comfortably within musicians' technique. To take another example, the more recent works of Babbitt thrust arduous responsibilities upon the performer, who must, as has been shown, play exactly the right pitches at the right time points for the right durations and at the right dynamic levels if the projection of the structure is not to be impaired.

These are all instances of extraordinary complexity achieved with conventional notation; there are of course problems of a quite different order in the performance of music which proposes new notations and new musical situations, perhaps requiring the executant to use his instrument or voice in an unprecedented manner, to work with electronic apparatus, to involve himself in some theatrical exercise, or to contribute to a more or less guided improvisation. It will already be apparent that such new situations have been energetically pursued by many composers during the period since 1960. Among the many factors responsible for this tendency has been the emergence of a generation of highly gifted performers anxious to extend the ranges and repertories of their instruments, as well as the need felt by many composers, whether for aesthetic or social reasons, that performing musicians should be involved more directly in the creation of music (though one may doubt whether, say, the flute part of *Le marteau sans maître* does not offer more of a challenge to a musician's skill, even his creative skill, than some graphic design or loose instruction). Thus it is that music has returned to something like its condition in the early 19th century, with composer-performers winning widespread acclaim, with works being created primarily as vehicles for virtuosity, and with a revival of the art of improvisation.

THE VIRTUOSO PERFORMER

So various have been the instrumental usages introduced during the last two decades, and so diverse the notations used to prescribe them, that it would be futile to attempt here anything more than a cursory survey before proceeding to the more central matter of how new playing techniques have been used in compositions, and how they have been allied with new concepts of the nature of musical performance. The possibilities of woodwind instruments have been greatly extended to encompass 'multiphonics' (i.e. chords) produced by novel fingerings or else by singing into the instrument, as well as percussive effects obtained from different parts of the instrument's body, microtones, and unusual sounds derived from more or less extreme alterations to the embouchure and mouthpiece. Many of these devices are also available on brass instruments. New sounds can be obtained from string instruments by using unusual bowing pressures, bowing unusual parts of the instrument, striking the instrument in various ways, and so on, while changes in the percussion department have been so numerous, both in the introduction of new instruments and in the use of new techniques, as to defy summary.

Faced with the abundant new riches of which orchestral instruments are capable, the composer may, to take the most straightforward instance, draw on them simply as extensions to his normal timbral resources without allowing them to influence the basic premises of his compositional thought. This is often the case in the music of Henze: in his *Heliogabalus imperator* (1971–2), for example, he uses woodwind multiphonics to create effects of festering decadence, the new sounds providing outlandish colours for what is otherwise a work in the conventional genre of the symphonic poem. Similarly, Henze's attitude to the solo performer, as evidenced in the Double Concerto for oboe, harp and strings (1966), the Concerto for double bass and chamber orchestra (also 1966) or the grandly symphonic Second Piano Concerto (1967), is essentially traditional, in that the relationship between soloist and ensemble is projected in continuous, developing forms as one of dialogue or confrontation.

The case is quite different in the music of Berio. Each of his many works for soloist, whether alone or in combination with a group, seems to arise in a very direct manner from the instrument or voice concerned and from the physical exercise of playing it. Hence, for example, the frenetic tremolo chords of his *Sequenza VI* for viola (1967), or the demanding requirements of carefully balanced chords linked by sensitively coloured lines in his *Sequenza IV* for piano (1965), or again the concentration in his *'Points on the Curve to Find . . .'* for piano and small orchestra (1973–4) on the piano's quite opposite characteristic of even and precise toccata-like enunciation. Berio has often made use of new performing techniques. especially in *Sequenza V* for trombone (1966), but always with such adroitness that the marginal effects produced do not stand out as dangerous, at least when his works are played by the virtuoso musicians for whom they were intended: the dedicatees of the *Sequenze* include many of those who have been most active in the presentation of new music, among them Severino Gazzelloni (*Sequenza I*, 1958), Cathy Berberian (*Sequenza III*, 1965) and Heinz Holliger (*Sequenza VII*, 1969).

Berio's solo pieces, besides being concerned with the physical activity of making music, sometimes require action of a more theatrical kind, this being particularly true of the works for voice and for trombone. The former is a setting of a short poem by Markus Kutter, but the main interest, as in the earlier electronic pieces *Thema* and *Visage*, is not in the communication of a verbal message but in the manifold ways in which that message may be distorted and in the whole spectrum of vocal behaviour from inarticulate noises to speech or song. Example 61, from near the opening of the piece, shows something of the variety of vocal styles required, and shows too Berio's characteristic use of psychological cues ('tense', 'urgent', etc.) as to the kind of style he requires. The rapid shifts from one

Ex. 61

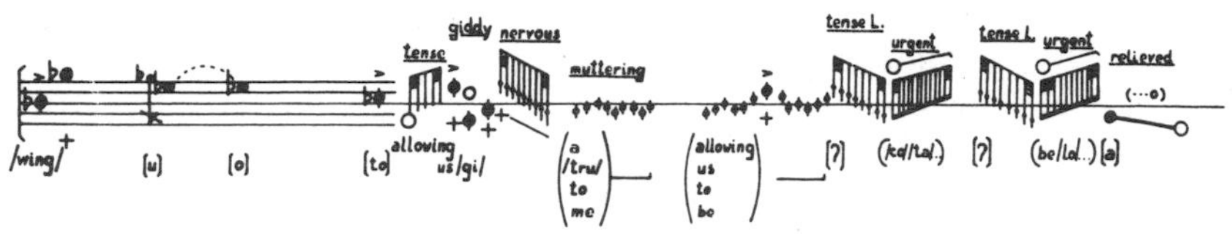

mode of expression to another are thus bound to give an impression of mental confusion, while the spectacle of a singer who does not just sing but engages in these other kinds of vocalization is immediately dramatic.

In the case of *Sequenza V* Berio has acknowledged a specific theatrical model for the clowning he demands of his trombonist, namely his memory of the clown Grock, and the player is required not only to produce new sonorities by singing into the instrument but also to vocalize and to gesture. So the piece becomes, if not a circus turn, at least a smart cabaret act. Both *Sequenza III* and *Sequenza VII* appear to have been designed by the composer not just as vehicles for their intended performers but equally as portraits, so that it may be difficult for a singer to avoid giving an imitation of Berberian's skill in assuming vocal disguises (a skill also exploited by Berio in those other works written for her, including *Epifanie* and *Recital I*) or for an oboist not to emulat Holliger's keen wit and his brilliance.

Yet the *Sequenze* also belong unequivocally to Berio's musical world. Not only does *Sequenza III* have a place with those other works of his which dwell at the frontiers between music and language, but each piece in the series shows his liking for hectic musical activity within closely defined harmonic limits, his obsession with repeated return, re-definition and re-elaboration. This is especially clear in the works for viola and for oboe, the former composed of lines that rapidly re-assort the same few pitches and of tremolo attacks on sustained chords, the latter a decoration of a single pitch which remains ever-present as a drone. In both these cases Berio was drawn to make new vertical elaborations of the original *Sequenza*, following the precedent of his *Chemins I* (1965), where the harp *Sequenza* is embedded in an orchestral tissue which develops in diverging directions the ideas contained in the solo piece. Writing of this work Berio has remarked that: 'A thing done is never finished. The "completed" work is the ritual and the commentary of another work which preceded it, of another work which will follow it. The question does not provoke a response but rather a commentary and new questions . . .'[1]

Sequenza VI has proved a particularly fruitful source of proliferating avenues, its perpetual workings over the same ideas transferred on to a wider plane of associated compositions. Berio first wrapped the viola solo in music for instrumental nonet to create *Chemins II* (1967) and then surrounded this work with orchestral divagations to make *Chemins III* (1968). A further, oblique route from *Chemins II* is taken in *Chemins IIb* (1969), an orchestral commentary from which the solo part has been removed, and this in turn gave rise to a daughter work, *Chemins IIc* (1972), which adds back the solo thread but now allots it to bass clarinet. The three directly linked works *Sequenza VI*, *Chemins II* and *Chemins III*, are related to each other, Berio has said, 'like the layers of an onion: distinct, separate, yet intimately contoured on each other: each new layer creates a new, though related surface, and each older layer assumes a new function as soon as it is covered'.[2] There is thus a centrifugal flow of musical thought from the original solo out into the progressively larger ensembles, a flow which may be one of clarification, as when latent harmonies become explicitly stated, or may alternatively be one of obscuring and distortion.

The same image of concentric musical layers is appropriate in the case of *Chemins IV* (1975), where the oboe *Sequenza* is joined by a web of music for ten strings; nor is it unhelpful in an approach to other concertante works of this period which, though not based on separate solo originals, share the commentary style of the *Chemins* pieces. For example, in *'Points on the Curve to Find . . .'* the ensemble fills out the harmonic potential in an almost exclusively monodic piano part; the brass, by providing sustained pitches and chords in what is otherwise a rapid, excited polyphony, underpin a nervous movement towards the resolution of the final unison D. The Concerto for two pianos and orchestra (1972–3) has a more complex but equally sure harmonic groundplan, beginning over an E pedal and coming in its second half to an increasingly firm definition of G as tonal centre, this finally affirmed by G major chords. However, the harmonic statements and processes in Berio's music are only unambiguous on the largest scale: at any moment they may be surrounded by alternatives which nudge at the music's basic principles and so serve to make clear the composer's concern with questions rather than answers.

Berio's view of the concerto format as implying an outward spreading from soloist to ensemble – a view again displayed in the Concerto for two pianos, notwithstanding those passages where roles are switched and the soloists start to accompany individuals from the orchestra – shows him very much in tune with his time. The same notion has already been observed at work in the music of Pousseur (*Les éphémerides d'Icare 2* and, on a smaller scale, *Madrigal III*), where it perhaps evolved from the more general idea, implicit in the European serialism of the 1950s, that musical composition involved an elaboration from simple elements to complex derivatives. Boulez has expressed this attitude in terms which call to mind the structure of the formant *Trope* from his Third Piano Sonata: 'When I have in front of me', he remarks, 'a musical idea or a kind of musical expression to be given to a particular text of my own invention, I discover in the text, when submitting it to my own kind of analysis and looking at it from every possible angle, more and more possible ways of varying it, transforming it, augmenting it and making it proliferate'.[3] This kind of thinking is especially clearly demonstrated in his most concerto-like work, *Domaines* for clarinet and six instrumental ensembles (1961–9) – perhaps too clearly, for he has spoken of revising the piece in order to make it less schematic.[4] In its 1969 version it presents a sequence of antiphonal exchanges between the simple ideas of the soloist and the more developed music of the ensembles, each of which is drawn in turn into a dialogue with the clarinet. First the clarinettist makes a tour of the ensembles (the idea of having performers move in order to dramatize musical structures had been introduced in two works of 1960: Berio's *Circles* and Schat's Improvisations and Symphonies); to each he offers a group of six elementary ideas which the ensemble then combine and cause to proliferate. Example 62 shows some simple instances of how the clarinet's 'domains' are further explored by the ensembles, this extract including one of the six structures from the soloist's 'Cahier E' and the opening of the corresponding music for oboe, horn and electric guitar: a unit of six neighbouring pitch classes is stated twice by the clarinet and imitated by the oboe, which then extends it to make a 12-note statement; also, the oboe's triplets are close echoes of that in the clarinet, and the other two instruments of the trio 'amplify' the soloist's opening pitch (horn) and interval (guitar). The second half of the work reverses the antiphonal layout of the first so that the ensemble replies come before the solo statements, but the techniques of liaison remain the same. Thus the work is, as it were, an analytic version of one of Berio's *Chemins,* with the commentary separated from its model and the two alternated in time instead of being superposed.

A quite different approach to solo–ensemble relationships is demonstrated by Barraqué's Concerto for clarinet, vibraphone and six instrumental trios (1968), despite that work's evident closeness to

Ex. 62

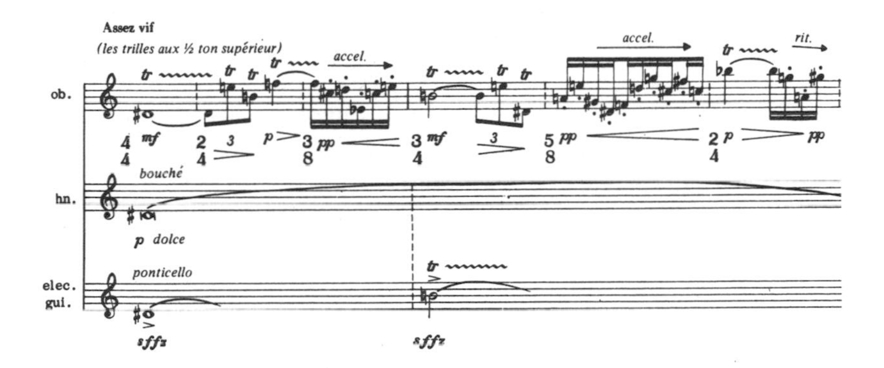

Domaines in disposition and even in details of instrumentation: for instance, Boulez's trio of oboe, horn and electric guitar is matched by Barraqué's of oboe, horn and harpsichord, both perhaps suggested by the scoring Debussy had intended for his fourth sonata. The Barraqué Concerto plays continuously, and the discontinuous formation is used not for effects of antiphony but to make available a wide spectrum of chamber groupings in which, at any particular moment, any instrument may be a soloist or a member of a small, diverse ensemble. Thus the composer has at his disposal the materials for a fluid stream of musical currents related to the continuing thread of the clarinet part (the vibraphone is silent for the first two-thirds of the work), but his Concerto does not partake of the static, concentric nature of Berio's concertante pieces; instead the thrust of his supple rhythm is no less purposefully directed than in the Piano Sonata, and the work is again in constant, searching, forward movement. One remaining feature shared by Boulez and Barraqué is a relative lack of interest in new instrumental techniques. Barraqué demands from his clarinet soloist the ability to make an abundantly lyrical and rhythmically mobile line but not any new effects, while Boulez offers opportunities for multiphonics, for example, but specifies only the principle pitch, so that the player need not be stretched beyond the bounds of his technique into awkward and dangerous territory.

Other composers have taken the opposite view and interested themselves in the hinterlands of technical possibility, and here those composers who are also performers, notably Globokar and Holliger, have done much of the most interesting work. Globokar's *Discours II* for five trombones or trombone and tape (1967–8) is typical of his output in its Berio-like concern with the physical activity of performance, and bears comparison with Berio's *Sequenza V* as a virtuoso comic turn. Again the trombone is made a vocal instrument by having the player sing into it and use various mutes to modulate the sound, so that the work becomes a discourse not only among the players (if all five parts are performed live) but also on the new nature of trombone playing, for it is based on a text – 'Numerous common factors exist between speech and trombone-playing . . .' – which is spoken through and with the instrument. But perhaps Globokar's distance from Boulez and Barraqué is most clearly shown in his *Ausstrahlungen* for soloist and 20 instruments (1969), where the similar disposition of forces (pointed in the commercial recording, where the all-purpose solo part is taken by a clarinettist) cannot disguise a very different musical orientation, a concern with instrumental dialogues which have the physical relish of conversation, for ebullient displays of virtuosity, and for sound combinations of a complex character suggestive of electronic transformation. These last, invented by a composer keen to prove that instrumentalists alone can equal if not surpass the products of technology, are also prominent in his works for homogeneous ensembles, including not only *Discours II* but also its successors for five oboes (1969) and three clarinets (1974), as well as *Fluide* for brass and percussion (1967).

Globokar's interests in expanding the range of instrumental sound, in stretching the capacities of performers and in finding new kinds of chamber musical discourse have been most freely expressed in his work with the New Phonic Art Ensemble, which he formed with the clarinettist Michel Portal, the pianist Carlos Alsina and the percussionist Jean-Pierre Drouet. With them he has been able to develop compositions, such as his *Correspondences* (1969), which allow a wide degree of choice (for instance, the score may supply a rhythmic pattern for which the player must supply pitches) and which call for creative reactions from each performer to the playing of the others. Such freedoms are common in the music of the late

1960s and early 1970s, but Globokar, as a performer himself, shows an unusual awareness that liberty is not to be used lightly. He has stressed the importance of providing an effective stimulus, whether in graphic designs or in broadly conventional notation, and of 'channelling' the performer's imagination in the service of the work; to do less is to throw the musician back on to his own resources, and therefore to evade the responsibility of being a composer. Globokar has also identified five modes of reaction which may be brought into play: imitating something, fusing one's sound or material with that of another player, hesitating in order to generate a tense silence, doing the opposite of what may be instructed or heard, and doing something different from that of another player.[5] In several of his later works the score consists more of directions of this kind, and of associated 'models' in graphic or traditional notation, than of conventional symbols.

Since the early 1970s Globokar has also been concerned with what he has described as the 'physical energy' of performance: with the relationships between bodily activity and musical sound, and with the intensity a sound may gain from being the result of a consuming mental and physical exercise. For instance, his oboe piece *Atemstudie* (1971), which he identifies as the first of his compositions to be stimulated by these matters,[6] requires sound to be produced without interruption (something made possible on the oboe by the 'circular breathing' technique introduced by Holliger, for whom the piece was written) and has the musician equipped with a contact microphone at the throat to amplify the sounds of his breathing and other vocal effects, thus bringing the physical exertions of performance directly into the sounding result. This line is pursued in two later works by Globokar for solo brass instrument, *Echanges* and *Res/as/ex/ins-pirer* (both 1973), whose titles indicate their preoccupations with, respectively, different mute effects and breathing as the source of music.

Holliger's compositions show something of the same interest in extreme virtuosity, in marginal effects and in the physical spin-off from performance, though where Globokar takes Berio as his point of departure, Holliger has been most influenced by his teacher Boulez and latterly by Kagel. The mark of Boulez is evident in the orchestration of his oboe concerto *Siebengesang* (1966–7) and also in that work's transposition of the form and feeling of a Trakl poem, *Siebengesang des Todes,* into instrumental music. This is a 'seven song' in having seven sections, orchestral groupings in sevens, sevenfold divisions of time and a seven-part female chorus to vocalize on syllables from the poem's last line in the final section; but the response is not only to the poet's numerology, for Holliger brings out also the imagery of death transfigured into a beautiful voyage, with the oboist here riding the 'shimmering torrents, full of purple stars' as he calls forth different orchestral ensembles to serve him either as foils (e.g. glockenspiel, celesta and two harps in the second section) or as assemblies of colleagues (e.g. alto flute, cor anglais, horn and viola in the fourth). The solo part requires multiphonics, quite extraordinary agility and, at the end, the ability to sustain a soft high A for about 50 seconds, while in the sixth section, with great dramatic effect, Holliger introduces an instrument with a microphone inserted into it and asks for playing techniques which enable the amplified oboe to imitate almost anything from disruptive staccatos in the brass to woodwind chords or the highest jitterings of the violins. His later works resemble those of Globokar in considering the physiology of performance, but with a touch of Kagel-like extrapolation to absurdity: the sounds of respiration become the main subject matter of *Pneuma* for wind orchestra with supplementary instruments (1970) and those of the performer's heart are amplified to take part in *Cardiophonie* for wind soloist (1971), while in his String Quartet (1973–4) Holliger demands unnatural breathing exercises from his players and waits for the effects, to be joined by all manner of new playing techniques.

ANTI-VIRTUOSITY

The careers of both Globokar and Holliger suggest a growing interest in the action of performing as much as in the acoustic results of musical performance: this is particularly clear in those works, such as the former's *Atemstudie* and the latter's *Cardiophonie*, where the physiological by-products of performance, breath sounds and heart beats respectively, become an important part of the music. Though some of Cage's works show a similar tendency, the more significant influence on these composers appears to be that of Kagel, who typically turns virtuosity against itself, either by asking the brilliant player to take part in musical situations which inevitably deflate his strenuous efforts, or else by asking him to devote his skills to quite unaccustomed activities. In his *Match* for two cellos and percussion

(1964), for instance, he satirizes the extreme exertions of the cellists, the difficulty of whose parts may be judged from Example 63, by having the piece presented as a duel umpired by the percussionist; this conception comes out most strongly in the composer's film version of the work. More fundamentally theatrical are such works as his *Tactil* for three pianos and plucked instrument (1970), which perpetrates the scandal of providing only accompaniment figures (derived from folk music) without a principal line, and then compounds the offence by having the performers stripped to the waist so that they may lazily undertake physical exercises in a satire on the view that fitness is a prerequisite of musical distinction. Many further examples of such anti-virtuosity are to be found among Kagel's works for solo instrumentalist and in his *Programm* (1971–2), a collection of unexpected 'conversations with chamber music'.

His *Unter Strom* for three performers (1969) provides a characteristic instance of a straight, even academic mode of composition applied to quite unusual materials, and hence another ironic inspection of the functions of music and musicians. The instruments heard at the beginning of this piece include an electric fan, to which is attached a strip of cloth which strikes the strings of a guitar at each rotation, three children's sirens amplified by a megaphone, and a hard rubber ball milled in an electric coffee grinder: the result may be rather ridiculous (it is also often quite beautiful), but Kagel makes the piece more ceremonial than comedy by asking for a controlled, almost hieratic manner of performance. And there is a serious point to be made. Writing about *Der Schall*, which is similarly scored for a small group using a variety of musical and non-musical instruments, Dieter Schnebel has noted that 'the debilitated or run-down or worn-out sounds, the notes of strange instruments and the noises of non-instruments are employed in a musical progression that radiates the aura of the great classical repertory; a symphony, composed as it were from the wreckage of the old symphonic school';[7] and Kagel himself has remarked that an essential aspect of his work is 'strict composition with elements which are not themselves pure'.[8] The composer ostentatiously and with intentional ironic humour gives his attention to phenomena that had been overlooked or spurned, whether the unusual instrumental resources of *Unter Strom, Der Schall, Musik für Renaissance-Instrumente, Exotica* and many other works, or the gestures of the players, or the routine of practising, or the basic assumptions of our musical culture. By contrast with most

Ex. 63

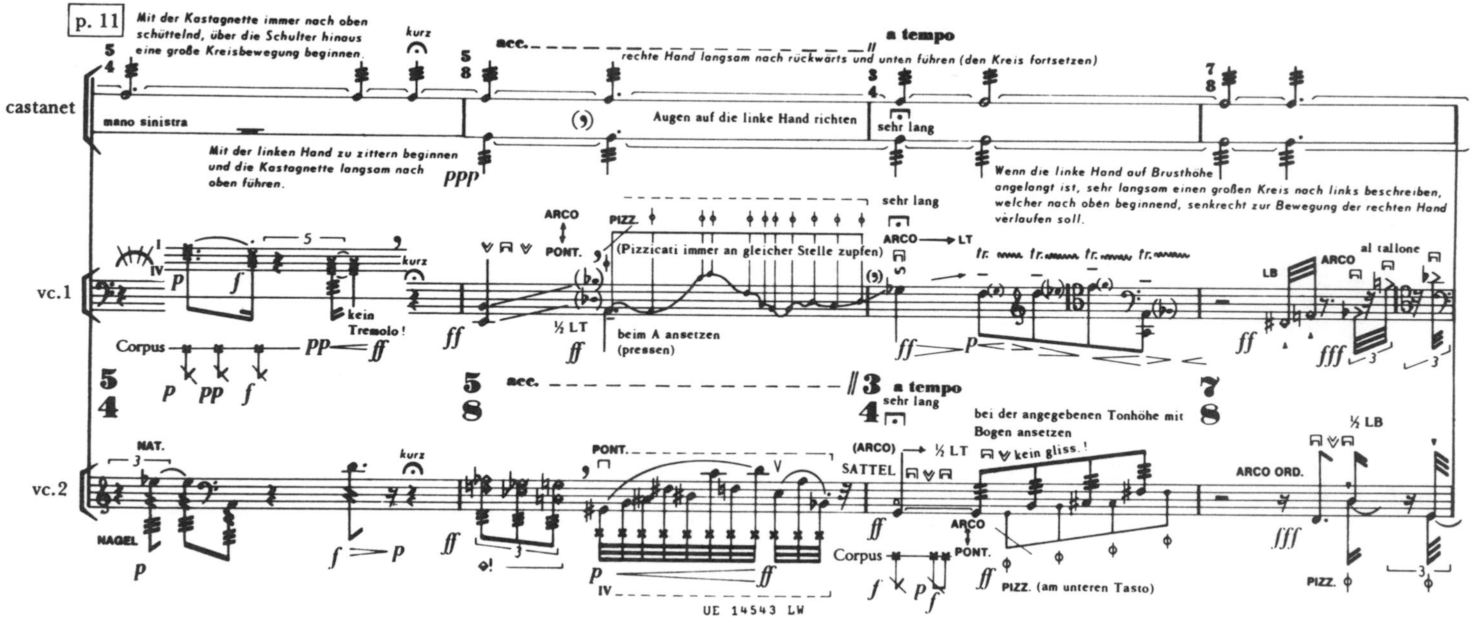

p. 11

castanet

Mit der Kastagnette immer nach oben schüttelnd, über die Schulter hinaus eine große Kreisbewegung beginnen.

mano sinistra

Mit der linken Hand zu zittern beginnen und die Kastagnette langsam nach oben führen.

kurz

acc.

rechte Hand langsam nach rückwärts und unten führen (den Kreis fortsetzen)

a tempo

Augen auf die linke Hand richten

sehr lang

Wenn die linke Hand auf Brusthöhe angelangt ist, sehr langsam einen großen Kreis nach links beschreiben, welcher nach oben beginnend, senkrecht zur Bewegung der rechten Hand verlaufen soll.

vc.1

Corpus

kein Tremolo!

ARCO PONT.

PIZZ.

(Pizzicati immer an gleicher Stelle zupfen)

½ LT

beim A ansetzen (pressen)

sehr lang

ARCO → LT

LB

ARCO

al tallone

vc.2

NAT.

NAGEL

kurz

PONT.

IV

(ARCO) → ½ LT

SATTEL

kein gliss.!

bei der angegebenen Tonhöhe mit Bogen ansetzen

Corpus

ARCO PONT.

PIZZ. (am unteren Tasto)

ARCO ORD.

½ LB

PIZZ.

UE 14543 LW

of the virtuoso compositions which have been considered above, Kagel's works can never score a success, whether for the composer or for the performer whose skill is diverted into unpromising avenues or else exploded in comedy. But then Kagel is not interested in success as much as he is in exposing the shakier foundations of contemporary musical practices, their elements of senselessness and degeneracy.

Examples of Kagel's examination of one particular cultural area are provided by three works which involve themselves with church music: *Hallelujah* for 16 voices (1967–8) and the organ pieces *Phantasie* (1967) and *Improvisation ajoutée* (1961–2), of which the first two figure in the film *Hallelujah* (together with the cinematic version of *Match*, this is perhaps an exception to the rule that Kagel's works do not present themselves as successful achievements). These three works all belong in the most orthodox of musical worlds, for organ works are inevitably most often performed in church and *Hallelujah* is a sacred work, yet each introduces the interference of everyday secular life. The choral piece appears more a rehearsal than a performance, showing Kagel's characteristic concern with the trials of preparation rather than with the perfection of execution, and the singers are also called upon to simulate vocal ailments; there is again the feeling, as in *Unter Strom* and numerous other works, that the composer is working in a run-down musical culture which has long outlived its useful life. *Improvisation ajoutée* has the organist indulging in activities – shouting, clapping, laughing, etc. – which appear quite out of place in a sacred building, and *Phantasie* introduces on tape 'scenes' from his daily life to commingle with his performance.

Schnebel, as both theologian and composer, has concerned himself like Kagel in the above works with church music for a time of doubt, ignorance and unbelief. His *Für Stimmen (. . . missa est)* (1956–68) is a cycle of choral and organ pieces in which the verbal message is obscured by an extraordinary variety of vocal sounds and textures: the effect is not one of analysis, as it might be in Boulez, nor one of dramatization, as it might be in a work of Berio's; instead the composer accepts the inevitability of confusion, a confusion more of randomness than of mystery. Schnebel also appears ready to countenance a degree of seeming purposelessness in other works which purport to be serious studies of vocal sound, such as his cycle of *Maulwerke* (1968–74), where small groups of performers concentrate on particular parts of the vocal apparatus and use amplification to bring out, often to bizarre or grotesque effect, the sounds they produce; in the piece *Atemzüge* from this series, for instance, the sounds of breathing are at issue. Since the unusual sonorities, and the unusual actions they require from the musicians, are not part of any evident expressive or formal design, the impression created by such pieces is bound to be one of confusion or mirth, as it is in so many works of Kagel.

In disconcerting his audience Schnebel has even gone further, following Cage, and removed sound from music. An example of his 'visible music' is *Nostalgie* for conductor alone (1962), made into a film by Kagel as *Solo*, and his *Mo-No* (1969) is a book of 'music for reading'. This latter work may perhaps be read as an ironic comment on that not insignificant body of contemporary music in which the score is unperformable as it stands, or is rather more aesthetically pleasing than any acoustic realization might be. Peter Hill has suggested[9] that Xenakis's writing for solo instruments, and particularly for the piano in his *Herma* (1960–64), *Eonta* with brass quintet (1963–4), *Synaphai* with orchestra (1969) and *Evryali* (1973), defies accurate performance: certainly Example 64, from *Evryali*, would appear unlikely ever to fit comfortably under two hands. In such cases, Hill proposes, the performer must decide what can be omitted as unimportant and what can be altered without severe detriment. But here there are difficulties. Xenakis's 'symbolic music', a variety introduced with *Herma* and further developed in *Nomos alpha* for cello (1965–6) and many later scores, is composed by the translation into music of theorems from set theory, and the listener will have

Ex. 64

little hope of comprehending the translations as such if they are compromised by approximations in execution. This may, however, be a less severe problem than might appear, for one must doubt that music can be understood as a branch of symbolic logic, despite Christopher Butchers's assertion that 'the music can be happily listened to in complete ignorance of the theory; for the logic of its operations is axiomatically the logic of the listener's every mental process'.[10] Even if that were a valid proposition, Xenakis's manner of writing – represented by the extreme rapidity of events in his piano parts, for instance, or the variety of special effects in *Nomos alpha*, which is a notoriously difficult essay in different types of tremolando, glissando and pizzicato – invites the listener to attend to global features, as in the composer's stochastic pieces, rather than to the outlines of pitch structures derived from set theory.[11] The score of *Herma* may be read as symbolic music; any performance is bound to impress itself above all as an exercise in dazzling virtuosity.

The above-mentioned works of Xenakis thus offer peculiarly neat demonstrations of the distinction between performance difficulty and musical difficulty, a distinction which has run as a sub-theme thoughout this section. Whereas the instrumental difficulties in Boulez or Barraqué, for instance, arise from the nature of the music and are necessary to that nature (with Boulez in *Domaines* allowing scope for optional extra displays of virtuosity), in Xenakis there is an antagonism between the ostensible musical form and the instrumental style. Nor is that antagonism ironically productive, as it is in the music of Kagel or Schnebel. Where all these composers, and others, concur is in allotting the performer a more demanding role than hitherto, whether in fulfilling more difficult technical tasks (e.g. Henze, Xenakis), in giving his attention to unprepossessing materials (Kagel, Schnebel) or in contributing creative ideas (Globokar). But this last eventuality, where virtuosity indubitably comes towards improvisation, has been most likely to arise in works where the performers have electronic equipment at their disposal.

THE ELECTRIC MUSICIAN

Though the works of Berio, Globokar and many others have vastly extended the range of instrumental and vocal possibilities, a completely new dimension of versatility is added when electronic means become available as well, as is graphically demonstrated in Holliger's

Siebengesang. Moreover, as has been noted, the difficulties in providing exact prescriptions for electronic contributions have encouraged the evolution of a more improvisatory art, though obviously this is not the case when the electronic component is merely music on tape: numerous examples have already been given of the combination of live with tape music (e.g. Stockhausen's *Kontakte* and works by Babbitt, Boulez, Pousseur and others), a combination which has proved of continuing interest if only because it alleviates the mummified and visually blank character of tape music. Instances of work in the more diverse field of live electronic music have also been noted, particularly with reference to the music of Cage and of American live electronic ensembles. This section will therefore consider more fully the new roles taken on by composer and performer in live music, and will centre on the works of a composer who has achieved more in this area than any other musician, namely Stockhausen.

Stockhausen's interest in solo virtuosity appears to have been indirect in the 1950s and 1960s: the technical demands of his piano pieces and the new vocal effects of *Momente*, for example, are motivated more by the needs of the musical structure than by a Berio-like wish to indulge and profit from the capacities of the performer. Even *Solo* (1965–6), a multi-purpose work available to any solo melody instrument, is well designed to curb the player's opportunities for display and to concentrate attention on the composer's workmanship, for the performer is deprived even of his distinction as soloist: his playing is recorded on a loop of tape by two assistants and combined with recordings from earlier in the performance, all according to instructions in the score, while a third assistant manipulates the controls of playback volume. There is thus, as in Kagel's *Transición II*, a fusion of musical tenses, the continuing present of the live solo being mixed with polyphonies of the near and distant past, and in this way a contrapuntal tissue is made to emanate from the monophonic source. Though the player may be dwarfed by the electronic apparatus, the work can be seen as a model of the benign interaction possible between man and technology, which enlarges his grasp and increases his power. A similar metaphorical reading is possible with the later *Spiral* for soloist (1968), in which the performer is asked to imitate and transform what he hears from a shortwave radio, even to the extent of going 'beyond the limits of the playing/singing technique that you have used up to this point and then also beyond the limitations of your instrument/voice'. The difference between *Solo* and *Spiral* – the one a composer's carefully determined scheme, the other a much more open invitation to the performer to excel himself – may be attributed to Stockhausen's intervening experience in the performance of live electronic music with his own ensemble.

His work in this area had its origins in *Mikrophonie I* (1964), in which a large tam tam is activated by two performers using a variety of objects while two others pick up the resulting vibrations with microphones and a further pair operate filters and volume controls. The score specifies the kind of sound required ('whispering', 'grunting', 'trumpeting' and so on), the means of production, the rhythm, the loudness and the electronic controls to be applied. Moreover, the work is formally determined, for though 'the order of structures may vary considerably from version to version', 'a strong and directional form' is, the composer says, guaranteed by a scheme of permitted connections among the structures.[12] *Mikrophonie I* thus offers an immediate contrast with most American live electronic music in its detailed prescriptions, its identity as a work. Stockhausen's concern here is not so much with performers as with sounds: the sounds are the actors, as they are in *Kontakte*, and the composition imposes itself more as a superior sort of *musique concrète* than as a piece of ensemble music. It is again a work in moment form, the moments being distinguished by one or more general characteristics, but unity on the large scale is enforced not only by Stockhausen's form plans but also by the use of a single instrument and hence of a connected, though extremely wide, net of resonances. As Robin Maconie has pointed out, 'a comparison may be made between the voice's constant modulation of a characteristic resonance [that of the vocal cavity], injecting percussive consonants at points of transition, and *Mikrophonie I*'s process of excitation, amplification and filtering'.[13] Heard in this way, the piece is a 'speech' in which the tam tam shows off the quite unexpected extent of its capabilities.

A large proportion of Stockhausen's subsequent output has required electronic equipment of some kind, the composer regarding the use of modern technology as a quite natural part of the process of composition. He has used ring modulators to transform performed sounds in the orchestral *Mixtur* (1964), in *Mikrophonie II* (1965) and in *Mantra* for two pianists (1970). Less drastically, he has used amplification as a means of achieving particular orchestral balances in *Trans* (1971) and *Inori* (1973–4), and has introduced electronic instruments in other orchestral scores, including *Ylem* (1972) and his own versions of his *Stop* (1965). He has also written specifically for microphone singing in *Stimmung* for six vocalists (1968), a work influenced by Young not only in being founded in pure consonant harmony (the piece can be understood, following the title, as an exercise in 'tuning', literally for the performers and mentally for the audience, to the overtones of a low B flat) but also in its use of different parts of the vocal cavity to secure specific resonances.

Several other works from this period, including *Prozession* (1967), the version of *Hymnen* with live participation by a group of soloists (1966–7), *Kurzwellen* (1968), *Pole* (1969–70) and *Expo* (1969–70), were written for the live electronic ensemble which grew out of the original *Mikrophonie I* sextet. In these works Stockhausen pursues a principle introduced with *Plus-Minus* (1963) of providing not a musical composition but a process which may be applied to materials chosen or discovered by the performers. The symbols of *Plus-Minus* detail sound qualities and processes in quite precise terms, though there is still enough latitude that musicians have been able to surprise the composer with their interpretations of the score.[14] Later works, destined in the first place for a familiar group of sympathetic musicians, are even freer. *Prozession, Kurzwellen, Spiral, Pole* and *Expo* are all notated largely in plus, minus and equals signs. Example 65 shows a representative passage from the tam tam part of *Prozes-*

Ex. 65

Elektronium gibt [R D 8] Bratsche gibt [G12]

Per Per + + +	+ +	Per +	+ + +	Per Per + + + +	–	– –	Per – –	– – –	– – – – –

sion, where the player must follow the lead of the electronium in register ('R') and duration ('D') for eight changes of event; the mathematical symbols are to be applied to the parameters of register, duration, volume and complexity (number of subsidiary sections), so that, for example, the fourth event here may be higher and longer (or longer and louder, etc.) than the third, while the 15th event will be, say, lower and softer and less subdivided than its predecessor; the sign 'Per' indicates an alteration in the direction of regular periodicity. *Prozession* thus makes possible 'chain reactions of imitation, transformation and mutation',[15] starting out from the players' memories of earlier Stockhausen works. *Mikrophonie II*, including taped 'windows' from *Gesang der Jünglinge*, *Carré* and *Momente*, had appeared to look back to more outgoing, public works in an effort at self-definition in a time of doubt; *Prozession*, by contrast, shows Stockhausen displaying enough confidence to allow his players to make their own forays within and around his musical world. There is also a marked contrast with *Mikrophonie I*, for *Prozession* encourages the players to engage in dialogues with each other as well as with the composer.

Kurzwellen takes a step further and opens the musicians to the whole universe of sounds offered to them by shortwave radios. The use of quite unpredictable source material coincided with a development in Stockhausen's musical metaphysics, for instead of attempting to embrace the 'music of the world', as he had in *Telemusik* and *Hymnen*, he asks the performers of *Kurzwellen* to be always alert to the call of the unknown; the work is a journey away from the self 'to the edge of a world which offers us the limits of the accessible', as Stockhausen has written.[16] The improvisatory *Spacecraft* developed by Musica Elettronica Viva at the same time was designed for similar ends, but where Rzewski and his colleagues were interested in a social journey from self-absorption to group commitment – and where the 'free improvisations' of the New Phonic Art Ensemble and other such groups were undertaken so that performers might be liberated from the dictatorship of composers – *Kurzwellen* is intended primarily as a spiritual journey in which enlightenment may come, for both players and listeners, from the channelling of impulses received from outside. From this period onwards Stockhausen becomes readier to see his music as having metaphysical properties and functions, or at least readier to declare that such is the case. *Stimmung* is a 'winged vehicle voyaging to the cosmos and the divine',[17] and the collections *Aus den sieben Tagen* (1968) and *Für kommende Zeiten* (1968–70), both consisting of prose poems couched largely in oracular language, are meditative exercises in improvisation, or, to use Stockhausen's preferred term, 'intuitive music'.

By the late 1960s improvisation had been a feature of contemporary music for several years; it had certainly had an important place in Cage's music for a decade, and an often under-estimated role in the graphic scores of Bussotti and others. But at the time of *Kurzwellen* its vogue had reached a high peak, perhaps under the influence of the more general political, social and religious revolutions of the period (the events of May 1968 in Paris, the rise of protest movements, the exploration of the mind by means of drugs and of meditative practices imported from the East). This was also the time of 'free improvisation', unlimited by any score, instructions or conventions other than those determined by the participants themselves. Globokar has enumerated the various reasons which might lead a performer to engage in free improvisation: 'a need for liberation, a search for a new musical aesthetic, a provocation, a wish to work collectively, to develop his instrument, to amuse himself, a political or social engagement, the wish to belong to an élite capable of improvising, a way of evaluating himself, a way of expressing himself not only through sounds but through his physical comportment, a need to create a contact (and that the most direct possible) with the audience, a need to give free rein to his imagination (without being obliged to spend hours of a reflection at a worktable), and many other things'.[18] All this is clear and unexceptionable, except where Globokar claims that free improvisation provides 'the most direct possible' contact with an audience, for without some framework of discourse, provided in most jazz or Indian music by recognized models and conventions, musical communication can exist only on a primitive level of surprise, allusion to other music, imitation of natural sounds, or suggestion of mood.

Stockhausen surmounted this problem in his earlier works for live electronic ensemble by having his players respond to each other in defined ways, so that the outline form of *Prozession,* for instance, provides for different kinds of musical conversation among members of the group, and by basing the music on defined material; his own music memorized in *Prozession,* his own tape played concurrently in *Hymnen,* or shortwave broadcasts in *Kurzwellen.* In the two sets of text pieces, however, he abandons these limitations for such vague pronouncements as those of *Verbindung* from *Aus den sieben Tagen,* where each player is asked to 'play a vibration in the rhythm of' his body, his heart, his breathing, his thinking, his intuition, his enlightenment and the universe. Stockhausen has said that his use of the term 'intuitive music' is intended 'to stress that it comes virtually unhindered from the intuition, and that as music, in the case of a group of musicians playing intuitively, it amounts to more, qualitatively speaking, than the sum total of individual "accidents", by virtue of a process of mutual "feedback". The "orientation" of musicians, which I call "accord", is not, I would emphasize, random or merely negative – in the sense of exclusive – musical thought, but joint concentration on a written text of mine which provokes the intuitive faculty in a clearly defined manner.'[19]

Yet there would appear to be more to it than that. Stockhausen has generally preferred to perform his text pieces with musicians who have had long experience of playing his more fully detailed music; the commercial recordings of *Aus den sieben Tagen* were made by a group based on his own live electronic ensemble. Inevitably, therefore, the players provide what they feel to be expected of a Stockhausen performance and even, perhaps unconsciously, refer to specific works, while the mere fact of similarity in the formation of the ensemble brings direct links with accredited performances of *Prozession* and *Kurzwellen*. Moreover, comparisons of different performances of the same text suggest that the composer in rehearsal stipulates rather more than is contained in the published instructions.[20] Globokar has remarked on the formal simplicity which seems unavoidable in group improvisation: 'Movements between action-reaction, simple-complex, tension-relaxation are made progressively, rarely in an abrupt manner. The form is often sinusoidal, each situation lasting until it has been exhausted. It is also for this reason that it goes slowly to extinction; brutal conclusions are rare.'[21] Slow growth and decay are indeed prominent features of the recorded performances of *Aus den sieben Tagen* and *Für kommende Zeiten*, but Stockhausen achieves also, whether by stimulating his players' intuitive faculties, drawing on their memories or laying down guidelines, a greater variety of form, gesture and atmosphere than might be expected, as well as, very often, an intensely concentrated feel that comes from the dedication of the performers and the quality not only of their playing but also of their listening to one another.

In practice, therefore, the pieces of the two text collections turn out to be a good deal more structured than the poetic instructions would lead one to suppose; and many of Stockhausen's subsequent works can be regarded as attempts to give a firmer shape to intuitive performance or else, in such fully notated compositions as *Mantra* and *Inori*, to provide determined vessels for the forces of enlightenment which he had hoped to conjure in his text pieces. *Aus den sieben Tagen* came, therefore, at the end of one line of development, that of progressive opening to the intuitive decisions of the performer (Piano Piece XI marks the line's origin), and also at the beginning of another, that of growing belief in music as in instrument of illumination. That belief had been fostered while his creative endeavours had been centred in his live electronic ensemble, for it had been an obvious extension to regard the musical trouvaille as a sign of a spritual enlightenment, but now the discovery of music's supernatural power could lead to more defined and larger works.

Sternklang (1971), for example, is a grand astrological ceremony designed for five ensembles playing intuitive music in a public park, and it comes with a carefully engineered formal plan as well as with basic harmonies, tempos, rhythmic incantations of constellation names and notations based on star patterns (as in Cage's *Atlas eclipticalis*). The intimate musical communications of the ensemble pieces must now be amplified to take place over a wide area, and this change increases the involvement of the audience, particularly when torch-bearing runners are dispatched from one group to another singing their musical messages. Improvisation as an exercise for a small group of adepts becomes performance as a public ritual, not on the old model of composer communicating through performers to listeners but on a new pattern requiring all to share in a collective contemplation. The composer is now, following the lesson of the text pieces, not so much a formulator of ideas as a guide who creates conditions favourable to intuitive leaps in performance, and who does so most efficaciously by giving a structure and a destination to the work.

REPERTORY

Barraqué: Concerto for clarinet, vibraphone and six instrumental trios (1968, Bruzzichelli).
Berio: *Sequenza II* for harp (1963, Universal).
——*Chemins I* for harp and orchestra (1965, Universal).
——*Sequenza III* for female voice (1965, Universal). Candide CE 31027, Philips 6500 631, Wergo 60021.
——*Sequenza IV* for piano (1965, Universal). Vox STGBY 637.
——*Sequenza V* for trombone (1966, Universal). DGG 137 005, Wergo 60021.
——*Chemins II* for viola and nine players (1967, Universal). RCA LSC 3168.
——*Sequenza VI* for viola (1967, Universal). RCA LSC 3168.

—— *Chemins III* for viola and orchestra (1968, Universal). RCA LSC 3168.
—— *Chemins IIb* for orchestra (1969, Universal), *IIc* for bass clarinet and orchestra (1972, Universal).
—— *Sequenza VII* for oboe (1969, Universal). Philips 6500 631.
—— Concerto for two pianos and orchestra (1972–3, Universal). RCA RL 11674.
—— *'Points on the Curve to Find . . .'* for piano and 23 players (1973–4, Universal). RCA RL 12291.
—— *Chemins IV* for oboe and ten strings (1975, Universal). RCA RL 12291.
Boulez: *Domaines* for clarinet with or without 21 players (1961–9, Universal, solo version only). RCA SB 6849 (with orchestra).
Globokar: *Fluide* for nine brass and three percussion (1967, Peters). Harmonia Mundi HMU 933.
—— *Discours II* for five trombones or trombone and tape (1967–8, Peters). DGG 137 005.
—— *Ausstrahlungen* for soloist and 20 players (1969, Peters). Harmonia Mundi HMU 933.
—— *Correspondences* for four players (1969, Peters).
—— *Discours III* for five oboes (1969, Peters).
—— *Atemstudie* for oboe (1971, Peters). Harmonia Mundi HMU 933.
—— *Echanges* for brass instrument (1973, Peters). Harmonia Mundi C 065 99712.
—— *Res/as/ex/ins-pirer* for brass instrument (1973, Peters). Harmonia Mundi C 065 99712.
—— *Discours IV* for three clarinets (1974, Peters). Harmonia Mundi C 065 99712.
Henze: Concerto for double bass and chamber orchestra (1966, Schott) DGG 139 456.
—— Double Concerto for oboe, harp and strings (1966, Schott). DGG 139 456.
—— Piano Concerto no. 2 (1967, Schott).
—— *Heliogabalus imperator* (1971–2, Schott).
Holliger: *Siebengesang* for oboe, female chorus, orchestra and electronics (1966–7, Schott). DGG 2530 318.
—— *Pneuma* for wind orchestra, four radios, organ and percussion (1970, Schott).
—— *Cardiophonie* for wind instrument and three tape recorders (1971, Schott).
—— String Quartet (1973–4, Schott).
Kagel: *Improvisation ajoutée* for organ (1961–2, Universal). Odyssey 3216 0158, Wergo 60033.

——*Match* for two cellos and percussion (1964, Universal). DGG 104 933, 2536 018.
——*Phantasie* for organ and tape (1967, Universal). DGG 137 003.
——*Hallelujah* for chorus (1967–8, Universal). DGG 643 544.
——*Der Schall* for five players (1968, Universal). DGG 2561 029.
——*Unter Strom* for three players (1969, Universal). DGG 2530 460.
——*Tactil* for three pianos and plucked instrument (1970, Universal).
——*Programm* for chamber ensembles (1971–2, Universal).
New Phonic Art Ensemble: Improvisation. Wergo 60060.
Schnebel: *Für Stimmen* (*. . . missa est*): 1 *dt 31*$_6$ for vocal groups (1956–8, Schott), 2 *amn* for seven vocal groups (1958–67, Schott), 3 *! (Madrasha 2)* for three vocal groups (1958–68, Schott), 4 *Choralvorspiele I-II* for organ, accessory instruments and tape (1970, Schott). DGG 643 544 (nos. 1–3), Wergo 60026 (no. 1), Wergo 60075 (no. 4).
——*Maulwerke* for three to eight vocalists (1968–74, Schott): 1 *Atemzüge* (1970–71), 2 *Kehlkopfspannungen*, 3 *Gurgelrollen*, 4 *Mundstücke*, 5 *Zungenschläge*, 6 *Lippendienst*. Wergo 60075 (no. 1).
Stockhausen: *Plus-Minus* for undetermined forces (1963, Universal).
——*Mikrophonie I* for tam tam and live electronics (1964, Universal). CBS 72647, DGG 2530 583.
——*Mixtur* for orchestra and live electronics (1964, Universal), also for small orchestra and live electronics (1967, Universal). DGG 137 012 (1967 version).
——*Mikrophonie II* for 12 voices, Hammond organ, ring modulators and tape (1965, Universal). CBS 72647, DGG 2530 583.
——*Stop* for small orchestra (1965, Universal). DGG 2530 442.
——*Solo* for melody instrument and tape recorders (1965–6, Universal). DGG 137 005.
——*Prozession* for live electronic ensemble (1967, Universal). DGG 2530 582, Vox STGBY 615.
——*Stimmung* for six vocalists (1968, Universal). DGG 2543 003.
——*Kurzwellen* for live electronic ensemble (1968, Universal). DGG 2707 045, Finnadar SR 9009.
——*Aus den sieben Tagen* for undetermined ensembles (1968, Universal). DGG 2720 073 (12 pieces from set of 14). Finnadar SR 9009 *(Setz die Segel zur Sonne)*, Musique Vivante MV 30795 *(Setz die Segel zur Sonne, Verbindung)*.
——*Spiral* for soloist (1968, Universal). DGG 2561 109, EMI C 165 02313–4, Wergo 325.
——*Pole* for two players (1969–70, Stockhausen). EMI C 165 02313–4.
——*Expo* for three players (1969–70, Stockhausen).
——*Für kommende Zeiten* for undetermined ensembles (1968–70, Stockhausen). Chrysalis 6307 573 *(Ceylon, Zugvogel)*, EMI C 165

02313–4 (*Japan, Wach*).
—— *Sternklang* for five undetermined ensembles (1971, Stockhausen). Polydor 2612 031.
—— *Ylem* for 19 players (1972, Stockhausen). DGG 2530 442.
Xenakis: *Herma* for piano (1960–64, Boosey). Adès 16005.
—— *Eonta* for piano and brass quintet (1963–4, Boosey). BV Haast 007.
—— *Nomos alpha* for cello (1965–6, Boosey). DGG 2530 562.
—— *Synaphai* for piano and orchestra (1969, Salabert). Decca HEAD 13.
—— *Evryali* for piano (1973, Salabert). BV Haast 007.

13 Opera → Music Theatre

Little cultivated in the fifties, when attention to musical fundamentals allowed avant-garde composers small room for compromise with other art forms, music for the theatre has since then burgeoned, and in several new directions. Indeed, so large a part have theatrical intentions played in music since 1960 – the year in which Cage aroused interest in new dramatic forms with his *Theatre Piece* and *Cartridge Music*, and when Nono began work on *Intolleranza*, the first opera of the new avant garde – that dramatic works have inevitably been considered in preceding chapters. One should conclude, Cage might argue,[1] that there is no longer any meaningful distinction between music and theatre, yet to deny music its own field of action is to deprive it of much of its force. Happily there have been other composers who, though not working in the conventional *genres* of opera and ballet, have found it possible to form new alliances, but not total fusions, between music and drama.

AROUND OPERA

Ligeti perhaps speaks for many of his colleagues in declaring: 'I cannot, will not compose a traditional "opera"; for me the operatic genre is irrelevant today – it belongs to a historical period utterly different from the present compositional situation. Yet by that I do not mean at all that I cannot compose a work for the facilities an opera house offers'.[2] In fact the 'Opernhaus-Stück' that Ligeti eventually came to write, *Le grand macabre* (1975–6), is by no means so far removed from 'traditional "opera" ' as are many works of the period; Kagel's *Staatstheater* (1967–70), for instance, is very much more 'a work for the facilities an opera house offers' without having any of the expected characteristics of narrative and continuity. Even so, *Le grand macabre* is sufficient to lend weight to Ligeti's expressed dissatisfaction with the genre. No doubt that dissatisfaction includes a certain measure of distaste for much of the standard operatic repertory and for the conditions under which opera is presented, but it is also founded in considerations of a more technical nature.

Opera has traditionally meant narrative; and narrative in music seems to require continuously evolving forms in which the passing of time is orderly and in which there is a definite sense of onward movement. Thematic, diatonic music is therefore ready ground for the narrative metaphor, but there have been notably few successful atonal operas; those which do exist (*Erwartung, Wozzeck, Lulu, Moses und Aron*) have generally found some alternative to diatonic harmony as fuel for continuous forward motion, or have retained sufficient diatonicism to guarantee a certain dynamism. The alternative approach, for a composer of atonal dramatic music, is to dispense more or less with narrative and look for models in theatrical traditions in which the story is relatively unimportant. Many composers since 1960 have thus been influenced by the ritual enactments of folklore, by oriental theatre (especially the nō drama, in which the momentary phenomena of comportment, gesture and delivery carry much more importance than the narrative thread), by the theatre of the absurd, or by the unstructured 'happenings' with which Cage associated himself.

A further problem facing the avant-garde composer writing for an opera house is that opera imposes a largeness of scale which he might prefer to avoid, for a variety of practical and aesthetic reasons. And from the point of view of the opera house, the costs of mounting a new work are such as to discourage commissioning more than one each season, if that. There is thus no opportunity for the runs of failures, imitations and near-misses with which composers of opera customarily began their careers in earlier centuries.

Perhaps it is significant that Henze, much the most successful composer of operas in the traditional mould, was fortunate enough to prove his theatrical flair from the first, though certainly his success has also been due to this ability to maintain enough thematic working and diatonic motivation to substantiate narrative forms. In *The Bassarids* (1965) he was even able to construct a full-length opera as a continuous symphony, extrapolating from Berg's example. As he has explained, the first movement is a sonata which establishes the

Ex. 66a

Ex. 66b

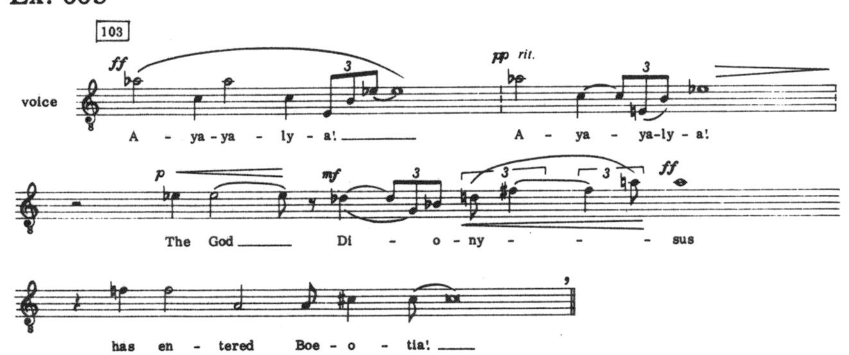

conflict between the two principals, Dionysus and Pentheus, in a musical opposition between Dionysus's call (Example 66*a*) and a trumpet signal (Example 66*b*).[3] The second movement is a scherzo in the form of a suite of Dionysian dances; the third, incorporating Dionysus's hypnotizing of Pentheus, is an adagio succeeded by a fugue; and the finale is a passacaglia.

In retrospect *The Bassarids* can be seen as the culmination of the sensuous, nostalgic style which Henze had pursued since his move to Italy more than a decade before. The symphonic structure, recalling not so much Berg in this respect as Mahler, is ample enough to include gestures made in diverse directions, from the wholesale, knowing pastiche of a Baroque French cantata in the vulgar intermezzo which interrupts the slow movement to quotations from Bach as an earlier master of the siciliana rhythm on which the opera floats, and as a source of references to support a parallel between the Crucifixion and the sacrifice of Adonis. The integration of varied materials and opposed themes, as displayed in *The Bassarids,* is in Henze's view a characteristic technique of the 'segregated' artist, the 'outlaw'. Undoubtedly he sees himself in this role, at odds both with bourgeois society and with the avant garde ever since he turned aside from the tentative approach to total serialism essayed in his Second Quartet. 'Never would he aim at an accord with the basic tendencies of his time', he writes of his chosen type; instead he must devote himself to a minority 'which merits his sympathy and which excites his sensual and spiritual substance'.[4]

Henze's concern with the individual as outcast and dreamer, and with the place of the individual within the sympathetic minority and the uncomprehending mass, is expressed in metaphorical terms in the concertos which followed *The Bassarids:* the chamber works for double bass and for oboe and harp, and most particularly the determinedly autobiographical Second Piano Concerto. But then this absorption in his own situation was joined by a commitment to the interests of all those ignored or oppressed by bourgeois society; to inwardness and nostalgia he added a fervent, public criticism of the social iniquities of the present and an optimistic expression of the egalitarian future promised by revolutionary socialism. The change came in the oratorio *Das Floss der 'Medusa'* (1968), dedicated to Che Guevara and dealing with the historical episode in which a group of shipwrecked men were abandoned to a raft by their officers, left to face the perils of sea and starvation. After the experience of its abortive premiere, lost amid the struggles of police and left-wing students, Henze spent a year in Cuba, writing his Sixth Symphony and there expressing his delight in the sonorities and rhythms of Cuban music as well as re-affirming his alignment with socialist causes, the elaborate polyphony including quotations from Vietnamese and Greek protest songs.

It was inevitable, given the theatrical focus of his previous output, that Henze's passionate political affiliation should soon find expression in a work for the stage, but at this point an opera might have necessitated too much of an accommodation to those bourgeois standards against which he was inveighing. He turned, therefore, to the composition of works which have their home in the small concert hall rather than the opera house, following a path from *Histoire du soldat* and *Pierrot lunaire* that had already been investigated by

Davies and others. *El Cimarrón* (1969–70), another work from his Cuban period, is described as a 'recital for four musicians' (baritone, flautist, guitarist and percussionist), who are called upon to use their creative imaginations in what may be seen, as in Pousseur, as an attempt at a more egalitarian relationship between composer and performers: the players may be required, for example, to improvise pitches to a given rhythm, and Henze has continued to use such moderate openness in subsequent scores. *El Cimarrón* is not explicitly theatrical, but the singer is cast in the role of runaway Cuban slave and the work presents itself more as a continuous dramatic recitation than as a song cycle. Here – and in the later *Voices* for two singers and small orchestra (1973), which quite definitely is a song cycle, on a variety of revolutionary subject matter – the composer uses the wide range of his eclectic palette to point up feelings of longing for a golden past (see Example 67*a*) or fierce involvement with present struggle (Example 67*b*).

Henze's celebration in *El Cimarrón* of the people's hero (contrasting with his vicious caricatures of those who represent the establishment or the past) is characteristic of his aesthetic interpretation of left-wing activism: the 'World Revolution' he has described as 'man's greatest work of art'.[5] This view obviously distances him from the ascetic dedication of such composers as Cardew, Rzewski and Wolff as much as from the efforts towards utopian musical structures made by Pousseur or Schat, and the differences appear more funda-

Ex. 67a

Ex. 67b

mental than the fact that all these composers found their political awareness sharpened by the radical tide of the late 1960s. Henze may, for example, share with Pousseur a striving towards integration, but in his case this means not the seeking of general harmonic solutions but the rather more heedless adoption of particular styles to be parodied or owned. Again, he has like Cardew submitted his earlier works to criticism, but instead of disowning them he has used his skills as a producer to attack, for instance, the self-obsession of the artist in his *Elegy for Young Lovers* and to place that opera's lyrical opulence in ironic quotation marks. His concern, in re-producing *Elegy for Young Lovers,* with his own situation as an artist suggests that he has by no means relinquished his earlier approach to music as a confessional, autobiographical art while using it also as an instrument of political propaganda; and that is borne out by his first revolutionary piece designed for stage presentation, the 'show' *Der langwierige Weg in die Wohnung der Natascha Ungeheuer* (1971), scored for baritone and several ensembles. The central problem in this work is that of the composer himself: can the left-wing intellectual justify a compromise which allows him to identify himself with the revolution in his work but to fight shy of active engagement in the class struggle? The music, like that of *El Cimarrón* and *Voices*, abounds in quotations and opportunities for more or less directed improvisation, as well as in musical–dramatic references which bring out the nature and force of the alternative siren songs which assail the artist–hero. There is a *Pierrot* quintet, dressed in hospital overalls, to represent the sick bourgeoisie; there is a brass quintet, whose police helmets mark them out as agents of the oppressive state machine; there is a pop group to provide the voice of the underground; and there are two instrumental soloists, the percussionist as revolutionary activist and the Hammond organist as plutocrat.

The contradictions exposed in this perhaps necessarily confused score are taken up again, on a more abstract level, in Henze's Second Violin Concerto (1971), which is also a work of music theatre. The soloist is here cast as the self-willed romantic virtuoso, trying at once to relate to the system (the orchestra) and to prove his independence, and the music is based on a poetic commentary by Hans Magnus Enzensberger on Gödel's theorem that any complex system contains meaningful propositions which can be neither proved nor refuted: the message is that 'freedom from contradiction is a defect', which might have surprised Gödel, and that any system – particularly musical and social systems, one is led to infer – must inevitably destroy itself.

Through all of Henze's political works there runs the unspoken suggestion that the real conflict is not between activism and cheering from the sidelines, as *Natascha Ungeheuer* would imply, but rather between the composer's felt need to identify himself with socialist revolution and his attachment to the sensuous romanticism of his earlier music, to which he reverts with seeming relief whenever the opportunity presents itself (see, for example, Example 67*a*). His Cuba, as revealed in his Sixth Symphony, in *El Cimarrón* and in the 'vaudeville' *La Cubana* (1973), is not that of Castro and of the struggles to build a socialist society but that of the tropical forest, of plantations lying under the beating sun, of seedy night life and exotic dance rhythms. His sympathies, as expressed in *Das Floss der 'Medusa', El Cimarrón, Natascha Ungeheuer* and *La Cubana,* are with the individual rather than the mass, which is usually presented as having a restraining influence on the flood of life and love in the individual's breast *(Der Prinz von Homburg)* or else as following blindly in the charismatic leader's wake *(The Bassarids)*. Henze's view of his own separateness as a gifted creator is, of course, not irrelevant here.

In *We come to the River* (1974–6) – a full-blown opera, though it avoids admitting as much by taking the sub-title 'actions for music', which came at the end of this period of experiment with music theatre and semi-dramatic forms – Henze's attachment to the old lyricism is such that the Emperor, though portrayed in his effeteness by a mezzo-soprano, is granted an aria whose weight and seductiveness mask any intended irony. No other character is so roundly presented; the sympathy for the common soldier is as generalized as the distaste for upper-class ladies is shrill. Henze is greatly more convincing in those works where, perhaps despite himself, he accepts his role as romantic artist rather than political activist: the symphonic poems *Heliogabalus imperator* and *Tristan,* and the group of chamber works which followed *We come to the River.* It is also noteworthy that his second major collaboration with Edward Bond, the committed left-wing librettist of the 'actions for music', was on the ballet *Orpheus,* marking a return after a 15-year gap to the genre in which he achieved his first successes in the theatre, and a return also to his abiding concern with the artist as individual, the individual as artist.

Long before *We come to the River* the usefulness of the operatic stage as a political platform had been realized more successfully, or at least with less doubt and delicious equivocation, by Nono in his *Intolleranza,* the work of a composer whose political radicalism had been more or less overtly expressed in almost all his scores. Having no bourgeois past to act as a lure, Nono has steadily pursued his political goals, and that pursuit has led him since the early 1960s to neglect the forms of established concert life. He has preferred the electronic medium, as in *La fabbrica illuminata* (1964), *Ricorda cosa ti hanno fatto in Auschwitz* (1966), *Contrappunto dialettico alla mente* (1967–8), *Musica-manifesto no. 1* (1969) and *Y entonces comprendio*

(1969–70), some of these works having vocal parts which can, if necessary, be added to the tape. In the studio the composer can work directly with actuality, for instance with the sounds of a metallurgical factory in *La fabbrica illuminata,* of political demonstrations in *Contrappunto* and *Musica-manifesto,* or of Castro reading a letter from Guevara in *Y entonces comprendio;* these works can therefore operate on one level as agit-prop, exciting revolt against the dehumanizing effect of factory life, sympathy with the aspirations of workers and students, or admiration for heroes of the revolution. Compositions of this kind can also be included in Nono's factory concerts without the incongruity that might be felt if a string quartet were to perform in such a setting, and the composer has reported how performances of *La fabbrica illuminata* have awakened workers to the political realities of their situation.[6]

Nono's works of the 1960s and 1970s continue to make use of the abstract constructive techniques he had developed in *Il canto sospeso* and other earlier compositions – particularly those behind his numerical organization of rhythm – but now the music is more broadly conceived. Such orchestral works as *Per Bastiana–Tai-yang cheng* (1967), which owes its sub-title to the disguised immersion in the music of the Chinese revolutionary song 'The east is red', or *Como una ola de fuerza y luz* (1971–2) emphasize the block clusters and the sustained, searing sonorities which had been growing in importance in his music since *Incontri,* and which seem to have been decisively liberated by his experience in the electronic studio: strident, anguished sounds are very much to the fore in *Omaggio a Vedova,* his first tape piece, and in *Ricorda,* with its intense choral wailings.

Apart from these matters of format and style, Nono's post-*Intolleranza* works are distinguished by the fact that none of them is abstract, and none has a programme which is anything but political. However, a second approach to opera appeared problematic. Nono has expressed a not unexpected dislike of the divisions imposed in traditional opera between cast and audience, voice and orchestra, word and music;[7] he has also preferred to find his audiences in the factory or the street. His admiration for the new techniques introduced by the Living Theatre led him to use part of their anti-Vietnam War play *Escalation* in *A floresta è jovem e cheja de vida* for voices, clarinet, bell plates and tape (1966), but finally he made a return to the opera house with *Al gran sole carico d'amore* (1972–4), though only when it had become clear that the cause of socialism in

Italy might be pressed even in such a bourgeois institution as La Scala. The new opera, like *Intolleranza,* is boldly and blockily scored for soloists, chorus, orchestra and tape, but it takes advantage of the methods Nono had developed in the intervening propaganda frescoes, and the libretto is now less a narrative than a documentary anthology focused on the plight of the one main character, an unnamed Mother. *Al gran sole* appears, indeed, as the work towards which most of Nono's compositions of the 1960s had been leading, not least in its projection of the solo female voice, against electronic or orchestral backcloths, as a 'symbol of life, of love, and of freedom from all new forms of oppression'.[8]

Berio, it will already be clear, has not been drawn to follow his compatriot in finding alternatives to traditional concert-giving; instead he has generally confined the expression of social or political views to works destined for the stage. *Passaggio* (1962), notable for its choral elaborations of the new vocal techniques developed in *Thema, Circles* and *Visage,* treats of a woman whose dehumanization to the status of object is presented on stage while the chorus, seated among the orchestra and the audience, represents the social forces by which she is degraded; *Traces* (1964), later withdrawn, concerned itself with racial equality. But the direct expression of a social message appears to have been uncongenial to a composer with Berio's growing taste for asking questions rather than providing answers, for bringing together quite separate and perhaps opposed strands of musical discourse. His *Laborintus II* (1965) still has a political substratum, in that Dante's Inferno is seen as a picture of capitalist society, but the work is much more an embroidery of musical and literary images around the continuing thread of a spoken text. The specific references, ranging from madrigalian euphony to jazz, are not made into dramatic symbols, as they might be in Henze, but set smoothly into a fluid stream. The subject is not so much the verbal content of the text as the labyrinth of connections to be drawn between words and music, and the narrator's speech, like the viola *Sequenza* in the dependent *Chemins,* gives birth to a variegated musical tissue within which it may be amplified, transformed and often obscured.

Berio's willingness to sacrifice straightforward verbal and theatrical messages to elaborate musical commentary is also evident in his *Opera,* whose very title declares a primary concern with the genre and its history. Again there is an underlying political theme, in that the work ostensibly proposes an analogy between the sinking of the *Titanic* and the decline of capitalism. Like Nono, Berio must have been impressed by the work of the new theatrical ensembles of the 1960s, for he takes this theme from the Open Theatre's *Terminal.* However, his overriding interest in what opera is, and what it can be, is expressed in his use of the whole range of musical–dramatic fusions available to the contemporary composer, and his historical consciousness in the fact that each act begins with an 'air' to a text from Striggio's *Orfeo* libretto, so that repeatedly the opera returns to the origins of the form and to the emergence of 'drama per musica' from pure vocal expression. The score also includes, apart from many other references to music from the past, quotations from and allusions to Berio's own creative history.

Pousseur similarly, but more clearly and pointedly, engages in self-examination in his opera *Votre Faust,* whose central character, Henri, shares his name not only with Dr Faust but also with the composer. Henri begins the opera with a lecture on contemporary musical problems taken from an article by Pousseur, and the composer's identification with his character is made explicit, as in *Lulu,* by self-quotation: in one scene Henri is observed analysing Webern's Second Cantata and then rehearsing a singer in his own, i.e. Pousseur's, *Trois chants sacrés,* the music establishing a link from Webern to the composer's own brand of post-Webernian serialism. More generally *Votre Faust* is a fabric of quotations, musical and literary, used to establish different dramatic situations and invoked in a scrutiny of the history of the Faust myth, of the operatic genre and of music as a whole. The fair of the first act, for instance, has four side-shows in four different languages, of which the 'little Faust' in French takes elements from the Faust works of Berlioz and Gounod, together with quotations from other French 19th-century operas, all treated in the manner of Milhaud, which itself suggests the 20th-century's obsession with reworking the past. As in other works by Pousseur, the quotations are linked and justified within connecting harmonic networks, his serial method allowing ramified developments into chordal territories of all kinds. 'I did not want', he has said, 'simply to trust myself to the hazards of juxtaposition, but to try to find, and not only on the harmonic level, a system sufficiently general that quotations find their places, as in crosswords, as in a chessboard of possibilities.'[9] The urge to connect is also present in Butor's libretto and in the dramatic presentation, which allows for instrumentalists to be involved in the action, thus abolishing the barrier between pit and stage. Even the audience is drawn into more than passive involvement, for this 'variable fantasy of operatic character', to quote the composer's generic definition of the piece, can take different courses depending on ballots and vocal interventions.

If *Votre Faust* suggests on one level that Henri's decision to write a Faust opera would be a selling of his soul, then there is some connection with Davies's *Taverner,* which more squarely confronts the issue of artistic truthfulness in conflict with worldly pressures. This is, of course, a venerable theme in 20th-century opera (see *Die glückliche Hand, Palestrina* and *Mathis der Maler*), but in *Taverner* the artist's betrayal of his creative impulse is seen more disturbingly as a rejection of the good in himself, opening him to the evil and the spiritually false which make the second act of the opera a nightmare parody of the first. And if parody can be seen as a form of betrayal, translation become traduction, then almost the whole of Davies's output is, as has been seen, implicated in the moral problems of his opera, not only those works which relate to the opera as earlier involvements with Taverner's music or provisional enactments of musical and spiritual betrayal. It is noteworthy that since the first production of *Taverner* he has moved away from its themes and methods. His second full-length stage work, *The Martyrdom of St Magnus* (1977), may be no less concerned with treason, but it deals more with politics than the soul, more with interpersonal relationships than with the intra-personal analysis of *Taverner*. Designed for performance in church, it is also more of a ritual pageant than the earlier opera, a fable rather than an attempt to bring psychological truths directly to the audience.

The works of Bussotti, another composer who has dealt in opera with his own situation as artist, show something of a contrast with the moral anxieties of Henze, Pousseur and Davies. Amplifying the already extravagant eroticism of his concert works, Bussotti creates a theatre of self-dramatization and exhibitionism, a world of sensuality in which he always has the starring role. His *La passion selon Sade* (1965–6) is a celebration of Eros featuring the composer as 'maestro di cappella', a mezzo-soprano identified with Sade's heroines Justine and Juliette, and an ensemble who must attack and cajole their instruments with as much carnal as musical passion, or almost. The work is a theatrical exaggeration of tendencies which had been present in much of his earlier music, and again the composer barely controls his creative intentions in a mixture of conventional notation and flamboyant disruptions. In turn *La passion selon Sade* gave rise to a whole series of extracts, paraphrases and developments, among which the *Rara* group reached its superb climax in *The Rara Requiem* for voices and orchestra (1969–70). Like the earlier *Torso* for voices and orchestra (1960–63), this is a work of sustained sensuousness, of highly mannered vocal and instrumental lines working in a framework of decadent harmony which may be overloaded but never heavy.

Though *The Rara Requiem* stands as proof that Bussotti can demonstrate the pleasures of Eros without any recourse to the stage, much of his output since the mid-1960s has had a more or less overt theatrical content. An abandoned 'concert play' dedicated to Italy gave rise to the *Cinque frammenti all'Italia* for vocal ensembles (1967–8), a cycle underlining his closeness to the Italian madrigalists of the late Renaissance. His operatic treatment of Musset's *Lorenzaccio* (1968–72) is an autobiographical fantasy on the most lavish and self-indulgent scale, the composer appearing here not only as principal actor (in the role of Musset) but as producer, designer, choreographer and film director; the last two acts quote *The Rara Requiem,* during which the opera magniloquently celebrates its own passing in a funeral ceremony for Eros. After this the ballet *Bergkristall* (1972–3) came as an escape to higher and purer realms, though still marked by Bussotti's excited filigree writing for large orchestra and by his will to impose himself, providing costume and scenic designs in the score, as supreme master of ceremonies.

NEW POSSIBILITIES

Some of the novel alternatives to opera have necessarily been mentioned in the foregoing section, and in particular the genre, if its diversity allows it so to be called, of music theatre. This term has generally been used to denote works for restricted forces which are to be performed with rudimentary staging on the concert platform: Henze's *Natascha Ungeheuer,* Berio's *Laborintus II* and Bussotti's *La passion selon Sade* provide examples, but the most prolific composer in this field has been Davies, whose first such work, *Revelation and Fall* for soprano and 16 players (1965–6), makes clear the roots of his music theatre in *Pierrot lunaire*. Setting a poem by Trakl, the work generates period atmosphere through its references to Schoenberg and also, with a characteristic love–hate attack on light music, to Lehár, while its highly disturbing presentation of the soloist as a nun in scarlet habit, screaming into a megaphone, set the tone for Davies's exploration of emotional extremes and, as in *Taverner*, blasphemous betrayal.

His adoption of expressionist violence, more fuelled than controlled by the rigorous post-medieval techniques which run through all his music, made possible on the one hand the exhibition of crazed, obsessive individuals in *Eight Songs for a Mad King* (1969) and *Miss Donnithorne's Maggot* (1974), and on the other a vituperative attack on religious dishonesty in *Missa super L'homme armé* (1968, revised 1971) and *Vesalii icones* (1969). All of these works are conceived for soloist – a male singer raised by madness to wild feats of virtuosity in *Eight Songs*, a similarly wracked mezzo-soprano in *Miss Donnithorne*, a spiteful priest in *L'homme armé* and a nude male dancer in *Vesalii icones* – accompanied by a *Pierrot* quintet plus percussionist, so that the dark shadow of the Schoenberg prototype hovers always in the background, encouraging Davies to vivid textures figured with intensely expressive instrumental gestures and to multiple levels of irony and satire.

If *Eight Songs* is the most spectacular of Davies's theatre pieces, casting the instrumentalists as birds in giant cages to witness and suffer the manic ravings of the soloist, *Vesalii icones* is the richest and most potent. The dancer, whose gestures refer both to the engravings in Vesalius's anatomy text and to the Stations of the Cross, lays bare the agonies of Christ while the instruments add further layers of analysis and distortion, Davies here using all his techniques of hidden and overt parody to keep the music on the disquieting border between commitment and mockery.[10] At the eighth Station, for instance, there is a complex masquerade of musical images to serve as commentary on the story of St Veronica's wiping of Christ's face and thus receiving the imprint of his features on her cloth. The opening, shown in Example 68, has the cello declaiming a theme from Davies's earlier *Ecce manus tradentis* for soloists, chorus and instruments (1965), itself based on the plainchant for those words: the chant of betrayal is thus doubly betrayed in the quotation. At the same time the piano decorates another plainsong theme in the style of a 19th-century salon piece. Subsequently the material is bent to allude to the scherzos from two Beethoven symphonies, to de la

Ex. 68

Rue's *L'homme armé* mass and to Davies's own *Missa super L'homme armé*. This last is also the source of the more blatant parodies of the sixth Station, where the mocking of Christ is the occasion for twisting the ancient tune into what Davies sees as the blasphemy of a comfortable Victorian-style hymn and later into a foxtrot, both played by the dancer on a honky-tonk piano. And at its conclusion the work, like the Second Taverner Fantasia, sharply and viciously deflates itself, for the Resurrection turns out to be that of Antichrist, triumphing to a horrendous development of the foxtrot.

Davies's relation to Schoenberg is paralleled by his colleague Birtwistle's dependence on Stravinsky, and in particular on the clear-cut forms of such works as the Symphonies of Wind Instruments and the rustic theatre of *Renard* and *Histoire du soldat*. Birtwistle's first major dramatic work was the chamber opera *Punch and Judy* (1966), which is based on the old puppet shows and presents a collection of characters who are half clown, half monster, all of them dancing in abrupt, grotesque movements as the composer pulls the strings of appalling passion and murderous savagery. His music is as piercing as Davies's in its violence of gesture, particularly when he forces the high woodwind into chords of screaching alarm which had their origin in his *Tragoedia* for ensemble (1965), but the cruelty is stylized by ritual necessity. The work is, like *Renard,* closed and cyclic, a rite of death and resurrection, night and day, winter and summer. Its very symmetrical structure includes, for example, four 'Melodramas' in which Punch traps his victims in word play, each followed by a 'Murder Ensemble' which is the celebration of a ritual execution, and these larger sections are filled with tiny, compact forms, strung together in patterns of verse and refrain.

Although *Punch and Judy* is nominally an opera it relates to the music theatre tradition not only in its links with *Renard* but also in its reduced scale and its dramatic style. The action is presented from a puppet booth, in which the characters go through their antics and in which a wind quintet is seated, the pit orchestra consisting of just ten further players. Moreover, as a cyclic ceremony the work discards narrative continuity, nor do the characters invite any kind of sympathy or identification; rather the work projects a schematic world in which emotions of ferocious hate and consuming lust can be played out safely in formal patterns. And however far removed from common experience those emotions may appear, the opera can be understood in terms of post-Freudian child psychology. Punch is the infant who has not yet learnt to adapt his needs to those of society. He uses language not to communicate but to ensnare; he demands instant gratification, symbolized in his quests for Pretty Polly, and when he does not get it his response is immediate, intense and murderous. For most human beings this is a passing phase, but *Punch and Judy* ends with the triumph of the barbarous child who has killed his father in executing Choregos and who, in tricking his way out of his own execution, has evaded that social intervention in personal development which is the only way to adulthood.

Birtwistle's next dramatic composition, *Down by the Greenwood Side* (1969), is again a ceremony of killing and rebirth with its roots in English folk legend, again a stylized assembly of bright fragments. The instrumental style of *Punch and Judy*, however, is pursued most powerfully not here but in *Veses for Ensembles* (1969), which, like *Tragoedia*, revels in the drama of antiphonal forms, and which gives that drama a physical presence by having the ensembles placed on different platforms. The three percussionists have one level for their noise instruments and another for their xylophones and glockenspiels; the five woodwind players are seated at the left when playing high instruments and at the right when using their lower equivalents; the brass quintet has its own platform, and there are also antiphonally separated desks for trumpet duets and for woodwind solos accompanied by the horn. Example 69 shows the opening of the first of two climactic sections of echoing and answer placed within the sequence of 'verses' for different groupings, sections which in their severe pulsation look forward to the time-measuring which underlies many of Birtwistle's works of the 1970s.

Verses for Ensembles, so arresting and dramatic in performance,

Ex. 69

(♩ = c 60) accel. (♩ = c.120)
trpt.
hn.
trbn.
f fff
(♩ = c.120)
picc.
E♭ cl.
ob.
cl.
bn.
(♩ = c.120)
hn.
2 trbn.
mf < ff > mf
sim.
(♩ = c.120)
3 xyl.
fff
(♩ = c.120)
3 xyl.
fff > f sim.
(♩ = c 160)
picc.
E♭ cl.
ob.
cl.
bn.
f fff

might be described as instrumental theatre, though that term is more usually confined to works in which the instrumentalist is required to act a part. Several examples have already been given from the output of Kagel, whose works since *Anagrama* have almost always had a theatrical content, even in those rare cases where no stage business is involved. *Match,* for instance, is most clearly a mimed entertainment, and so too is *Der Atem* (1970), in which Kagel takes up a long-standing concern with the pathology of musical performance. According to the composer's description: 'A retired wind player devotes himself to the continual repetition of the same thing: maintaining his instruments. At each moment he goes to the cupboard, opens the cupboard, takes out the instruments and puts them back, oils them, blows into them, wipes the saliva traps, warms the reeds and the mouthpieces, silently does some exercises; often he talks to himself while polishing away all the time. Occasionally he happens to play, properly speaking'.[11]

Inevitably Kagel has cast his amused, ironic eye upon the genres of opera and music theatre, and his staged works often show his findings. *Staatstheater* uses all the resources of an opera house – principals, chorus, orchestra, corps de ballet, scenery and costumes – in activities which satirize, ignore or overturn their customary purposes, the soloists being brought together in a mad ensemble, the dancers put through their paces in gymnastic exercises. But not all Kagel's theatrical works are so absurd, nor so unstructured. In *Tremens* (1963–5) he considers the effects of hallucinogenic drugs on aural experience: the subject is presented in a hospital cubicle, where he is forcibly encouraged by a doctor to listen to tapes of music which a live ensemble distorts, as if projecting his imagined versions. And in *Mare nostrum* (1973–5) he has the nice idea of showing a party of Amazonians trying to make sense of Mediterranean culture, pointing out at once the relativity of accepted norms, musical and social, and the patronizing attitude inherent in anthropological research.

Kagel's exposure of the theatre implicit in musical performance has had its effect on Stockhausen, but in Stockhausen's works dramatic gesture is used not in an ironic sense but in order to clarify the composer's intentions, to give a visual focus for visionary creations, or to assist in the demonstration of the physical and metaphysical powers of sound. Before *Aus den sieben Tagen* Stockhausen had composed only one theatrical work, *Originale,* but since 1971 almost all his works have been in some measure dramatic: even

'Atem gibt das Leben . . .' (1974), originally composed as a simple piece for amateur chorus, was later revised as a 'choral opera'. *Trans* (1971) and *Inori* (1973–4), two of the most substantial of Stockhausen's later compositions, are also two in which the dramatic apparatus is most precisely conceived and economical in effect. In *Trans* the audience is offered the awe-inspiring spectacle of a string orchestra seated in close rows behind a magenta-lit gauze, solemnly unfolding a sequence of still, dense harmonies. From behind come the amplified but indistinct sounds of wind and percussion groups in marching chords or swirling melodies, this background music oblivious of the implacable crashes of a weaving shuttle, heard at irregular intervals from loudspeakers, to which the strings respond with a change of chord. All this, like Kagel's *Match,* came to the composer in a dream, and there is a further connection with Kagel in the four moments of surreal comedy which are superimposed on the rest: the first of these has a viola player performing a virtuoso cadenza, 'like a little wound-up toy instrument'[12] switched on by a marching drummer.

In *Trans* orchestral music is made theatre, but not with the self-dramatizing intentions of Berlioz's *Lélio,* which seems in this respect an ancestor rather of Bussotti's creations. The work is, Stockhausen has said, 'transpersonal music',[13] not willed by him but accepted as a dictation from beyond. *Inori* is comparable in its powerful communication of a mystic vision and its massive orchestral sonorities, mapping out the development of a melody through phases that concentrate on rhythm, dynamics, melody, harmony and polyphony as if in a résumé of musical history. Here the theatrical element is provided by a mime who goes through various positions of worship taken from disparate cultures, and who seems to have her prayerful gestures amplified by the orchestra. This, at least, was how *Inori* appeared in its first performances. The solo part is in fact denominated simply 'Beter' (worshipper) in the score, and is notated as a melodic line; it may be played or sung, though the use of a mime, with a basic gesture for each pitch of the part, would seem essential to the work's appeal as ceremonial. Example 70 shows a simplified extract in which the 'Beter' is assigned the last three of the principal melody's five sections, harmonized by strings, brass, bassoons and percussion; the soloist's dynamics are notated numerically on a scale from one to 60.

Leaving aside *Herbstmusik* (1974), a somewhat naïve essay in

Ex. 70

612
= 75.5 molto rit.
42.5 acc.
53.5
85
63.5
high ww.
vn. I: 1-4
antique cymbals
Beter
45
5
45
15
55
brass
bns.
str.
pf.
vib.
rin
gongs
= 90
80
90
80
63.5
60
50
60
50
= 71 poco rit.
63.5
35
15
10
1

sound conservation which brings autumnal country pursuits to the concert platform, Stockhausen's other works of music theatre have been concerned with the powers of sound. *Alphabet für Liège* takes the unusual form of an exhibition, with demonstrations of the effects of acoustic vibrations on fish, on fine powder scattered on metal plates (Chladni's experiment), on the yeast in dough and on the physical and mental faculties of human beings. 'Sounds can do anything', Stockhausen has said: 'They can kill. The whole Indian mantric tradition knows that with sounds you can concentrate on any part of the body and calm it down, excite it, even hurt it in the extreme'.[13] In *Musik im Bauch* (1975), a mimed children's fable, he shows this discovery being made by three percussionist brothers who find the secret of ordered music in some music boxes hidden in the stomach of a giant dummy. And *Harlekin* (1975), for clarinettist dressed in appropriate costume, would appear to be a portrait of a benign Pied Piper.

The realization that the basic parameters of sound are linked – that insight which had been celebrated in *Kontakte* – seems to have developed in Stockhausen's mind to the extent that he feels able to encompass creatively other and vaster cycles of vibration: those of light, of the days, months and years, even (though in an astral future) of the galaxies.[14] Music alone is no longer sufficient, certainly not for the cosmic play of St Michael, Lucifer and Eve on which Stockhausen is engaged in *Licht* (1977–), a cycle of musical–dramatic works intended for performance over seven consecutive evenings and apparently due to absorb his creative energies until the early 1990s.

REPERTORY

Berio: *Passaggio* for soprano, two choruses and small orchestra (1962, Universal).

—— *Traces,* scenic oratorio (1964, withdrawn).

—— *Laborintus II* for speaker, three female voices, eight actors, 18 players and tape (1965, Universal). RCA SB 6848.

—— *Opera,* opera (1969–70, revised 1977, unpublished). RCA ARL 10037 (two concert excerpts).

Birtwistle: *Tragoedia* for wind quintet, harp and string quartet (1965, Universal). Argo ZRG 759.

—— *Punch and Judy,* chamber opera (1966, Universal). Decca HEAD 24–5.

—— *Down by the Greenwood Side* for soprano, five actors and nine players (1969, Universal).
—— *Verses for Ensembles* for 12 players (1969, Universal). Decca HEAD 7.
Bussotti: *Torso* for three voices and orchestra (1960–63, Universal).
—— *La passion selon Sade* for female voice, actors and instrumental ensemble (1965–6, Ricordi). Wergo 60054 (derived work *0* for female voice).
—— *Cinque frammenti all'Italia* for vocal sextet or chorus (1967–8, Ricordi). DGG 2561 110.
—— *The Rara Requiem* for four singers, vocal sextet, chorus and orchestra (1969–70, Ricordi). DGG 2530 754.
—— *Lorenzaccio,* opera (1968–72, Ricordi). DGG 2531 011 (symphony from the work).
—— *Bergkristall,* ballet (1972–3, Ricordi). DGG 2531 011.
Davies: *Revelation and Fall* for soprano and 16 players (1965–6, Boosey). HMV ASD 2427.
—— *Missa super L'homme armé* for speaker and six players (1968, revised 1971, Boosey). L'Oiseau-Lyre DSLO 2.
—— *Eight Songs for a Mad King* for male voice and six players (1969, Boosey). Unicorn RHS 308.
—— *Vesalii icones* for dancer and six players (1969, Boosey). Unicorn RHS 307, Nonesuch H 71295.
—— *Miss Donnithorne's Maggot* for soprano and six players (1974, Boosey).
—— *The Martyrdom of St Magnus,* opera (1977, Boosey).
Henze: *Elegy for Young Lovers,* opera (1959–61, Schott). DGG 138 876 (excerpts).
—— *The Bassarids,* opera (1965, Schott).
—— *Das Floss der 'Medusa'* for soprano, baritone, speaker, chorus and orchestra (1968, Schott). DGG 139 428–9.
—— *El Cimarrón* for baritone and three players (1969–70, Schott).
—— *Der langwierige Weg in die Wohnung der Natascha Ungeheuer* for baritone, 16 players and tape (1971, Schott). DGG 2530 212.
—— Violin Concerto no. 2 for violin, bass-baritone, 33 players and tape (1971, Schott). Decca HEAD 5.
—— *La Cubana,* 'vaudeville' on operatic scale (1973, Schott).
—— *Voices* for mezzo-soprano, tenor and chamber orchestra (1973, Schott). Decca HEAD 19–20.
—— *We come to the River,* opera (1974–6, Schott).
—— *Orpheus,* ballet (1979, unpublished).
Kagel: *Tremens* for two actors and five players (1963–5, Universal).
—— *Staatstheater* for operatic forces (1967–70, Universal). DGG 2707 060.

—— *Der Atem* for wind player and tape (1970, Universal). EMI C 061 28808.
—— *Mare nostrum* for countertenor, baritone and six players (1973–5, Universal).
Ligeti: *Le grand macabre,* opera (1975–6, unpublished). Wergo 60085.
Nono: *La fabbrica illuminata* for soprano and tape (1964, unpublished). Wergo 60038.
—— *A floresta è jovem e cheja de vida* for voices, clarinet, bell plates and tape (1966, unpublished). Arcophon AC 6811, DGG 2531 004, Harmonia Mundi MV 30767.
—— *Ricorda cosa ti hanno fatto in Auschwitz* on tape (1966, unpublished). Wergo 60038.
—— *Per Bastiana–Tai-yang cheng* for orchestra and tape (1967, Ricordi). Wergo 60067.
—— *Contrappunto dialettico alla mente* on tape (1967–8, unpublished). DGG 2561 044.
—— *Musica-manifesto no. 1* (1969, unpublished): 1 *Un volto, del mare* for voices and tape, 2 *Non consumiamo Marx* on tape. I Dischi del Sole DS 182 4 CL, Philips 6521 027.
—— *Y entonces comprendio* for voices and tape (1969–70, unpublished). DGG 2530 436.
—— *Como una ola de fuerza y luz* for soprano, piano, orchestra and tape (1971–2, Ricordi). DGG 2530 436.
—— *Al gran sole carico d'amore,* opera (1972–4, Ricordi).
Pousseur: *Votre Faust,* opera (1960–67, unpublished).
Stockhausen: *Trans* for orchestra and electronics (1971, Stockhausen). DGG 2530 726.
—— *Alphabet für Liège* for various solos and duos (1972, Stockhausen), from which *'Am Himmel wandre ich . . '* for two singers (1972, Stockhausen). DGG 2530 876 (*'Ah Himmel . . .'*).
—— *Inori* for soloist and orchestra (1973–4, Stockhausen).
—— *'Atmen gibt das Leben . . .'* for chorus (1974, Stockhausen), revised as choral opera for chorus and orchestra or tape (1977, unpublished). DGG 2530 641 (1974 version).
—— *Herbstmusik* for players (1974, Stockhausen).
—— *Musik im Bauch* for six percussion (1975, unpublished), from which *Tierkreis* for undetermined forces (1975, Stockhausen). DGG 2530 913 (both works).
—— *Harlekin* for clarinet (1975, Stockhausen). DGG 2531 006.
—— *Licht,* cycle of dramatic works (1977–, unpublished): 1 *Der Jahreslauf* for dancers and orchestra (1977), 2 *Michaels Reise um die Erde* for trumpet and orchestra (1978), 3 *Michaels Jugend* for three singers, three dancers, four players and tape (1978–9).

14 Series → Melody

When Stockhausen returned, in *Mantra* (1970), to explicit notation, and even to the continuous and progressive development of something very like a theme, the result appeared an extraordinary volte-face after a period of gradual relaxation of control which had culminated in the text scores of *Aus den sieben Tagen*. Seen from a later viewpoint, however, *Mantra* and subsequent works by Stockhausen take their place in a general movement during the 1970s towards clear, unique structure, often on the basis of simple elements. If the music of Reich and Glass shows this tendency at its most extreme, the trend is hardly less clear in that of such diverse European contemporaries as Boulez, Stockhausen, Birtwistle and Ligeti, all of whom have found new interest in phenomena and procedures earlier judged outdated, including most conspicuously the phenomenon of melody (or, in the case of Pousseur and Schat, schematic harmonic methods). Whereas the development of serial thinking in the 1950s had encouraged composers to build from undisclosed, deeply hidden musical units, with the primacy of melody came the placing of the foundations squarely and openly in the body of the work.

EUROPEAN SERIALISM

It has already been established that the mainstream development of European serialism was seriously disrupted in the late 1950s, principally by reactions to the innovations of Cage. However, some composers maintained their allegiance to the methods they had elaborated from the serial idea, to a serial style rather than to ever broader definitions of the serial principle. Chief among them was Barraqué, whose music shows nothing of the tendency to replace serial by melodic formulae (he died in 1973 and had completed his last finished work in 1968) but rather demonstrates the continuing range and power of the style he had developed in his Piano Sonata and in *Séquence*.

After completing his revision of the latter score, in 1955, Barraqué devoted himself to what was intended to be a vast system of musical commentaries on Broch's novel *The Death of Virgil*, whose dense meditations on death, on the act and purposes of creation, and on the necessity of incompletion were close to his own preoccupations. 'All goes, all dies . . .', he wrote. 'Every trustee of creation must accept that as he accepts his own death. Even on the technical level his art must evolve towards death; it must be completed within "incessant incompletion".'[1] Barraqué's omission of final bar lines in his later scores is thus no empty idiosyncrasy but a true need, for each work is not only part of a larger whole but also a desperate act in travail with silence at every point, and not just at its close. There is an ambiguity, too deep to be called ironic, between the composer's fully determined intentions, inscribed on a high plane of musical endeavour where nothing is left to chance, and his awareness, strongly to be felt, that these are insufficient, partial and transitory.

La mort de Virgile was planned as a work in five books, one for each part of the Broch novel and a fifth of commentary, but only three compositions from the second book were brought to definitive form: *Le temps restitué* for soprano, chorus and small orchestra (1957–68), *. . . au delà du hasard* for soprano, female chorus and four instrumental groups (1958–9) and *Chant après chant* for soprano, piano and percussion sextet (1966). In each of these Broch's thoughts on the vanity of creative effort, and on the artist's compulsion to destroy what he has made, are considered in a surge of musical and poetic disquisition. *. . . au delà du hasard*, for instance, takes only a short quotation from the novel – 'Blinded by the dream and made by the dream to see, I know your death, I know the limit which is fixed for you, the limit of the dream, which you deny. Do you know it yourself? Do you want it so?' – which is set in one of the 13 sections, the others using a fragmentary text by Barraqué himself. The presentation of the quotation is made with an imposing gesture: a long orchestral passage is suddenly cut off and the music stops for 15 seconds; there is then an immense orchestral crescendo in two phases and a further 15-second emptiness before the untuned percussion loudly usher in the sybilline utterance of Broch's words. Such magniloquence, within a context of impatience and despair, is typical of Barraqué's rhetoric, which is always inwardly directed by the composer's, and indeed the music's, self-questioning.

More frequently the anxious introspection of . . *au delà du hasard* is conducted in a richly figured and strongly dynamic polyphony, which is a genuine polyphony of individual but interdependent lines, bound by serial and motivic links as well as by the flexible cellular rhythm Barraqué had called upon in his earlier works. Since the score is laid out for distinct groupings – the first of brass, saxophones and vibraphone, the second of tuned percussion, the third of untuned percussion, the fourth of four clarinets and the fifth of voices – a polyphony at two levels is possible. Generally, the connections between lines are close within groups, while the groups are bound together by more tenuous liaisons. The largeness of the music makes it difficult to select intelligible extracts, but Example 71 has at

Ex. 71

least the virtue of relative simplicity, not only of texture but also of serial usage. It is clear, for example, that the polyphonic lines are made up largely from 12-note statements, though there is often no obvious relation among the several series presented (Barraqué referred to his use of 'proliferating series' in his later works, but one can do no more than speculate as to the processes of derivation he employed). The vibraphone of the first group unfolds forms of four different series, marked *A–B–C–D* in the example, which appear quite unrelated. There is, however, a close connection with the other instrumental lines here, for the vibraphone and xylophone of the second group begin their music with a retrograde inversion of A and an inversion of B, while the clarinet has an inversion of A, an inversion of B and a prime transposition of C (the Webernian symmetry of this series allows the statement to be interpreted also as a retrograde inversion). Barraqué provides further for more detailed and evident relationships, whether of pitch (e.g. the registral fixing of G in the last five bars of the example), of rhythm (e.g. the triplet semiquavers in the sixth bar, which stand out in a context of such irregularity) or of both (e.g. the focusing on F sharp before and at the soprano's 'décidé', which is intensified by the vibraphone of the first group). And within this network there is room for the clearest word-painting, as when the clarinet falls from a high point in the sixth bar or the vibraphones come to a halt on a trilling 5th shortly before.

Each part of *La mort de Virgile,* both in its snatches of verbal expression and in its musical substance, protests against its own existence, against the necessity of creation, but at the same time sets itself implacably against anything facile, any evasion of artistic duty. There is nothing superfluous in Barraqué's tumultuous floods of musical imagery, where fully achieved beauty beckons as the artist's inescapable obligation but also as a perfection that can only be false, because untrue to the impermanent condition of man and his works, and where silence waits on the other hand as the only unequivocal statement but also as the ultimate evasion. Example 72, from *Chant après chant,* shows a passage where these 'seas of silences' threaten and lure and are fended off by a forceful crescendo. In structural terms there are parallels with Example 71: the soprano has a 12-note series while a different series (with one pitch class repeated) unfolds in the piano, the two being tied in the third bar by the xylophone. The example also gives some hint of Barraqué's interest in resonance phenomena, an interest that is prominent in a score laid out for a wide variety of instruments, ranging from those with long resonance (e.g. the metal instruments of the first half of the example) to those with little (e.g. such wooden instruments as maracas and claves), the skin drums of the second half of the example standing at an intermediate point. The sung phrase of Example 72 comes to rest on a note joined by its sixth harmonic, an image of the text's 'childlike voice' but perhaps also a momentary glimpse of that 'pre-echo of the ultimate achievement' which is present in the text printed at the front of the score but which has been suppressed in the composed version. This high B, before falling through five octaves to become the subject of the ensuing crescendo, is left to linger through a long silence, and so here, as so often in the work, resonances reach out from the music being played to another music of intangible echo and dissolution, from the spectacular instrumentarium to the spaces of nothingness.

Ex. 72

Boulez's orchestral *Eclat/multiples* (begun 1965), one of the many works left incomplete since *Pli selon pli,* is also concerned with resonance phenomena. The concertante group of nine players on pitched percussion instruments, an enlargement of the ensemble used in the first two *Improvisations sur Mallarmé* (and also of that employed by Barraqué in . . . *au delà du hasard*), is placed against a sextet of wind and strings in the first section, which enjoys separate

existence as *Eclat*; the subsequent 'multiples' introduce further groupings of sustaining instruments in generally homogeneous formations, the second section, for instance, adding a basset horn and nine violas. With this antinomy between resonators and non-resonators Boulez is able to create 'a kind of "suspended" musical space in opposition to very dynamic ideas' and hence to develop a contrast between 'a contemplative attitude towards the phenomenon of sonority – demanding a different way of listening, attentive to what is happening within the resonance itself – and an active effort of thought occupying itself still more with the thought connecting the musical events and which makes them take a determined direction'.[2] Example 73, taken from towards the end of

Ex. 73

Eclat, shows this contrast in action, the sustaining group being locked in firmly directed music, and almost exclusively in parallel chords, while the percussion are devoted largely to extracting from these chords the pitch B flat/A sharp whenever it appears, together with one or two chromatic neighbours from those available. To the contrast of sonority between the groups, therefore, is added a

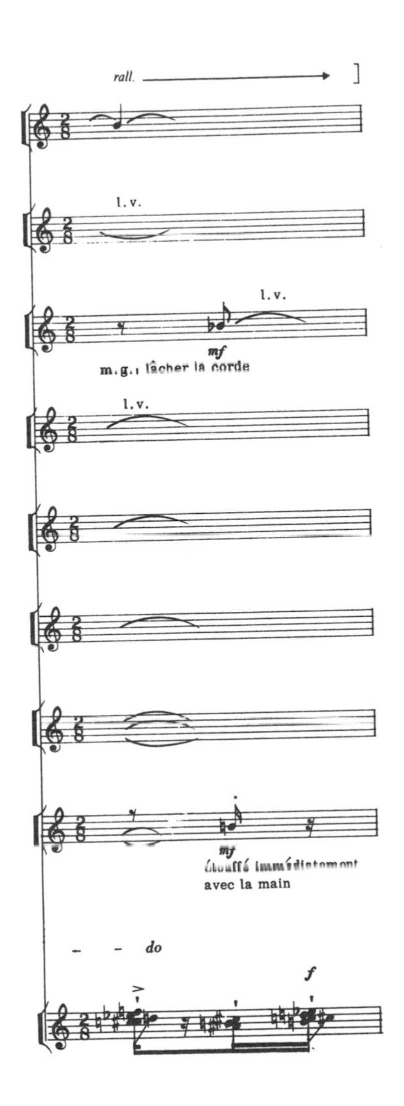

contrast of pitch material (though with an essential link) and of rhythm, the quintet jerking in what Boulez terms 'striated time'[3] while the percussion present in 'smooth time' the B flat/A sharp as an object of changing colour and interference.

Boulez has described *Eclat/multiples* as 'a succession of mirror images in which developments reflect each other; or, so to speak, the multiple reflections of the original musical images interfere with each other and create divergent perspectives, such as Paul Klee imagined in certain of his paintings'.[4] In this light Example 73 may be interpreted as offering the divergent perspectives of a pivotal pitch in the percussion and a constant harmony in the sustaining group; but reflections of musical images are most readily observed in the slow central portion of *Eclat,* where the composer plays on his percussion ensemble as on a giant keyboard, calling upon different groupings to colour each suspended resonance. Example 74 shows the pitch

Ex. 74

materials in the opening of this passage, where a 12-note series is divided into five harmonic units (marked *a–e*). The latter part of the example is based on the same series of harmonic units, rotated to begin with the second, and with each repeated two or three times in new dispositions. One pitch alone, C, remains fixed in register and is always confined to the tubular bells; its importance is further emphasized by the fact that it completes the chromatic total at the beginning of the passage. This element of fixity, in a context of seeming improvisatory character despite the close harmonic control, provides a clear focus, an exemplary instance of Boulez's use of registral fixing and chromatic complementation to generate harmonic polarities.

The richer chords more characteristic of the work may frequently be analysed in terms of Boulez's technique of 'multiplication', which he first described in his 1952 article 'Eventuellement . . .', and which appears to have had a substantial role in the composition of *Pli selon pli* and subsequent scores. Two pitch-class sets are deemed to be multiplied when one is transposed on to every degree of the other to generate a new, larger set as product. For example, the product of chords *b* (a statement of the pitch-class set [0,1] to follow the notation of Forte)[5] and *c* (or [0,4,5,6]) in Example 74 will clearly be the set [0,1,4,5,6,7], which is expressed in the piano part of

Ex. 75

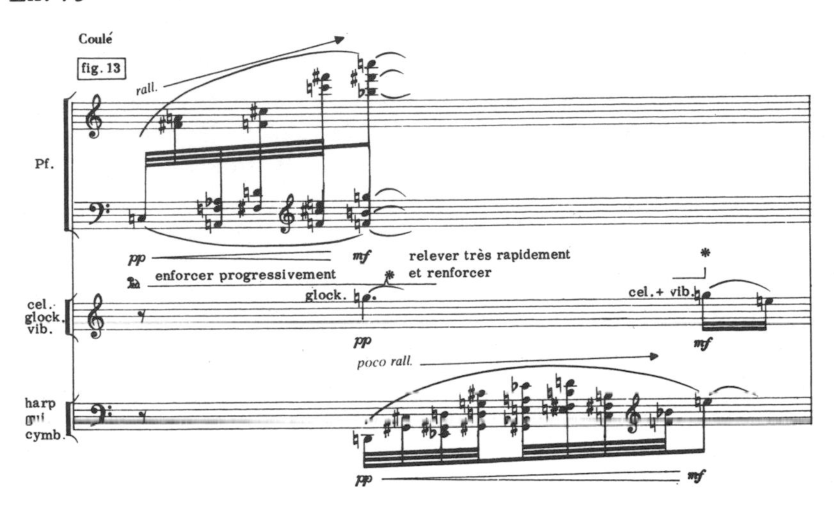

Example 75, where it is gradually built up from the inside outwards, as it were. Following this the harp, guitar and cymbalom asymmetrically build and dismantle a five-note set, [0,1,5,6,7], a defective version of the piano's set. It is also noteworthy that both the brilliant, fluid gestures in this example are based on stable, symmetrical harmonies, which becomes clear if they are transcribed as intervallic distances in semitones:

				6	6
			8	8	8
pf:	[0]	3	3	3	3	3
			8	8	8	8
						6

			6	6	6				
harp, gui, cymb:	[0]	5	5	5	5	5	5	5	[0]
				6	6	6	6		
					2	2			

Boulez thus has at his disposal various oppositions – between pulsed and pulseless motion, fixed and mobile register, fixed and mobile interval content, and so on – which can be brought into play in the modulation between glacial stasis and darting movement which is characteristic of *Eclat/multiples*.

His next full orchestral work, *Rituel* (1974–5), is very much more straightforward and solid, even monumental in construction, being based not on a vast ensemble of more or less closely related harmonic units but on a single formula set. The piece is, in Boulez's appropriately liturgical terms, a sequence of 'verses and refrains'[6] for a congregation of homogeneous instrumental groupings (solo oboe, clarinet duo, flute trio, violin quartet, woodwind quintet, string sextet, woodwind heptet and 14 brass), each accompanied by unpitched percussion to beat out the time. Example 76 shows the

Ex. 76

first verse and hence the first statement of the tritone-rich melodic formula. In succeeding verses, which bring more and more of the groups into heterophonic combination, the formula is extended, developed, rearranged and transposed, but its identity and its centrality are never in doubt. It also governs the chordal refrains, these being constructed from the inversion of the seven-note formula set. The awesome grandeur of *Rituel,* which appears at this mature stage in Boulez's career as a curious throwback to the world of Messiaen (particularly the latter's *Et exspecto resurrectionem mortuorum*), is a function of the severe alternation of heterophonic verses and block-harmonic refrains, and also of the emergence of the single melodic idea as determining factor. If the work can be termed a serial composition at all, it is only because its variation techniques and its habit of projecting melodic lines harmonically had their origins in the much more fluid and flexible universe of *Pli selon pli* and *Eclat/multiples*.

MELODIES

The fact that Ligeti could in 1971 give the title '*Melodien*' to an orchestral piece signals not only the general renewal of interest in melody but also his own retrieval of those discriminations which had been thoroughly dissolved in *Atmosphères*. Several of his works from the 1960s, including the large-scale *Requiem*, the unaccompanied *Lux aeterna* and the orchestral *Lontano*, continue his 'micro-polyphonic' style in which clusters glide and slowly evolve; but there are also more defined features in the pictorial 'Dies irae' from the *Requiem*, for instance, and in the sense in *Lontano* of a harmonic substructure which remains usually as a concealed current but which rises occasionally to the surface when the chords thin out towards octaves.[7] Writing of the harmonic procedures in his music since the mid-1960s Ligeti has said that: 'There are specific predominant arrangements of intervals, which determine the course of the music and the development of the form. The complex polyphony of the individual parts is embodied in a harmonic-musical flow, in which the harmonies (i.e. the vertical combinations of intervals) do not change suddenly, but merge into one another; one clearly discernible interval combination is gradually blurred, and from this cloudiness it is possible to discern a new interval combination taking shape'.[8]

Ligeti's later compositions also admit a greater variety of texture than previously, with extremes represented by the static coloured clusters of his early music and the precise, puppet-like movements of *Aventures*. The two are separately presented in the Cello Concerto (1966), where he follows his compatriot Bartók in treating the same material in quite different ways in a pair of movements, the abstract comedy of the second movement contrasting with the still flow of the first. In many later scores, however, the two kinds of music are made to combine and to grow out of one another: this is particularly the case in the aptly titled *Clocks and Clouds* for female chorus and orchestra (1972–3) and in the Double Concerto for flute, oboe and orchestra (1972). This latter work also develops those tremulous repeating patterns which had been introduced in *Continuum* for harpsichord (1968) and *Coulée* for organ (1969), and whose proximity to the world of Reich and Riley is acknowledged in the central piece of the two-piano triptych of 1976, *Selbstportrait mit Reich und Riley (und Chopin ist auch dabei)*. The incessant repetition of small fragments brings about a blurring within which Ligeti's processes of gradual harmonic change may be carried out with ease. An alternative resource is that of microtonal deviation, as in the Second String Quartet (1968), *Ramifications* for two string groups tuned a quarter-tone apart (1968–9) and again the Double Concerto, where 'normal' and 'abnormal' harmonies shimmer and merge in glassy brilliance.

All of these techniques – the reduction of harmonic potency by the addition of neighbouring pitches in cluster formation, the repetitions which obscure, the microtones which introduce doubt – are exquisitely calculated to veil the music's underlying processes. Similarly, the bundles of melodies in *Melodien* or *San Francisco Polyphony* for orchestra (1973–4) defy any effort to take note of them all. The secret and magical but at the same time ironic aspect of Ligeti's music, which justifies his quotation from Lewis Carroll in the score of his Ten Pieces for wind quintet (1968), depends very much on the creation of music which withholds as much as it reveals, and of works which appear as fragments of continuing wholes, stealing away, like *Lontano*, to other realms as their physical sound fades. *Monument–Selbstportrait–Bewegung*, however, is not of this type, for it ends with a chorale in the form of 'an eight-voice mirror canon which contracts like a telescope' and which is 'the common coda of all three pieces'.[9] It is also quite clearly the quintessence of those canonic workings trapped amid the lustrous figuration of the earlier part of *Bewegung*. Example 77*a* shows a passage from this earlier part, whose canonic content is revealed in Example 77*b*.

Berio sometimes shows something of the same interest in obscuring essentially simple musical structures, in modulating between the most rudimentary and the most complex harmonies (in this respect, if in this respect alone, *Nones* relate to *Lontano*) and even in using minimalist-like cascades of repetitive figuration, these in such pieces as *Agnus* for two sopranos, three clarinets and drone (1970–71). This work also shows his use of a definite melody rather than a set as musical generator, a technique which had appeared for the first time in his music in *O King* for mezzo-soprano and quintet (1968), later orchestrated to form the second movement of the *Sinfonia*. Here a vocal cantus firmus is lightly hidden by staggerings and decorations in the instrumental parts. Berio's ballet *Linea* for two pianos, vibraphone and marimba (1973) also weaves patterns of allusion and divergence around a melody which is sometimes clearly discernible, as in the opening section, and at other times submerged in half-memories.

Melody in Birtwistle's later music has a privileged place in the construction of forms which seem to mirror natural processes of birth and gradual change. Indeed, with reference to his orchestral work *The Triumph of Time* (1972) he has mentioned his interest in working with different rates of change, drawing attention to a cor anglais melody which never alters and to a soprano saxophone signal which is similarly fixed until it suddenly flowers near the end of the

Ex. 77a

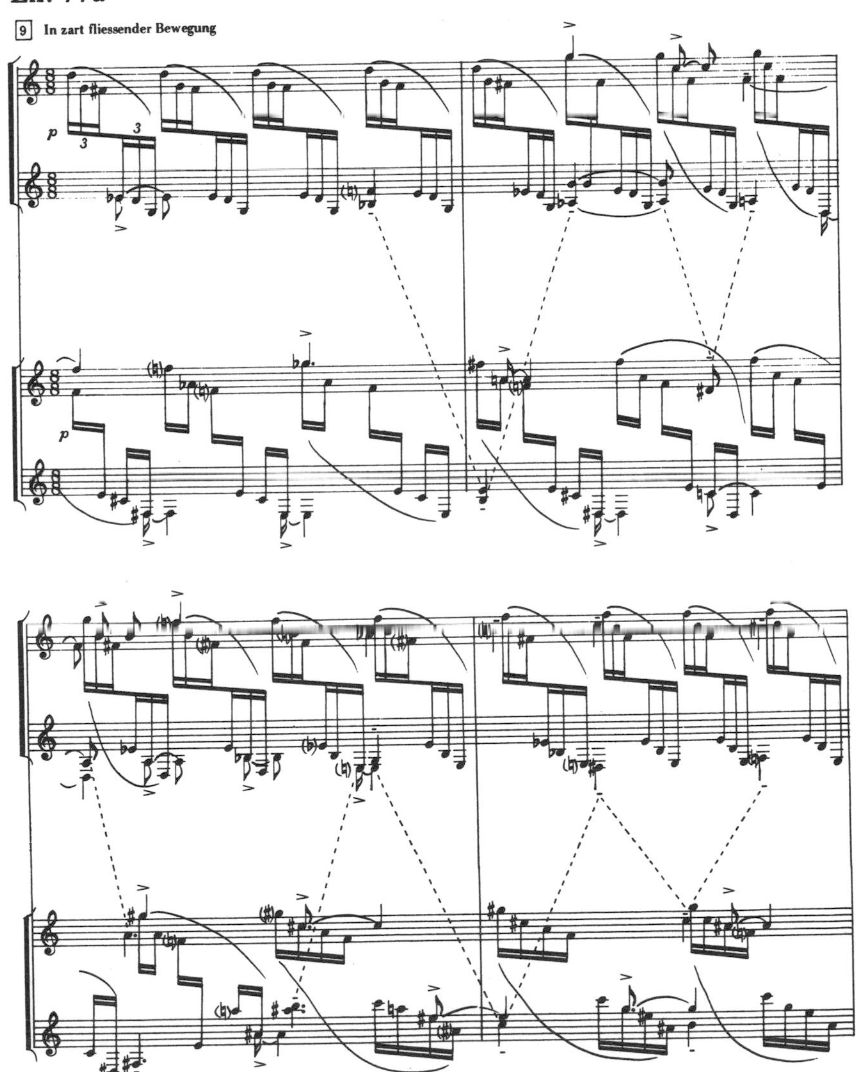

Ex. 77b

piece.[10] Birtwistle's melodies often give prominence to groups of neighbouring pitch classes, whether in meandering through small intervals or in jagged leaps, and often too they develop as if emerging, in somewhat Varèsian fashion, from a sustained or reiterated note: thus the elaborate textures of *Melencolia I* for clarinet, harp and two string orchestras (1976), for instance, are drawn through the mediation of the wind soloist from a single held A. The rhythmic complement of this procedure is the evolution of the most complex patterns from a regular pulse, or, as in *Silbury Air* for chamber orchestra (1977), from a 'labyrinth' of interconnecting pulses. In both domains, those of pitch and of rhythm, Birtwistle has engaged himself with the basic materials of the art while also concerning himself with its poetic origins in his opera *Orpheus*, to which many of his works of the 1970s relate as studies or pendants (it is highly characteristic of him that musical objects should be shifted from one work to another, and so find a new environment in which to grow). *Nenia: The Death of Orpheus* for soprano and five players (1970) was the first of his Orphic works, and the first to show song emerging from speech, asymmetry from regularity and melody, in the shape of a long line on the clarinet, from the calling of the demi-god's name.

Stockhausen's *Mantra* for two pianists, dating from the same year, displays a very much more systematic and conscious melodic technique than any work discussed hitherto in this section. Everything in it, as in Boulez's *Rituel,* is derived not from a series or a set but from a definite melody, the 'mantra', which is subjected to melodic and rhythmic expansions or contractions. Example 78 shows the 'mantra' as it appears at the beginning of the work: the right-hand melody has four 'limbs', as Stockhausen calls them,[12] while the left hand plays an inverted variant with the 'limbs' crossed over (i.e. in the order 2–1–4–3). The rhythmic alteration of the 'mantra' by regular augmentation or diminution is straightforward; more unusual is Stockhausen's technique of melodic variation, which depends on a scheme of 12 artificial scales ranging from the chromatic to one in which only 25 notes on the keyboard are used. When the 'mantra' is played in one of these scales, each semitone becomes a scalar interval, which in the most extreme case will be a major or minor 3rd, and so the melody is more or less regularly expanded like a drawing on an inflated rubber balloon. Example 79 shows a passage where the maximal expansion is in operation for the right-hand part in the first piano, and where the durations are halved. The major 6th chords

Ex. 78

Ex. 79

here are prompted by a verticalization of the first two notes of the 'mantra' in the current expansion.

The 'mantra' further determines the large form of the composition, in that there are 13 principal sections, each centred on one of the skeleton notes of the original formula (A–B–G sharp–E, F–D, G–E flat–D flat–C, B flat–G flat–A). Each note of the 'mantra' has a different character (rapid repetition for the first, sharp final attack for the second, and so on), and these characters in turn dominate the various phases of the work. Each note also provides a focal pitch for its daughter section, a pitch to which each pianist tunes his sine-wave generator, the first following the sequence of the basic melody while the second has that of its inversion. Since the piano tones are ring modulated against these sine tones, Stockhausen thereby obtains a new method of harmonic differentiation. At the beginning, for instance, both sine-tone generators are tuned to A = 220 Hz, and so the first and last notes of the right-hand melody of Example 78, having the same fundamental frequency, will produce a simple ring-modulated product: the ring modulator produces sums and differences of the frequencies submitted to it, so that in these cases it will generate frequencies of 440 Hz (i.e. the A an octave higher) and zero, and the sound will therefore be consonant. The last note of the first limb is the E close to 330 Hz, and so here the product will contain frequencies close to 110 Hz (i.e. the A an octave below the sine tone) and 550 Hz (i.e. something near the C sharp on the treble staff), and again the result will be consonant. But clearly the ring-modulated product will be dissonant if the piano tone is not in a simple frequency ratio with the sine tone, or nearly so, and thus in Stockhausen's terms 'one perceives a continual "respiration" from consonant to dissonant to consonant modulator-sounds'.[12] The situation is complicated by the fact that the pianos produce inharmonic partials, but the effect of these is muted by circuitry specially designed by the composer for this work. Thus the effect of the ring modulation, apart from giving an aura of Cage's prepared piano, is to provide a quite new means of projecting harmonic relationships. Since the 'tonic' is imposed from outside, the composer is not limited by any need to maintain a consistent tonality in the music, and the artificial scales act to lay the piece open to a wide range of harmonic characters, from Hindemithian quartal harmony to exotic pentatonicism.

Yet although the function of ring modulation in this work is primarily harmonic – the search for new sounds, which Stockhausen had undertaken in *Mixtur* and *Mikrophonie II*, is secondary – the composer characteristically takes advantage of the spectacular gestures which present themselves, as at one point where the players scan massive piano chords with sweeping glissandos in the sine-wave generators. And there are other points where the music leaves the confines of its scheme, where the two pianists fight for possession of a motif (bars 218–28), where they stand to call to each other in the manner of nō percussionists (bar 639) or where the composition breaks off in its final phase for a résumé of all the 'mantra' transformations in flurries of even semiquavers. These, however, are all exceptional moments which serve to point the ceremonial continuity of the rest, where a melody is made to engender what Stockhausen has with some justice likened to a galaxy of different shapes.[13]

The melody of *Mantra* also served to stimulate a gift for melodic composition which Stockhausen has put to effect in inventing similarly haunting lines for *Japan* (1970) from the collection *Für kommende Zeiten*, for the 12 Zodiac melodies of *Tierkreis* (1975), which are available in various instrumental and vocal arrangements by the composer as well as in their original musical-box forms, and for the five clarinet pieces of the set *Amour* (1976). The first of these, 'Ein Vöglein singt an Deinem Fenster', may be quoted to illustrate both the conscious structuring in Stockhausen's melodies and their graphic imagery. The piece begins with a 'bird melody' (Example 80*a*) which in three stages of compression is converted into a 'human melody' (Example 80*b*) retaining the same pitch classes and the same durations, except for a final adjustment. Like the 'mantra' of the two-piano work, the melody is an expression of a 12-note set with internal repetition and with a 13-note return to the origin (in the seventh bar), but here it continues with a varied repeat of its opening 'limb'. Equally characteristic is the diversity of rhythmic values and, for all the individuality of style, the background presences of Schoenberg and Messiaen.

Most of Stockhausen's larger works since *Mantra* have also been based on germinal melodies. The orchestral *Inori* (1973–4) offers a close parallel to *Mantra* in being founded on the transformations of a formula which allows a wide variety of chordal materials to be gathered together (see Example 70 on p.267). *Sirius* for soprano, bass, trumpet, bass clarinet and tape (1975–6) uses four of the melodies of *Tierkreis* to build a work lasting for more than an hour and a half and representing a seasonal cycle: the tape carries the main continuity and the four soloists are superposed as embodiments of the four seasons, the four elements, the four cardinal directions, the four phases of the day and what Stockhausen sees as the four kinds of

Ex. 80a

Ex. 80b

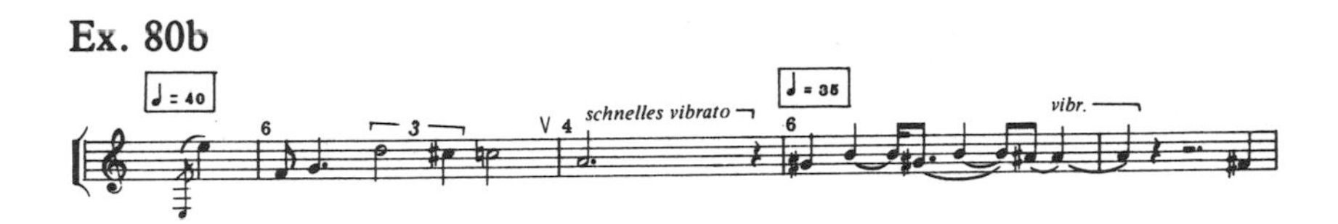

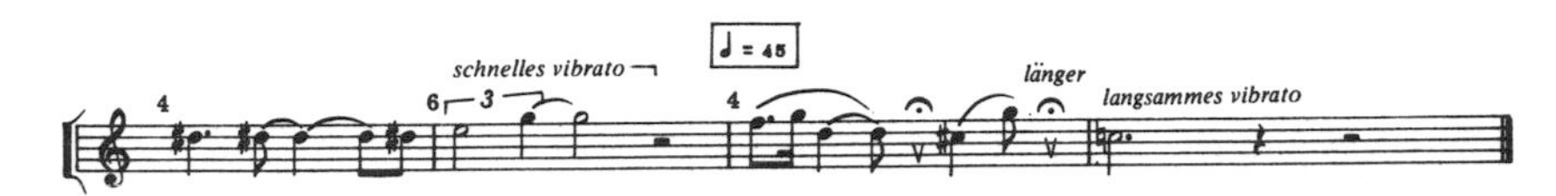

human being (man, adolescent, woman, lover). The music theatre sequence *Licht* is similarly planned to revolve around three principal melodies, each associated with one of the main characters: Michael (impersonated by tenor and trumpet), Lucifer (bass and trombone) and Eve (soprano and basset horn). Melody, it would appear, has become central to the solid grandeur of Stockhausen's most recent works and projects, superseding the serial considerations which had governed his earlier music. And yet he has insisted that his works of the 1970s represent no break with the serial past but rather an extension, and he has spoken with confidence not only of his own future[14] but also of the future of serial composition. 'Composition with series of proportions', he writes, 'has now for many years been applied not only to individual tones, to their individual attributes, but also to groups and collectives. What was once hierarchical thought at every level of music has been expanded to serial thought and will now remain authoritative for many centuries.'[15]

REPERTORY

Barraqué: . . . *au delà du hasard* for soprano, female chorus and 20 players in four groups (1958–9, Bruzzichelli).
—— *Chant après chant* for soprano, piano and percussion sextet (1966, Bruzzichelli). Valois MB 951.
—— *Le temps restitué* for soprano, chorus and small orchestra (1957–68, unpublished).
Berio: *Agnus* for two sopranos, three clarinets and drone (1970, Universal). RCA ARL 10037.
—— *Linea* for two pianos, vibraphone and marimba (1973, Universal). RCA RL 12291.
Birtwistle: *Nenia: The Death of Orpheus* for soprano, three clarinets, piano and percussion (1970, Universal). Decca HEAD 7.
—— *The Triumph of Time* for orchestra (1972, Universal). Argo ZRG 790.
—— *Melencolia I* for clarinet, harp and two string orchestras (1976, Universal).
—— *Silbury Air* for chamber orchestra (1977, Universal).
—— *Orpheus*, opera (1974–).
Boulez: *Eclat* for 15 players (1965, Universal), extended as *Eclat/multiples* for orchestra (1966–).
—— *Rituel* for orchestra (1974–5, Universal).
Ligeti: *Requiem* for soprano, mezzo-soprano, chorus and orchestra (1963–5, Peters). Wergo 60045.
—— Cello Concerto (1966, Peters). Wergo 60036.
—— *Lux aeterna* for chorus (1966, Peters). DGG 2530 392, DGG 137 004, EMI C 063 29075, Wergo 60026.
—— *Lontano* for orchestra (1967, Schott). Wergo 60045.
—— *Continuum* for harpsichord (1968, Schott). Wergo 60045.
—— String Quartet no. 2 (1968, Schott). DGG 2530 392, DGG 2543 002, Wergo 60079.
—— Ten Pieces for wind quintet (1968, Schott). EMI 4 E 061 34091, EMI 4 E 031 34047, Wergo 60059.
—— *Zwei Etüden* for organ: 1 *Harmonies* (1967, Schott), 2 *Coulée* (1969, Schott). DGG 137 003 (1), DGG 2530 392 (1), Wergo 60076 (complete).
—— *Ramifications* for string orchestra (1968–9, Schott). Wergo 60059.
—— *Melodien* for orchestra (1971, Schott). Decca HEAD 12.
—— Double Concerto for flute, oboe and orchestra (1972, Schott). Decca HEAD 12.
—— *Clocks and Clouds* for female chorus and orchestra (1972–3, Schott).
—— *San Francisco Polyphony* for orchestra (1973–4, Schott). Wergo 60076.

—— *Monument–Selbstportrait–Bewegung* for two pianos (1976, Schott). DGG 2531 102.
Stockhausen: *Mantra* for two pianos and electronics (1970, Stockhausen). DGG 2530 208.
—— *Sirius* for soprano, bass, trumpet, bass clarinet and tape (1975–6, unpublished). DGG 2707 122.
—— *Amour* for clarinet (1976, Stockhausen).

Postlude

It should be clear, particularly from the second part of this book, that any attempt to summarize the present state of music would be vain in the extreme. The history of the art since 1945 has been one not only of rapid and far-reaching developments but also of continuous forking by which the comparatively unified effort of the late 1940s and early 1950s, when composers as diverse as Babbitt and Stockhausen, Boulez and Nono appeared to share similar aims and to some degree similar methods, has evolved into the current tangle of endeavours. If composers could once be placed with some certainty on a straight line from indeterminacy to serial determination, they must now be considered within a multi-dimensional space of vast and various possibilities which grow ever more so. Since 1952, when the whole range of music appeared to have been contained between the extremes of Cage's *4′ 33″* and Boulez's *Structures I*, new vistas have repeatedly been opened to show that this was not the case, until the avant garde has lost whatever defining features it may have had. Attempts to draw up new distinctions, between 'avant garde' and 'experimental', 'bourgeois' and 'revolutionary', 'post-serial' and 'minimalist', may offer useful signposts, but no borders may be firmly drawn in the heterogeneous musical commonwealth of today.

Nevertheless, it is possible to find one respect in which the music of the 1970s has an identity that sets it apart from that of the 1950s, and that is the concern not so much with musical composition in the abstract as with the effect of music on the listener. Even Babbitt, whose methods might appear to betoken an interest much more in the musical artefact than in problems of communication, has been obliged by his experience in the electronic studio to give attention to the reach of musical understanding, for in his view the electronic revolution has effected 'a transfer of the limits of musical composition from the limits of the nonelectronic medium and the human performer, not the limits of this most extensive and flexible of media but to those more restrictive, more intricate, far less well understood limits: the perceptual and conceptual capacities of the human auditor'.[1]

Babbitt, of course, is interested in the mental limitations on the nature and complexity of musical structures which the composer may propose, but other composers have concerned themselves rather with musical effects which the listener imposes, with those acoustic analogues of optical illusions and more generally with phenomena resulting from the physiological and psychological mechanisms of hearing. Reich has spoken of the 'impersonal, unintended, psychoacoustic by-products of the intended process', these including 'submelodies heard within repeated melodic patterns, effects due to listener location, slight irregularities in performance, harmonics, difference tones, etc'.[2] An important part of the musical experience may thus be provided by the listener: the composition is not an object with a clear identity but a source of opportunities for the listener to make and analyse his own perceptions. Using very different techniques, such spatially conceived works as Stockhausen's *Gruppen* also offer themselves to some degree as unique experiences for each individual, for the simple reason that what is heard will depend on where one is seated, and at the same time the music begins to change its field of action from the objective, being considered from outside, to the subjective, being experienced from within.

When the sound is both enveloping and highly repetitive, as in the music of La Monte Young, then the invitation is all the greater to a personal exploration of the phenomena rather than to an analysis of the composer's intentions. It is not so surprising, therefore, that Young, like Stockhausen, should speak of his work with reference to its physical and metaphysical effects, expressing the hope that he may be able to retrieve a presumed lost knowledge concerning the emotional and spiritual states to be excited by combinations of frequencies. Since Cage wrote his *Sonatas and Interludes,* Indian music has had a special place in the minds of Western composers as the repository of this wisdom. 'The mere fact', Young has said, 'that they have the means to classify the moods of the different ragas, in whatever poetic way, means they have something that has almost disappeared from Western music.'[3] And Stockhausen adds: 'The whole Indian mantric tradition knows that with sounds you can concentrate on any part of the body and calm it down, excite it, even hurt it in the extreme. There are also special mantras, naturally, that can lift the spirit of a person up into supernatural regions so that he leaves his body'.[4]

The capacity of music to exert specific effects on the human subject is also accepted, at least by implication, by those composers who would make the art serve more mundane functions in the furthering of political change. It may be argued that music can be politically effective only by virtue of the force it lends to a political text, and indeed most examples of revolutionary socialist music, whether by Henze or Nono, Cardew or Pousseur, Schat or Wolff, have used words to focus the message, or else have used musical elements of latent verbal content, such as the protest songs invoked in various works by Pousseur, Cardew, Nono and others. Yet Pousseur has argued eloquently that musical forms themselves carry the burden of inherent world-pictures and hence may be used to propose alternative social systems or to point out limitations, contradictions and ambiguities within existing ones.[5]

If the role of music in stimulating religious or political enlightenment still remains doubtful, despite the high claims made by particular composers, its ability to affect perceptions within its own special domain, that of time, has long been established, and few composers working since 1945 have not taken note of the new means of temporal ordering which become available when metrical regularity is obliterated or severely challenged, and when tempos can range from the hectic speeds of *Le marteau sans maître* to the motionlessness of Young's early pieces. Much music has been stimulated by the possibility of fusing a Western conception of time as regularly passing from one point to another with an Eastern notion of cyclical phases, of combining dynamic, goal-directed movement with circular return or stasis; this is particularly, but by no means exclusively, a characteristic of works written by Boulez and Stockhausen from the late 1950s onwards. Other composers have worked with time palpably moving in irregular quantities (e.g. Perle and Wuorinen) or have concerned themselves with pulsations which collide and interact (e.g. Reich and, in a very different manner, Birtwistle), in either case imposing new mental images of temporal progress on the metronomic model of clock time which we are inclined to accept as normal.

When thus acting upon its own element music can take on a primary role, independent of outside reference, but a great deal more music of the last 20 years has adopted a secondary role as commentary, whether referring to itself (as most explicitly, for example, in Berio's *Chemins* series or Boulez's *Domaines*) to the music of other times and places (as in the wide repertory of compositions mentioned in Chapter 11) or to other arts, principally literature. In their approach to words many composers since 1945 have preferred to couch their contribution in this commentary form, so that the eventual work does not absorb the text, as in most earlier vocal music, but instead allows it a separate existence as the fount of musical extrapolations. Paradoxically, the identity of the text is best preserved when it is omitted, as in large parts of Boulez's *Pli selon pli*, so that the music presents itself wholly as a gloss upon words the listener is presumed to have assimilated. And that the mode of commentary can be very much more than a self-regarding pose, even when the work reflects on its own creative origins and purposes as it unfolds, is unequivocally demonstrated by the compositions of Barraqué, while Stockhausen has shown in several works that found objects, whether texts, expressions of alien musical cultures or given instruments, can be accommodated along with the newly invented, each taking a new meaning from the other.

It may be, however, that the future development of music will depend not only on research into psychoacoustics, not only on the evolution of new techniques for fusion and assimilation, but also on further work in basic fields of compositional method and technology. Six decades after Schoenberg's first serial essays there still remain many difficulties in the elaboration of a coherent serial discourse, and undoubtedly the procedures of 12-note music will be refined and reinterpreted. Meanwhile, the more recent works of Reich and Glass suggest that repetitive music may be leaving its minimal origins behind and venturing into more demanding realms of thought which open the prospect of a quite new kind of tonality. In the technological area, work on computer synthesis promises unprecedented precision and flexibility in the handling of electronic sound, while at Boulez's research establishment, the Institut de Recherche et Coordination Acoustique/Musique, composers and technicians are exploring, among other things, new kinds of instrument and new ways of linking conventional instruments with electronic apparatus. Boulez has attributed the shallowness of much contemporary music to the absence of a general store of musical knowledge which might direct, limit and fertilize the composer's invention, and it may well be that it is the relative lack of ground rules which makes a second-rate piece composed in 1980 less likely to be of interest than one written in 1880. The works of a Raff, for instance, may show a modest individual approach to the language of the time and may help to form the background against which greater music may be measured, but Raff's successors are offered no language, only sets of personal solutions. Babbitt's serial methods are unusual in offering guidelines sufficiently general that they may be appropriated by other composers without imitation, but they go no more than a small way in establishing a framework of discourse.

If a new common language is to be found, whether at IRCAM or elsewhere, it seems likely that it will not be able to ignore the recent past, and that it will therefore have to be a synthesis of the most diverse means and methods. Perhaps it is more probable that the present condition will persist, and that new directions in music will forever fork more than they intertwine.

Notes to the Text

Prelude: Music in 1945

1 'Où en est-on?', *Revue musicale,* no. 276–7 (1971), 7–9; p.7.

2 Igor Stravinsky and Robert Craft: *Dialogues and a Diary* (New York, 1963), pp.51–2.

Chapter 1: Paris, 1945–8

1 'Hommage à Messiaen', *Melos,* xxv (1958), p.387.

2 Joan Peyser: *Boulez: Composer, Conductor, Enigma* (London, 1977), pp.32–3.

3 ' "J'ai horreur du souvenir!" ', *Roger Desormière et son temps,* ed. Denise Mayer and Pierre Souvtchinsky (Monaco, 1966), 134–58; p.144.

4 Antoine Goléa: *Rencontres avec Pierre Boulez* (Paris, 1958), p.20.

5 Ibid., p.20.

6 *Conversations with Célestin Deliège* (London, 1976), p.30.

7 See René Leibowitz: 'A New French Composer: André Casanova', *Music Survey,* ii/3, pp.148–55.

8 See Goléa: op. cit., p.38.

9 See ibid., p.28.

10 See Paul Griffiths: *Boulez* (London, 1978), p.10.

11 Reprinted in his *Relevés d'apprenti* (Paris, 1966), pp.235–40.

12 Reprinted in ibid., pp.65–74.

13 Ibid., p.68.

14 Ibid., p.68.

15 See *Conversations,* pp.40–41.

16 See Griffiths: op. cit., p.15.

17 See *Conversations,* p.41.

18 See Robert Sherlaw Johnson: *Messiaen* (London, 1975), pp.92–3.

19 *Conversations,* p.21.

20 Goléa: op. cit., p.99.

21 ' "Sonate, que me veux-tu?" ', *Perspectives of New Music,* i/2 (1963), 32–44; p.34.

22 *Relevés,* p.74.

23 *Conversations,* p.53.

24 See Pierre Schaeffer: *A la recherche d'une musique concrète* (Paris, 1952).

Chapter 2: New York, 1948–50

1 *Relevés d'apprenti* (Paris, 1966), p.74.

2 See Joan Peyser: *Boulez: Composer, Conductor, Enigma* (London, 1977), pp.60–2.

3 'The Future of Music: Credo', *Silence* (Middletown, Conn., 1961), pp.3–7, also in *John Cage,* ed. Richard Kostelanetz (London, 1971), pp.54–7.

4 'For More New Sounds', Kostelanetz: op. cit. 64–6; p.65.

5 Ibid., pp.77–84.

6 Ibid., pp.81–2.

7 Ibid., p.85.

8 Preface to the score.

9 *John Cage,* p.129.

10 Ibid.

11 *Relevés,* p.177.

12 Sleeve note, CRI 138.

13 *Serial Composition and Atonality* (London, 1962, 4th edition 1978), pp.99–101, 135–6, 139–41.

14 'Some Aspects of Twelve-Tone Composition', *The Score,* no. 12 (1955), pp.53–61.

15 Sleeve note, CRI 138.

16 See Peter Westergaard: 'Some Problems Raised by the Rhythmic Serialism in Milton Babbitt's Composition for Twelve Instruments', *Perspectives of New Music,* iv/1 (1965), pp.109–18.

17 See Merton Shatzkin: 'A Pre-Cantata Serialism in Stravinsky', *Perspectives of New Music,* xvi/1 (1977), pp.139–43.

18 'Perle', *Dictionary of 20th Century Music,* ed. John Vinton (London, 1974), p.568.

Chapter 3: Darmstadt/Paris, 1951–2

1 *Relevés d'apprenti* (Paris, 1966), p.254.

2 Ibid., p.253.

3 *The Score,* no. 6 (1952), 18–22; reprinted in *Relevés,* pp.265–72.

4 Ibid., p.271.

5 (Paris, 1947), also English translation (New York, 1949).

6 Claude Samuel: *Entretiens avec Olivier Messiaen* (Paris, 1967), p.183.

7 Richard Toop: 'Messiaen/Goeyvaerts, Fano/Stockhausen, Boulez', *Perspectives of New Music,* xiii/1 (1974), 141–69; pp.150–52.

8 Karl H. Wörner: *Stockhausen: Life and Work* (London, 1973), p.81.

9 Ibid.

10 See Toop: op. cit., p.162.

11 For analytical notes see ibid., pp.152–8.

12 See Peter Westergaard: 'Webern and "Total Organization": an Analysis of the Second Movement of the Piano Variations, Op. 27', *Perspectives of New Music,* i/2 (1963), pp.107–20.

13 For analytical notes see Jonathan Harvey: *The Music of Stockhausen* (London, 1975), pp.14–20; Robin Maconie: *The Works of Karlheinz Stockhausen* (London, 1976), pp.21–7; and Toop: op. cit., pp.159–64.

14 *Texte,* i (Cologne, 1963), p.21.

15 See Karlheinz Stockhausen: 'Schlagquartett', *Texte,* ii (Cologne, 1964), pp.13–18.

16 Review, *Contact,* no. 12 (1975), 45–6, p.46.

17 György Ligeti: 'Pierre Boulez', *Die Reihe,* no. 4 (1958, English edition 1960), pp.36–62.

18 See Toop: op. cit., p.165.

19 *Conversations with Célestin Deliège* (London, 1977), p.55.

20 See Ligeti: op. cit.; and Paul Griffiths: *Boulez* (London, 1978), pp.22–3.

21 Wörner: op. cit., p.229.

22 In Jean Barraqué: 'Rythme et développement', *Polyphonie,* no. 9–10 (1954), 47–74; pp.71–2; and Antoine Goléa: *Rencontres avec Pierre Boulez* (Paris, 1958), pp.141, 143.

23 *Conversations,* p.58.

24 *Relevés,* pp.147–82.

25 Ibid., p.149.

26 See Richard Toop: notes with EMI EMSP 551.

27 *La musique depuis Debussy* (Paris, 1961), p.173.

28 Sleeve note, RCA VICS 1313.

Chapter 4: New York, 1951–3

1 Benjamin Boretz: 'Babbitt', *Dictionary of 20th Century Music,* ed. John Vinton (London, 1974), pp.43–8.

2 Sleeve note, Nonesuch H 71202.

3 *Silence* (Middletown, Conn., 1961), p.59.

4 *I Ching: Book of Changes,* translated by Cary Baynes.

5 See 'To Describe the Process of Composition used in *Music of Changes* and *Imaginary Landscape no. 4*', *Silence,* pp.57–9.

6 Preface to the score.

7 From a note on the work by Cage in *John Cage,* ed. Richard Kostelanetz (London, 1971), p.109.

8 Paul Griffiths: 'Morton Feldman', *Musical Times,* cxiii (1972), 758–9; p.758.

9 Michael Nyman: *Experimental Music* (London, 1974), p.42.

10 Ibid., p.42.

11 See footnote 23 to Heinz-Klaus Metzger: 'Essay on Prerevolutionary Music', published with EMI C 165 28954–7.

12 Nyman: op. cit., p.45.

13 Griffiths: op. cit., p.759.

14 Ibid., p.758.

15 Nyman: op. cit., p.48.

16 Ibid.

17 See footnote 29 to Metzger: op. cit.

18 'The Question of Order in New Music', *Perspectives of New Music,* v/1 (1966), 93–111; p.95.

Chapter 5: Cologne 1953–4

1 *Relevés d'apprenti* (Paris, 1966), pp.165–7.

2 no. 212 (1952).

3 See his 'Musique concrète', *Relevés,* pp. 285–6.

4 See Karlheinz Stockhausen: 'The Origins of Electronic Music', *Musical Times,* cxii (1971), 649–50.

5 See Richard Toop: 'Stockhausen's *Konkrete Etüde*', *Music Review,* xxxviii (1976), pp. 295–300, and 'Stockhausen and the Sine Wave: the

story of an Ambiguous Relationship', *Musical Quarterly,* lxv (1979), 379–91. This second article throws doubt on the chronology given here, which is based on Stockhausen's own account.

6 See Stockhausen's analysis 'Komposition 1953 Nr. 2', *Texte,* ii (Cologne, 1964), pp.23–36.

7 See preface to the score, reprinted in *Texte,* ii, pp.37–42.

8 'What is Electronic Music?', *Die Reihe,* no. 1 (1955, English edition 1958), 1–10; p.10.

9 For a note on this version, and a page of the score, see Robin Maconie: *The Works of Karlheinz Stockhausen* (London, 1976), pp.51–3.

10 See Dieter Schnebel: 'Karlheinz Stockhausen: "Kontra-Punkte" oder "Morphologie der musikalischen Zeit" ', *Denkbare Musik* (Cologne, 1972), 213ff.

11 See Maconie: op. cit., pp.55–6.

12 *Texte,* i (Cologne, 1963), p.37.

13 Op. cit., p.63.

14 'Karlheinz Stockhausen', *Die Reihe,* no. 4 (1958, English edition 1960), pp.121–35.

15 *The Music of Stockhausen* (London, 1975), pp.24–6.

16 Op. cit., pp.64–5.

17 Karl H. Wörner: *Stockhausen: Life and Work* (London, 1973), p.32.

18 See Karlheinz Stockhausen: 'Gruppenkomposition: Klavierstück I', *Texte,* i, pp.63–74.

19 Op. cit., p.67.

20 *Texte,* i, p.47.

Chapter 6: The Avant-garde Achievement 1954–8

1 *Relevés d'apprenti* (Paris, 1966), pp.27–32.

2 Ibid., p.20.

3 Ibid., p.30.

4 Ibid., p.32.

5 See Piero Santi: 'Luciano Berio', *Die Reihe,* no. 4 (1958, English edition 1960), pp.98–102.

6 See Reinhold Schubert: 'Bernd Alois Zimmermann', *Die Reihe,* no. 4, pp.103–13.

7 See his 'Webern's Organic Chromaticism', *Die Reihe,* no. 2 (1956, English edition 1958), pp.51–61.

8 See Gottfried Michael Koenig: 'Henri Pousseur', *Die Reihe,* no. 4, pp.14–28.

9 See his 'Outline of a Method', *Die Reihe,* no. 3 (1957, English edition 1959), pp.44–8.

10 *Die Reihe,* no. 7 (1960, English edition 1965), pp.5–19.

11 'Some Aspects of Twelve Tone Composition', *The Score,* no. 12 (1955), 53–61; p.53.

12 'Music and Speech', *Die Reihe,* no. 6 (1960, English edition 1964), pp.40–64.

13 See Rudolph Stephan: 'Hans Werner Henze', *Die Reihe,* no. 4, pp.29–35.

14 'Son et verbe', *Relevés,* 57–62; p.58.

15 See 'Sprechen, singen, spielen', *Werkstatt-Texte* (Frankfurt and Berlin, 1972), 124–41; p.138.

16 See ' "Sonate, que me veux-tu?" ', *Perspectives of New Music,* i/2 (1963), 32–44; p.34.

17 See, for example, his note on *Telemusik* in Karl H. Wörner: *Stockhausen: Life and Work* (London, 1973), pp.57–8.

18 See 'Sprechen, singen, spielen', p.137.

19 See *Boulez on Music Today* (London, 1971) for some indication of the range of his serial methods.

20 *Relevés,* p.62.

21 Ibid., p.297.

22 'Music and Speech', p.64.

23 See Stockhausen's 'Actualia', *Die Reihe,* no. 1 (1955, English edition 1958), 45–51; and his 'Music and Speech', pp.57–64.

24 'Actualia', p.50.

25 'Music and Speech', p.49.

26 Ibid., p.48.

27 *Die Reihe,* no. 3, pp.10–40.

28 *Relevés,* pp.165–7.

29 *The Music of Stockhausen* (London, 1975), pp.59–61; see also Gottfried Michael Koenig: 'Commentary', *Die Reihe,* no. 8 (1962, English edition 1968), pp.80–98.

30 See, for example, John Backus: '*Die Reihe:* a Scientific Evaluation', *Perspectives of New Music,* i/1 (1962), pp.160–71.

31 See his 'Twelve-tone Rhythmic Structure and the Electronic Medium', *Perspectives of New Music,* i/1 (1962), pp.49–79.

32 *Gravesaner Blätter,* no. 1 (1955), 2ff.

33 'The Question of Order in New Music', *Perspectives of New Music,* v/1 (1966), pp.93–111.

34 *Formalized Music* (Bloomington and London, 1971), p.9.

35 *Texte,* i (Cologne, 1963), p.235.

36 'Edgard Varèse: a Few Observations of his Music', *Perspectives of New Music,* iv/2 (1966), pp.14–22.

37 See Arnold Whittall: 'Varèse and Organic Athematicism', *Music Review,* xxviii (1967), pp.311–15.

38 See, for example, *John Cage,* ed. Richard Kostelanetz (London, 1971), plate 38.

Chapter 7: Chance and Choice

1 'To Describe the Process of Composition used in "Music for Piano 21–52" ', *Die Reihe,* no. 3 (1957, English edition 1959), pp.41–3.

2 Directions on the verso of the printed music.

3 For a different approach to Markovian music see Iannis Xenakis: *Formalized Music* (Bloomington and London, 1971), pp.43–109.

4 Jonathan Cott: *Stockhausen: Conversations with the Composer* (London, 1974), p.70.

5 Antoine Goléa: *Rencontres avec Pierre Boulez* (Paris, 1958), p.229.

6 *Perspectives of New Music,* iii/1 (1964), 42–53; p.45.

7 See *Relevés d'apprenti* (Paris, 1966), p.30.

8 ' "Sonate, que me veux-tu?" ', *Perspectives of New Music,* i/2 (1963), 32–44; p.37.

9 See *Boulez on Music Today* (London, 1971), pp.73–4, and Iwanka Stoïanowa: 'La *Troisième sonate* de Boulez et le projet mallarméen du livre', *Musique en jeu,* no. 16 (1974), pp.9–28.

10 ' "Sonate, que me veux-tu?" ', p.41.

11 See Iwanka Stoïanowa: 'Pli selon pli. Portrait de Mallarmé', *Musique en jeu,* no. 11 (1973), pp.75–98.

12 See Boulez's article 'Wie arbeitet die musikalische Avantgarde?', *Werkstatt-Texte* (Frankfurt and Berlin, 1972), pp.179–200, and also his *Conversations with Célestin Deliège* (London, 1976), pp.94–5.

13 *Die Reihe,* no. 5 (1959, English edition 1961), 84–120; p.116.

14 Sleeve note, Time 8009; reprinted in *John Cage,* ed. Richard Kostelanetz (London, 1971), pp.144–5.

15 Sleeve note, Mainstream 5009.

16 Feldman quoted in Michael Nyman: *Experimental Music* (London, 1974), p.59.

17 See Wolff's article 'On Form', *Die Reihe,* no. 7 (1960, English edition 1965), pp.26–31.

18 Quoted in 'Wolff', *Dictionary of 20th Century Music,* ed. John Vinton (London, 1974), p.820.

19 'Musik und Graphik', *Texte,* i (Cologne, 1963), pp.176–88.

20 Dore Ashton: 'Cage, Composer, Shows Calligraphy of Note', *New York Times* (6 May 1958); reprinted in Kostelanetz: op. cit., p.126.

21 Richard Toop: note with EMI EMSP 551.

22 See Kagel's sleeve note, Mainstream 5003, and also his articles 'Tone, Clusters, Attacks, Transitions', *Die Reihe,* no. 5, pp.40–55, and 'Translation–Rotation', *Die Reihe,* no. 7, pp.32–60.

23 Jean-Yves Bosseur: 'Dossier Kagel', *Musique en jeu,* no. 7 (1972), 88–126; pp.91–2.

24 Note by Stockhausen in Karl H. Wörner: *Stockhausen: Life and Work* (London, 1973), p.42.

25 See his article 'Wie arbeitet die musikalische Avantgarde?'.

26 Sleeve note, RCA SB 6850.

27 Ibid.

28 Henri Pousseur and Michel Butor: 'Répons', *Musique en jeu,* no. 4 (1971), 106–11; p.107.

29 *Formalized Music,* pp.112–13.

30 See ibid., pp.131–54.

31 See Hiller and Isaacson: *Experimental Music* (New York, 1959).

Chapter 8: Moments of Parting

1 *Boulez on Music Today* (London, 1971), p.26.

2 Boulez: 'Où on est-on?', *Revue musicale,* no. 276–7 (1971), 7–9; p.7.

3 *Boulez on Music Today,* pp.20–34.

4 See his article 'La crise de la musique sérielle', *Gravesaner Blätter,* no. 1 (1955), pp.2ff.

5 *Die Reihe,* no. 7 (1960, English edition 1965), pp.5–19.

6 Ibid., p.15.

7 *Die Reihe,* no. 4 (1958, English edition 1960), pp.36–62.

8 For the text of a staged version see *Aventures & Nouvelles aventures,* ed. Ove Nordwall (Stockholm, 1967).

9 See John Casken: 'Transition and Transformation in the Music of Witold Lutosławski', *Contact*, no. 12 (1975), pp.3–14.

10 See Michael Nyman: *Experimental Music* (London, 1974), pp.60–74.

11 See Dave Smith: 'Following a Straight Line: La Monte Young', *Contact*, no. 18 (1977–8), pp.4–9.

12 See Cardew's article 'Report on Stockhausen's "Carré" ', *Musical Times*, cii (1961), pp.619–22, 698–700.

13 Jonathan Cott: *Stockhausen: Conversations with the Composer* (London, 1974), p.31.

14 'Die Einheit der musikalischen Zeit', *Texte*, i (Cologne, 1963), pp.211–21.

15 Sleeve note, Vox STGBY 638.

16 See 'Die Einheit der musikalischen Zeit' and other articles of this period.

17 See Karl H. Wörner: *Stockhausen: Life and Work* (London, 1973), p.110.

18 Ibid., pp.46–7.

19 See also his article 'Momentform', *Texte*, i (Cologne, 1963), pp.189–210.

20 Programme note for the world première at the 1962 Donaueschingen Festival.

21 On the two versions see Robin Maconie: *The Works of Karlheinz Stockhausen* (London, 1976), pp.173–5.

22 See his note on *Momente* in Wörner: op. cit., pp.48–53 for insights into the philosophical thinking on which this synthesis was in part based.

23 See various statements by the composer in *Luigi Nono: Texte, Studien zu seiner Musik*, ed. Jürg Stenzl (Zurich, 1975).

24 Sleeve note, Adès 16001.

Chapter 9: American Serialim → Computer Music

1 *Contemporary Music Catalogue* issued by C. F. Peters Corporation (New York, 1975), p.4.

2 'On *Relata I*', *Perspectives of New Music*, ix/1 (1970), pp.1–22.

3 'Milton Babbitt: String Quartet no. 3', *Contemporary Music Newsletter*, viii/1 (1974), pp.1–2.

4 Sleeve note, Turnabout TV 34515.

5 'On *Relata I*', p.21.

6 Ibid., p.22.

7 Sleeve note, Turnabout TV 34515.

8 See his article 'An Introduction to the R.C.A. Synthesizer', *Journal of Music Theory,* viii (1964), pp.251–65.

9 'Twelve-Tone Rhythmic Structure and the Electronic Medium', *Perspectives of New Music,* i/1 (1962), 49–79; p.79.

10 See, for example, his article 'Towards a Twelve-tone Polyphony', *Perspectives of New Music,* iv/2 (1966), pp.90–112.

11 See ibid.

12 See William Hibbard: 'Charles Wuorinen: *The Politics of Harmony*', *Perspectives of New Music,* vii/2 (1969), pp.155–66.

13 Sleeve note, Nonesuch H 71225.

14 Ibid.

15 Sleeve note, Nonesuch H 71245.

16 *Perspectives of New Music,* viii/i (1969), pp.1–74; viii/2 (1970), pp.49–111; ix/1 (1970), pp.23–42; ix/ii–x/1 (1971), pp.232–70; xi/1 (1972), pp.146–223; xi/2 (1973), pp.156–203.

17 See J. K. Randall: 'A Report from Princeton', *Perspectives of New Music,* iii/2 (1965), pp.84–92.

Chapter 10: Indeterminacy → Changing the System

1 *Experimental Music: Cage and Beyond* (London, 1974), p.3.

2 Quoted in ibid., p.110.

3 Frederic Rzewski, quoted in ibid., p.110.

4 Quoted in ibid., p.111.

5 Quoted in ibid., p.112.

6 Mumma, quoted in ibid., p.87.

7 Lucier, quoted in ibid., p.91.

8 Young: sleeve note, Shandar 83 510.

9 Ibid.

10 *Writings about Music* (Halifax, Nova Scotia, 1974), p.40.

11 Keith Potter and Dave Smith: 'Interview with Philip Glass', *Contact,* no. 13 (1976), 25–30; p.29.

12 Ibid., p.30.

13 *Writings,* p.9.

14 Ibid., p.10.

15 Ibid., p.50.

16 Ibid., p.53.

17 Ibid., p.58.

18 Cornelius Cardew, ed.: *Stockhausen serves Imperialism* (London, 1974), p.86.

19 *Treatise Handbook* (London, 1971).

20 Cardew: 'A Scratch Orchestra: Draft Constitution', *Musical Times,* cx (1969), p.617.

21 See *Stockhausen serves Imperialism.*

Chapter 11: Quotation → Integration

1 IRCAM press brochure (Paris, 1974), pp.6–7.

2 'Rythme et développement', *Polyphonie,* no. 9–10 (1954), pp.47–73.

3 'Notes on the Performance of Contemporary Music', *Perspectives of New Music,* iii/1 (1964), 10–21.

4 Stephen Arnold: 'The Music of *Taverner*', *Tempo,* no. 101 (1972), 20–39; p.29.

5 Claude Samuel: *Entretiens avec Olivier Messiaen* (Paris, 1967), p.11.

6 *Conférence de Notre-Dame* (Paris, 1978), p.3.

7 See Arnold: op. cit., p.22.

8 Programme note for concert at the Queen Elizabeth Hall, London, 9 December 1969; quoted in Arnold: op. cit., p.21.

9 'Returns and Departures: Recent Maxwell Davies', *Tempo,* no. 113 (1975), 22–8; p.25.

10 Review, *Contact,* no. 19 (1978), pp.26–9.

11 Preface to the score.

12 *The Music of Stockhausen* (London, 1975), pp.118–21.

13 *Texte,* i (Cologne, 1963), p.21.

14 *Werkstatt-Texte* (Frankfurt and Berlin, 1972), p.183.

15 Sleeve note, Adès 16001.

16 ' "Sonate, que me veux-tu?" ', *Perspectives of New Music,* i/2 (1963), 32–44; p.34.

17 'Aléa', *Perspectives of New Music,* iii/1 (1964), 42–53; p.51.

18 Programme note for a concert at the Severance Hall, Cleveland, 5 December 1970.

19 *Texte,* iii (Cologne, 1971), p.79.

20 Ibid., p.76.

21 Ibid., p.75.

22 Ibid., p.80.

23 Ibid., p.76.

24 *The Works of Karlheinz Stockhausen* (London, 1976), p.210.

25 Quoted in Michael Nyman: *Experimental Music* (London, 1974), p.83.

26 *Dictionary of Twentieth-Century Music,* ed. John Vinton (London, 1974), p.491.

27 Sleeve note, Nonesuch H 71255.

28 'The Music of George Crumb', *Contact,* no. 11 (1975), 14–22; p.16.

29 Ibid., p.15.

30 Kagel, quoted in Werner Klüppelholz: ' "Ohne des Wesentliche der Ideen unkenntlich zu machen." Zu Kagels "Variationen ohne Fuge . . ." ', *Die neue Musik und die Tradition,* ed. Reinhold Brinkmann (Mainz, 1978), 114–29; p.128.

31 Programme note, *Clés pour la musique,* no. 24 (1970), p.15.

32 Stockhausen, quoted in sleeve note, DGG 139 461.

33 Preface to the score.

34 Ibid.

35 Ibid.

36 *Musique/Sémantique/Société* (Tournai, 1972), pp.75–6.

37 See, for example, his article 'Ecoute d'un dialogue', *Musique en jeu,* no. 4 (1971), pp.73–82.

38 Programme note for a concert at the Palais des Beaux-Arts, Brussels, 20 December 1968.

39 *Musique/Semantique/Société,* p.66.

40 See Richard Witts: 'Report on Henri Pousseur', *Contact,* no. 13 (1976), pp.13–22.

41 'Stravinsky by Way of Webern: the Consistency of a Syntax', *Perspectives of New Music,* x/2 (1972), 13–51; p.16.

42 J.-Y. Bosseur and P. Torrens: 'Midi-minuit Stravinsky à Liege', *Musique en jeu,* no. 6 (1972), pp.104–5.

43 Ibid.

44 'Stravinsky by Way of Webern: the consistency of a Syntax (II)', *Perspectives of New Music,* xi/1 (1972), 112–45; p.126.

45 See Dick Witts: 'Pousseur's "L'éffacement du Prince Igor" ', *Tempo,* no. 122 (1977), pp.10–17.

46 Schat: 'The Reason of a Dream', *Key Notes,* no. 4 (1976), 41–5; p.43.

47 Sleeve note, Nonesuch H 71283.

48 'The New Image of Music', *Perspectives of New Music*, ii/1 (1963), 1–10.

49 Sleeve note, CRI 231 USD.

Chapter 12: Virtuosity → Improvisation

1 Programme note for a concert at the Palais des Beaux-Arts, Brussels, 18 December 1966.

2 Sleeve note, RCA LSC 3168.

3 *Conversations with Célestin Deliège* (London, 1976), p.15.

4 Ibid., p.88.

5 'Réagir . . .', *Musique en jeu*, no. 1 (1970), pp.70–77.

6 Sleeve note, Harmonia Mundi HMU 933.

7 *Mauricio Kagel: Musik, Theater, Film* (Cologne, 1970).

8 Quoted in Josef Häusler: 'Kagel', *The New Grove*.

9 'Xenakis and the Performer', *Tempo*, no. 112 (1975), pp.17–22.

10 'The Random Arts: Xenakis, Mathematics and Music', *Tempo*, no. 85 (1968), pp.2–5.

11 See Paul Griffiths: 'Xenakis: Logic and Disorder', *Musical Times*, cxvi (1975), pp.329–31.

12 Sleeve note, CBS 72647.

13 *The Works of Karlheinz Stockhausen* (London, 1976), p.187.

14 See his *Texte*, iii (Cologne, 1971), pp.42–3.

15 Karl H. Wörner: *Stockhausen: Life and Work* (London, 1973), p.64.

16 Ibid., p.69.

17 Ibid., p.67.

18 'Ils improvisent . . . improvisez . . . improvisons', *Musique en jeu*, no. 6 (1972), 13–19; p.14.

19 *Texte*, iii, pp.123–4.

20 See Paul Griffiths: *A Guide to Electronic Music* (London, 1979) for a comparison of two versions of *Verbindung*, and Harald Bojé: 'Aus den sieben Tagen: "Text"-Interpretation', *Feedback Papers*, no. 16 (1978), pp.10–14, for notes on performance by musicians closely associated with Stockhausen.

21 'Ils improvisent . . .', p.18.

Chapter 13: Opera → Music Theatre

1 See, for example, *John Cage,* ed. Richard Kostelanetz (London, 1971), pp.22–3.

2 Ursula Stürzbecher: *Wekstattgespräche mit Komponisten* (Cologne, 1971), p.43.

3 See 'The Bassarids: Hans Werner Henze talks to Paul Griffiths', *Musical Times,* cxv (1974), pp.831–2.

4 *Essays* (Mainz, 1964), p.32.

5 Quoted in Robert Henderson: 'Henze', *The New Grove.*

6 See *Luigi Nono: Texte, Studien zu seiner Musik* (Zurich, 1975).

7 See ibid.

8 Sleeve note, Wergo 60067.

9 Quoted in Dominique and Jean-Yves Bosseur: 'Collaboration Butor/Pousseur', *Musique en jeu,* no. 4 (1971), 83–111; p.85.

10 See Michael Taylor: 'Maxwell Davies's *Vesalii icones*', *Tempo,* no. 92 (1970), pp.22–7.

11 'Atem pour un instrument à vent (1969–1970)', *Musique en jeu,* no. 7 (1972), p.95.

12 Jonathan Cott: *Stockhausen: Conversations with the Composer* (London, 1974), p.63.

13 Ibid., p.59.

14 See Jill Purce: 'Stockhausen', *Sound International* (October–December 1978).

15 See ibid.

Chapter 14: Series → Melody

1 *Courrier musical,* no. 26 (1969).

2 Programme note for the first performance of *Eclat/multiples,* at the Festival Hall, London, 21 October 1970.

3 *Boulez on Music Today* (London, 1971), p.89.

4 Ibid.

5 *The Structure of Atonal Music* (New Haven and London, 1973).

6 Programme note for the first performance, at the Festival Hall, London, 2 April 1975.

7 See Helmut Lachenmann: 'Bedingungen des Materials', *Darmstädter Beiträge,* no. 17 (1978), 93–9; p.98.

8 Ligeti's note with Decca HEAD 12.

9 Programme note for the first British performance, at the Queen Elizabeth Hall, London, 8 May 1977.

10 Note with Argo ZRG 790.

11 See Jonathan Cott: *Stockhausen: Conversations with the Composer* (London, 1974), p.227.

12 Sleeve note, DGG 2530 208.

13 Ibid.

14 See Jill Purce: 'Stockhausen', *Sound International* (October–December 1978).

15 'Zur Situation', *Darmstädter Beiträge,* no. 14 (1974), 19–23; p.19.

Postlude

1 'Twelve-Tone Rhythmic Structure and the Electronic Medium', *Perspectives of New Music,* i/1 (1962), 49–79; p.49.

2 *Writings about Music* (Halifax, Nova Scotia, 1974), pp.10–11.

3 Quoted in Dave Smith: 'Following a Straight Line: La Monte Young', *Contact,* no. 18 (1977–8), 4–9; p.7.

4 Jonathan Cott: *Stockhausen: Conversations with the Composer* (London, 1974), p.81.

5 *Musique/Semantique/Société* (Tournai, 1972), pp.32–77.

Bibliography

Since *The New Grove* contains comprehensive bibliographies for the composers and principal terms mentioned in this book, it has seemed necessary only to list here the most important volumes relating to the period. References to articles are included among the notes to the text.

Bibliographies

A. P. Basart, *Serial Music: a Classified Bibliography of Writings on Twelve-tone and Electronic Music* (Berkeley and Los Angeles, 1961).

L. M. Cross, *A Bibliography of Electronic Music* (Toronto, 1967).

General texts in English

J. Appleton and R. Perera, eds., *The Development and Practice of Electronic Music* (Englewood Cliffs, N.J., 1975).

J. Beauchamp and H. von Forester, eds., *Music by Computers* (New York, 1969).

M. Cooper, ed., *The New Oxford History of Music, x: The Modern Age 1890–1960* (London, 1974).

H. Davies, ed., *Repertoire international des musiques électroacoustiques/ International Electronic Music Catalog* (Cambridge, Mass., 1968).

D. Ernst, *The Evolution of Electronic Music* (New York, 1977).

L. Foreman, ed., *British Music Now* (London, 1975).

P. Griffiths, *A Guide to Electronic Music* (London, 1979).

L. Hiller and L. Isaacson, *Experimental Music* (New York, 1959).

R. S. Hines, ed., *The Orchestral Composer's Point of View* (Norman, Oklahoma, 1970).

A. Hodeir, *Since Debussy* (New York, 1961).

P. H. Lang, ed., *Problems of Modern Music* (New York, 1962).

P. H. Lang and N. Broder, eds., *Contemporary Music in Europe* (New York, 1965).

H. Lincoln, ed., *The Computer and Music* (Ithaca, N.Y., 1970).

M. V. Mathews, *The Technology of Computer Music* (Cambridge, Mass., 1969).

M. Nyman, *Experimental Music: Cage and Beyond* (London, 1974).

E. Schwartz, *Electronic Music: a Listener's Guide* (New York, 1973).

R. Smith Brindle, *The New Music* (London, 1975).

J. Vinton, ed., *Dictionary of Twentieth-Century Music* (London, 1974).

A. Whittall, *Music since the First World War* (London, 1977).

W. Zimmermann, *Desert Plants: Conversations with 25 American Composers* (Vancouver, 1977).

General texts in other languages

K. Boehmer, *Zur Theorie der offenen Form in der neuen Musik* (Darmstadt, 1967).

U. Dibelius, *Moderne Musik 1945–1965* (Munich, 1966).

—— ed., *Musik auf der Flucht vor sich selbst* (Munich, 1969).

H. Eimert and H. U. Humpert, *Das Lexikon der elektronischen Musik* (Regensburg, 1973).

A. Gentilucci, *Guida all'ascolto della musica contemporanea* (Milan, 1969).

—— *Introduzione alla musica elettronica* (Milan, 1972).

W. Gieseler, *Komposition im 20. Jahrhundert* (Celle, 1975).

E. Karkoschka, *Das Schriftbild der neuen Musik* (Celle, 1966).

C. Samuel, *Panorama de l'art musical contemporain* (Paris, 1962).

D. Schnebel, *Denkbare Musik* (Cologne, 1972).

R. Stephan, ed., *Die Musik der sechziger Jahre* (Mainz, 1972).

U. Stürzbecher, *Werkstattgesprache mit Komponisten* (Cologne, 1971).

H. Vogt, *Neue Musik seit 1945* (Stuttgart, 1972).

Musique et technologie [= *Revue musicale* no. 268–9] (Paris, 1971).

Boulez

P. Boulez, *Penser la musique aujourd'hui* (Paris, 1963), English translation as *Boulez on Music Today* (London, 1971).

—— *Relevés d'apprenti* (Paris, 1966), English translation as *Notes of an Apprenticeship* (New York, 1968).

—— *Werkstatt-Texte* (Frankfurt and Berlin, 1972).

—— *Anhaltspunkte* (Stuttgart and Zurich, 1975).

—— *Par volonté et par hasard: entretiens avec Célestin Deliège* (Paris, 1975), English translation as *Conversations with Célestin Deliège* (London, 1977).

A. Goléa, *Rencontres avec Pierre Boulez* (Paris, 1958).

P. Griffiths, *Boulez* (London, 1978).

J. Peyser, *Boulez: Composer, Conductor, Enigma* (London, 1977).

Cage

J. Cage, *Silence* (Middletown, Conn., 1961).

—— *A Year from Monday* (Middletown, Conn., 1967).

—— *M* (Middletown, Conn., 1973).

R. Kostelanetz, ed.: *John Cage* (London, 1971).

Cardew

C. Cardew, *Treatise Handbook* (London, 1971).

—— ed.: *Nature Study Notes* (London, 1971).

—— *Scratch Music* (London, 1972).

—— *Stockhausen serves Imperialism* (London, 1974).

Henze

K. Geitel, *Hans Werner Henze* (Berlin, 1968).

H. W. Henze, *Undine: Tagebuch eines Balletts* (Munich, 1959).

—— *Essays* (Mainz, 1964).

C. H. Henneberg, ed., *El Cimarron: ein Werkbericht* (Mainz, 1971).

D. de la Motte, *Hans Werner Henze: Der Prinz von Homburg* (Mainz, 1960).

E. Schnabel, *Das Floss der Medusa: Text zum Oratorium von Hans Werner Henze: zum Untergang einer Uraufführung – Postscriptum* (Munich, 1969).

Kagel

D. Schnebel, *Mauricio Kagel: Musik, Theater, Film* (Cologne, 1970).

Ligeti

O. Nordwall, *Det omöjligas konst: anteckningar till György Ligetis musik* (Stockholm, 1966).

—— ed., *Ligeti-dokument* (Stockholm, 1968).

O. Nordwall, *György Ligeti: eine Monographie* (Mainz, 1971).

E. Salmenhaara, *Das musikalische Material und seine Behandlung in den Werken 'Apparitions', 'Atmosphères', 'Aventures' und 'Requiem' von György Ligeti* (Helsinki and Regensburg, 1969).

Lutosławski

O. Nordwall, ed., *Lutosławski* (Stockholm, 1968).

B. A. Varga, *Lutosławski Profile* (London, 1976).

Messiaen
A. Goléa, *Rencontres avec Olivier Messiaen* (Paris, 1961).

R. S. Johnson, *Messiaen* (London, 1975).

O. Messiaen, *Technique de mon langage musical* (Paris, 1944).

R. Nichols, *Messiaen* (London, 1975).

C. Samuel, *Entretiens avec Olivier Messiaen* (Paris, 1967).

Nono
J. Stenzl, ed., *Luigi Nono: Texte, Studien zu seiner Musik* (Zurich, 1975).

Pousseur
H. Pousseur, *Fragments théoriques sur la musique experimentale*, i–ii (Brussels, 1970, 1972).

—— *Musique/Sémantique/Société* (Tournai, 1972).

Reich
S. Reich, *Writings about Music* (Halifax, Nova Scotia, 1974).

Schaeffer
M. Pierret, *Entretiens avec Pierre Schaeffer* (Paris, 1969).

P. Schaeffer, *A la recherche d'une musique concrète* (Paris, 1952).

—— *Traité des objets musicaux* (Paris, 1966, 2nd edition 1977).

—— *De la musique concrète à la musique même* [= *Revue musicale* no. 303–5] (Paris, 1977).

Stockhausen
J. Cott, *Stockhausen: Conversations with the Composer* (London, 1974).

J. Harvey, *The Music of Stockhausen: an Introduction* (London, 1974).

R. Maconie, *The Works of Karlheinz Stockhausen* (London, 1976).

K. Stockhausen, *Texte*, i–iv (Cologne, 1963, 1964, 1971, 1978).

K. H. Wörner, *Karlheinz Stockhausen: Werk und Wollen* (Rodenkirchen, 1963), English translation, enlarged, as *Stockhausen: Life and Work* (London, 1973).

Xenakis
I. Xenakis, *Musique formelles* [= *Revue musicale* no. 253–4] (Paris, 1963), English translation as *Formalized Music* (Bloomington, Indiana, 1971).

—— *Musique-architecture* (Tournai, 1971).

Young
L. Young and M. Zazeela, *Selected Writings* (Munich, 1969).

L. Young and J. MacLow, *An Anthology* (Munich, 2nd edition 1970).

Index

Numbers in bold type refer to music examples, those in italic to entries in the 'Repertory' sections.